Postcolonial Overtures

Irish Studies

James MacKillop, *Series Editor*

Other titles from Irish Studies

All Dressed Up: Modern Irish Historical Pageantry
Joan FitzPatrick Dean

Compassionate Stranger: Asenath Nicholson and the Great Irish Famine
Maureen O'Rourke Murphy

Irish Women Dramatists: 1908–2001
Eileen Kearney and Charlotte Headrick, eds.

Joyce/Shakespeare
Laura Pelaschiar, ed.

Memory Ireland: Volume 3: The Famine and the Troubles
Oona Frawley, ed.

Memory Ireland: Volume 4: James Joyce and Cultural Memory
Oona Frawley and Katherine O'Callaghan, eds.

Representing the National Landscape in Irish Romanticism
Julia M. Wright

The Urban Plays of the Early Abbey Theatre: Beyond O'Casey
Elizabeth Mannion

Syracuse, New York 13244-5290

First Edition 2015
15 16 17 18 19 20 6 5 4 3 2 1

∞ The paper used in this publication meets the minimum requirements of the American National Standard for Information Sciences—Permanence of Paper for Printed Library Materials, ANSI Z39.48-1992.

For a listing of books published and distributed by Syracuse University Press, visit our website at www.SyracuseUniversityPress.syr.edu.

ISBN: 978-0-8156-3400-3 (cloth) 978-0-8156-5349-3 (e-book)

Library of Congress Cataloging-in-Publication Data
Obert, Julia C.
Postcolonial overtures : the politics of sound in contemporary Northern Irish poetry / Julia C. Obert. — First edition.
pages cm — (Irish studies)
Includes bibliographical references and index.
ISBN 978-0-8156-3400-3 (cloth : alk. paper) — ISBN 978-0-8156-5349-3 (e-book)
1. English poetry—Irish authors—History and criticism. 2. English poetry—20th century—History and criticism. 3. Sound in literature. 4. Northern Ireland—In literature. 5. Carson, Ciaran, 1948—Criticism and interpretation. 6. Mahon, Derek, 1941—Criticism and interpretation. 7. Muldoon, Paul—Criticism and interpretation. I. Title.
PR8781.S75O23 2015
821'.9109357—dc23 2015027643

Manufactured in the United States of America

POSTCOLONIAL OVERTURES

The Politics of Sound in Contemporary Northern Irish Poetry

Julia C. Obert

Syracuse University Press

For Nevin, who makes all things possible

CONTENTS

ACKNOWLEDGMENTS

THIS BOOK began as a dissertation project at the University of California, Irvine. I gratefully acknowledge the assistance, financial support, and intellectual encouragement that I received at UCI. I am particularly indebted to my wonderful dissertation committee, Rajagopalan Radhakrishnan, Laura O'Connor, and Carrie Noland, who nurtured and challenged my ideas and who graciously shepherded this project forward. Thanks are also due to Richard Cavell of the University of British Columbia, who first asked me to consider "the fate of the acoustic," as well as to Annie Moore, Peter Leman, Mia McIver, and Judy Joshua, who all went beyond the call of duty as readers when I most needed their keen eyes and kind words. Financial support for the early stages of the project was generously provided by the University of California, Irvine's Murray Krieger Endowed Fellowship in Literary Theory, as well as by a Social Sciences and Humanities Research Council of Canada doctoral fellowship.

As I revised, rewrote, and reshaped the work, my dear friends and colleagues at the University of Wyoming provided me with a great deal of moral and intellectual support. I have very much appreciated the lunches, the listening ears, and the engaged discussions, all of which have sustained me during the last few years. Thanks are particularly due to Antoinette DeNapoli for sharing her materials and thoughts with me as I embarked on the process of submitting book proposals. I am also extremely thankful for the support of friends and mentors affiliated with the American Conference for Irish Studies, the Canadian Association for Irish Studies, and the Keough-Naughton Notre Dame Centre's Irish Seminar. This book would not exist without the kindness, the scholarly guidance, and the good humor of those individuals. I am especially grateful to Richard

Rankin Russell, who has been an incredibly generous and encouraging correspondent since we first met in 2012.

I have enjoyed working with the wonderfully thoughtful and hugely capable editors at Syracuse University Press: Jennika Baines (whom I wish well in her new position in Indiana), Deb Manion, and Jim MacKillop. I thank all three for their patience, their help, and their good cheer. I also appreciate the feedback offered by SUP's three anonymous reviewers; the book is far clearer and richer for their careful and considered advice.

Above all, I would like to express my love, admiration, and appreciation for Dr. Nevin Aiken, the best personal and professional partner imaginable. Here's to the buddy system, now and always.

All quotations from Derek Mahon's *New Collected Poems* (2011), Alan Gillis' *Hawks and Doves* (2007) and *Somebody, Somewhere* (2004), Paul Muldoon's *General Admission* (2006), and Ciaran Carson's *The Irish for No* (1987) appear by kind permission of The Gallery Press, Loughcrew, Oldcastle, County Meath, Ireland. Quotations from Ciaran Carson's *Belfast Confetti* (1989) appear courtesy of The Gallery Press and Wake Forest University Press. Passages from Paul Muldoon's *Poems, 1968–1998* (2001) appear courtesy of Faber & Faber. Quotations from Leontia Flynn's *Profit and Loss* (2011) are reprinted by permission of The Random House Group Ltd.

Portions of chapters 2 and 3 of this book appeared as "Sounding the City: Ciaran Carson and the Perceptual Politics of War" in *Textual Practice* 26, no. 6 (2012) and are reprinted here with permission of Taylor & Francis (http://www.tandfonline.com). Portions of chapters 6 and 7 appeared in *Éire-Ireland* 46, no. 3–4 (2011) as "Paul Muldoon: Becoming Opera" and are reprinted here with permission of the Irish-American Cultural Institute. A short excerpt from chapter 8 appeared in "Shared Space: A Belfast Soundscape Study" in *New Hibernia Review* 18, no. 1 (2014) and is reprinted here with permission of the Center for Irish Studies at the University of St. Thomas. I thank the publishers and editors of these journals for their generosity.

Postcolonial Overtures

1

OF HOMING REFRAINS

Out of Place: Ulster's Unbelongings

Poet Ciaran Carson evocatively describes Troubles-era Belfast as a "demolition city" (1989, "Schoolboys and Idlers of Pompeii" 54). Decades of violence, Carson suggests, gradually unmade Belfast's built environment, "swallow[ing home] in the maw of time and trouble" (1989, "Question Time" 63). Much of his work hinges on this predicament: throughout his collections, bombings and blitzes destroy local landmarks and defamiliarize the cityscape. Carson also notes that the geographical sectarianism accompanying the conflict has left the city anxiously fragmented. Even today, almost twenty years after the Belfast Agreement, Northern Ireland is carved up along partisan lines; the places where people live, go to school, shop, and socialize remain divided (Hughes et al. 2007). Moreover, particularly in contentious "interface" regions of Derry/Londonderry and Belfast (incendiary border zones where Catholic and Protestant communities collide), these places are cluttered with sectarian symbols. Flags, murals, paramilitary graffiti, and painted curbstones declare allegiance to either the Tricolor or the Union Jack, complicating locals' feelings of belonging and hindering efforts at conciliatory community-building. As Carson (1997, 258) describes in his memoir, *The Star Factory*, "Protestant territory . . . proclaim[s] itself by small details of street furniture: graffiti, obviously; more subtly, the galvanized iron flagholders bolted to the walls of terrace houses, defunct for that part of the year which [i]s not the marching season. Even the colours of the flower displays in front windows c[an] be read as code, these pansies of bruise-blue and black, those clustered reds of sweet William."[1]

As the region's physical contours have been disorientingly reshaped, so too have its psychic contours: a phenomenon that Edna Longley (1994, 88) terms Ulster's "inhospitality." With familiar spaces forever slipping from its residents' grasp, "as if in recoil from organic unity" (Graham 2003, 154), the "Troubled" North poses unique challenges to deep-seated senses of rootedness, place-consciousness, and belonging. For this reason, says Carson, "even the little piggy who stayed at home [throughout the conflict] will sometimes feel lost" (1989, "Question Time" 57); even the longtime local can feel insecure, unsettled, and out of place. As Carson's concerns indicate, contemporary Northern Irish writers, particularly those who came of age during the Troubles, have been left to reckon with the country's "unhomely moment" (Bhabha 1994, 9). In response, many of these authors take discomfort and dislocation as their driving themes. Derek Mahon, for instance—who, like Carson, was born and raised in Belfast—readily admits to being "*terrified* of home" (2002, 109). Nevertheless, if Sara Ahmed's (2004, 89) assertion that "being at home is a matter of how one feels or fails to feel" holds true, we might also be able to excavate authors' attempts to remedy these painful structures of feeling.

This book explores the work of three Northern poets—Ciaran Carson, Derek Mahon, and Paul Muldoon—who try to reimagine belonging and community-building as they seek comfort or consolation (if not quite

1. Although overt violence has mostly been quieted in the North since the 1998 signing of the Belfast Agreement, some paramilitaries, such as the Real IRA (RIRA) and the Continuity IRA (CIRA), remain active. Communities throughout the North are almost entirely segregated, and levels of mutual distrust and animosity are still disconcertingly high among residents. Parade season, during which Catholic and Protestant groups commemorate previous victories, still frequently devolves into violent riots. Moreover, nationwide studies since 1998 have shown that as much as 30 percent of Northern Ireland's population meets the diagnostic criteria for post-traumatic stress disorder (Fey et al. 1999, 11). Living for thirty years with the ever-present possibility of violence, it seems, does physiological and psychological damage that even a peace agreement cannot cure, and Northern Ireland's social rifts seem nearly irreparable even in the absence of a collective appetite for conflict.

compensation) in the wake of conflict. Crucially, what unites these three poets in their search is a peculiar attunement to sound: an effort to engage the heard world in their work. By way of careful listening, their collections respond to "geographical violence" (Said 1993, 225): to "demolition," segregation, and sectarian symbolism, all-too-visible reminders of the North's "inhospitality." In other words, when alienated from home turf, these writers turn from the eye to the ear, reconsidering landscape as *sound*scape, an immersive auditory field. This strategy suggests sound's political and affective potential: music, accent, and even familiar white noise can help otherwise unmoored subjects feel at home. Acoustic cues, moreover, can slip across borders that bodies cannot or will not cross; they transgress strictly policed visual divides (including the North's fortified "Peace Walls") and debunk the tribal myths of purity on which these divides depend. The work to come is therefore wired for sound; it eavesdrops on these ear-minded poets and argues for their acoustic attunements as efforts to counteract visual estrangement. When seeing no longer means believing, sound at least sometimes satisfies.

Several critics of Irish literature have considered single-author acoustics: Seamus Heaney's "auditory imagination" has received concerted attention (Bilbro 2011, 321), and Carson's "aural sign system" (McCracken 1995, 365) and Mahon's "attentive[ness] to oral history" (Longley 1995, 283) have been mentioned in passing. However, the surprising prevalence of sound in contemporary Northern poetry has never been studied systematically. This book serves as a provocation to deep literary listening; the forthcoming chapters perk their ears to the poetry and consider the verses' "homing refrains" (Deleuze and Guattari [1987] 2004, 343) as efforts to remedy histories of displacement and dislocation.[2]

Although I tried to comprehensively address the Northern acoustic in this book, I did apply some degree of selectivity. Carson, Mahon, and

2. Of course, this is not to say that sound is never violent or coercive. Hitler, after all, infamously claimed that he conquered Germany thanks to the loudspeaker, and sound (plus infrasound and ultrasound) today serves as a destructively clandestine weapon for the international war machine. That said, the undertheorized perceptual and emotional possibilities that local soundscapes provide are worth investigating.

Muldoon are relatively close in age, have spent significant portions of their lives in Belfast (which seems a kind of crucible for their shared interest in sound), and are all keen listeners. Place is mediated by the ear in their work more than by any other sense. The younger Belfast poets discussed in the concluding chapter, Leontia Flynn, Alan Gillis, and Gearóid Mac Lochlainn, inherit this interest in local soundscape and meditate together on the role that sound might play in the ongoing work of reconciliation in their city.

The figures most obviously absent from this book are Seamus Heaney, Michael Longley, and Medbh McGuckian—marvelous (and canonical) Northern poets all three. Heaney's work, however, often dominates the critical scene, and his soundscapes have already been explored extensively by other authors. These analyses might be usefully read alongside this volume to more fully register the relationship of rural to urban sound-spaces in Northern Irish poetics (see Bilbro 2011, Rankin Russell 2010, and Tyler 2013). Longley's poetry of place, insofar as Belfast is concerned, is often filtered through the distancing lens of classical allusion or the magnifying effects of the intensely personal, so his engagement with urban space is less direct than that of the poets examined in this book. The soundscape of Carrigskeewaun, County Mayo, which becomes audible in Longley's poetry, warrants further study, particularly as it relates to his self-professed poetic "burble" (see Sean O'Brien's "A Hundred Doors by Michael Longley," *The Guardian*, April 8, 2011). Finally, although McGuckian's writing is wonderfully engaging and richly textured, it is also intensely mythopoetic and often more engaged with interior than exterior spaces, which sets it apart from the work of Carson, Mahon, and Muldoon. Heaney, Longley, and McGuckian all use poetic sound effects in inventive and even virtuosic ways. However, it is an engagement with *environmental* sound—poetry nourished by the choppy drone of helicopter rotors, the clanging of cranes, the caws of gulls, the cadences of pub talk—to which this book turns a listening ear.

All Ears: The Perceptual Turn

Carson, Mahon, and Muldoon's shared concern with the sensations of place—the body's intimacy with lived space—suggests phenomenology's currency as a critical approach to belonging and community-building.[3] Our encounters with the tastes, textures, and timbres of the phenomenal world clearly affect our feelings of rootedness in that world. However, very few phenomenologists discuss environmental acoustics in depth; most defer to the eye as a primary conduit to place. Don Ihde (2007) responds to this critical myopia in his acclaimed book, *Listening and Voice: Phenomenologies of Sound*; he asserts that surround sound is central to a stable sense of place. Ihde argues that vision has long been privileged as our most objective sense, and he traces this bias back to pre-Socratic jurisprudence (Heraclitus' belief in "eyewitness accuracy") and through Enlightenment epistemologies equating sight with scientific insight. Ihde (2007) suggests that even our language reflects this perceptual presumption, noting that vision remains our "root metaphor for thought": we "see the light" in our "Eureka moments"; we daydream in the so-called "mind's eye"; we even frame pedagogy as "illumination" or "enlightenment" (8). This "visualism," Ihde believes, has increasingly impoverished Western approaches to perception. When the eye is treated as a conduit to the "real," the relationships of our other senses to the experience of being-in-the-world (and of feeling at home in the world) are too easily neglected.[4] His work

3. Although long out of favor, phenomenology has returned to the theoretical table in recent years, with many writers pioneering what might be called a "post-poststructuralist phenomenology." Indeed, the "affective turn" (Clough 2007, 1), a cluster of renewed investments in emotion and embodiment, suggests that post-structuralism and phenomenology can hang together. This conjunction hinges on the fact that feeling isn't fantasy; one can question the seeming immediacy or transparency of primary experience even while acknowledging that there is something we experience as such—a feeling-state—that is fundamental to our way of being-in-the-world. As Rei Terada describes in *Feeling in Theory* (2001, 89), "If we have emotions because we can't know what to believe"—if we (rightfully) can't accept the immediacy of primary experience—"then we have emotions even though we can't know which emotions we ought to have." I take Terada's sentiments to heart in this book, questioning embodied essentialisms but at the same time valuing sensations and emotions as such.

4. For a sociological approach to the same point, see Michael Bull and Les Back's *The Auditory Culture Reader* (2003, 3). Bull and Back argue that "[t]he dominance of the visual has often meant that the experience of the other senses . . . has been filtered through

therefore tries to recuperate the ear; his turn to the "auditory dimension" serves not as a simple changing of variables, but rather as a decentering of a dominant tradition and an effort to recover "the richness of primary experience" (13). In pursuit of "reflective listening" (57), Ihde asks us to submit the ways in which we are involuntarily *moved* by sound to conscious awareness and to concede the importance of learned perception to lived experience.

As to the ways in which we are moved by sound, particular auditory cues exert predictable embodied effects. Toes tap reflexively to a catchy tune, the startle reflex is triggered by sudden loud noises, and bodies are literally stunned by the shockwaves emitted by low-frequency infrasound. On the other hand, some perceptual experiences require social framing. Many of these semanticized sound-states are relatively generalizable, such as the idea that auditory grain can reveal whether a truck or a car has passed below your window or the notion that hearing can reveal invisible interiors, as when you knock on a melon to reveal its ripeness. Other sound-states, though, are intimately personalized: Ihde's (2007, 68) ability to "hear surfaces" in the hallway outside his office (he "can tell if it is Leslie in her heels or Eric in his tennis shoes [passing by]") assumes both domestic familiarity and social learning based on patterned behavior. With respect to both autonomic and socially contextualized ways of being moved by sound, Ihde's experiments are revelatory. We can, he says, conclusively hear shapes (e.g., by rolling an object inside a box), spaces (via echolocation), and textures (e.g., a blind man's tapping cane gives his landscapes an "auditory surface-aspect"), and these encounters affect our understanding of the world (61–71).[5] We can even hear the very materiality

---

a visualist framework. [This] reduction . . . has placed serious limitations on our ability to grasp the meanings attached to much social behavior, be it contemporary, historical or comparative."

5. Barry Blesser and Linda-Ruth Salter's (2006) work on aural architecture explains the cognitive bases for these auditory understandings of space. Strategies for "decoding spatial attributes," for instance, use such cues as "the difference in time, amplitude, and spectrum between the sounds arriving at the two ears, as well as detection of changes in

of being, as in the wheezing of a person with emphysema—a sound that "bespeaks the interior state of the body and its pathology" (195).[6]

I propose Ihde's acoustic phenomenology as a potential counterweight to Northern Ireland's apparent "unhomeliness." If this unhomeliness is rooted primarily in topographical violence—in histories of colonial "dominion . . . made visible" (Ramazani 2009, 145) and in the Troubles' violent destruction of long-standing landmarks and streetscapes—then it might be useful to reimagine home beyond visual coordinates as a series of aural cues. This is not to say that close listening somehow fully compensates for loss, nor is it to deny that conflict can involve invasive cacophony. Nevertheless, if place becomes illegible, it might yet whisper toward audibility. For example, landscapes' characteristic "earmarks," whether they be biophonic (gulls cawing), geophonic (waves crashing), or anthrophonic (clocks ticking), link us intimately to our lived spaces (Krause 2012, 157). These "keynote sounds," the acoustic backgrounds against which our lives unfold, are often dismissed as no more than white noise, but they in fact exert "deep and pervasive influence on our behaviour and moods" and

---

the expected spectral and temporal attributes of familiar sounds" (36). Moreover, when decoding the aural architecture of, say, a streetscape, "[e]ach traffic sign, parked automobile, or telephone pole has a surface that produces both sonic reflections when the sound source is in front of it and acoustic shadows when it is behind. A reflection may be heard as an echo if the sound is impulse-like and the surface is more than 10 meters (33 feet) away, or as tonal coloration if the source is continuous and the surface is nearby. A sonic shadow may be diffuse and blurred for low frequencies, or sharp and clear for high frequencies" (42). The innate ability to hear and make sense of these "reflections" and "shadows," that is, to convert binaural cues into spatial schemas, explains why human beings can develop very sophisticated modes of echolocation. Many blind people and even some blindfolded sighted ones can learn to ride bikes and navigate obstacle courses without aid by way of "close listening" (39–40).

6. Ihde's (2007, 83) work suggests that sometimes hearing is our *only* reliable conduit to believing. For example, he cites the making of Stanley Kubrick's *2001: A Space Odyssey* (1968, Beverly Hills, CA: Metro-Goldwyn-Mayer), during which cinematographers discovered that their spaceship's slow drift across the screen could not be perceived as movement without the benefit of the film's background music.

help root us in place (Schafer 1977, 9). As Belfast poet Tom Paulin (2003a, 35–36) explains, offering the local example of the wind blowing off Belfast Lough, such sounds carry "ontological meaning" and convey a sense of "dwelling in the world," and their absence is felt as profound sensory impoverishment. For Paulin, the wind's whines and whistles fundamentally define home, providing an aural sense of security even amidst Belfast's unnerving visual stratifications.

Similarly, a soundscape's distinctive foreground "signals"—sounds that demand our conscious attention (e.g., Cape Town's noon gun, Vancouver's ship horns, which daily sound the opening bar of "O Canada" over the Strait of Georgia, or London's Big Ben and its resonant Cambridge chimes)—make the acoustic life of a particular place unique, expressing something of its texture and character (Schafer 1977, 9).[7] Although these sounds are not necessarily soothing in and of themselves, their recurring rhythms often provide reassuring continuity. For example, many people in Belfast today mention "missing" the choppy drone of helicopter rotors and the throbs of Chinooks "chuckling comfortingly" over the city (McLiam Wilson 1996, chap. 1), despite the fact that these sounds signified incessant army surveillance during the Troubles.

Finally, "centripetal sounds" like church bells can "attract and unify" local ears, defining a community and briefly uniting local listeners in sensory experience (Schafer 1977, 54–55). In addition, a familiar vocal lilt or a few bars of a childhood tune can send one back in time, evoking a

7. These examples suggest that the soundscape in which one feels most intimately immersed need not be national in scope. This insight is especially important in Northern Ireland, where the notion of the (contested) nation remains an almost obsessive preoccupation. For example, Paulin's (2003a, 35–36) sense of the howling wind as an "essence of Belfast," an index of "dwelling" for the city's pedestrians, links sound to a regionalism that (perceptually if not always conceptually) transcends ties to either Britain or the Irish Republic. That said, there also exist chimes between distant soundscapes that can conjure feelings of inhabitancy. Those who live below Table Mountain in Cape Town might be reminded more of home in Vancouver than in Johannesburg because of the proximate frequencies of the noon gun to Vancouver's nine o'clock cannon. Regionalisms, then, can be relational, suggesting that homemaking might be structured by allegiances both within and beyond the nation-state.

profound sense of belonging.[8] As these observations suggest, sound can be a salve for those otherwise out of place. Familiar earmarks activate subconscious pathways of association and reshape affect, enabling a "politics of good feeling" in a seemingly "inhospitable" space (Carter 2001).

Acoustic Space

The work of reimagining "homeplace" isn't simply a matter of realigning modes of perception; it also requires re-envisioning the concept of space itself. The term "space," insofar as most Western cultures are concerned, refers to a horizon of visibility: a sense of surroundings defined by what the eye can see. As I have suggested, many of Northern Ireland's visual spaces, particularly in its contested urban centers, have been overtaken by either nervous fortification or intergroup aggression—by barbed wire or angry graffiti. However, following Marshall McLuhan and Edmund Carpenter's (1960) pioneering essay "Acoustic Space," I suggest that space is not only spectacle, it is also an immersive auditory field.[9] Lived landscape

8. R. Murray Schafer, a Canadian composer, became interested in environmental acoustics in the late 1960s while working at Simon Fraser University in Vancouver. Curious about performance venues' effects on audience perception of his music, he began exploring ambient sound as an important phenomenon in its own right. His work on the interactions of ecological and manmade noise, and on the effects of these interactions on lived experience, led to the Vancouver Soundscape Project, a 1973 audio recording of the city's "sound-map." The project, re-released on compact disc with an update on the changing cityscape in 1996, involved locational sound recordings designed to raise listener consciousness of the city's sonic environment and to investigate how our soundscapes provide us with a sense of place and how we might design sustainable soundscapes in urban spaces. These pioneering recordings inaugurated the field of acoustic ecology, a discipline that today systematically studies how surround sound mediates relationships between living beings and their environments. Acoustic ecology quickly developed an international profile among academics and activists, and institutes of sound studies are now aggregated by the World Forum for Acoustic Ecology (WFAE) and unified by the field's seminal journal, *Soundscape*. See http://wfae.proscenia.net for details.

9. "Acoustic Space" proceeds from McLuhan's ethnographic finding that many Inuit communities encounter and define space primarily by way of the ear. In white-out conditions, for example, a landscape's acoustics can reveal distances, contours, and

is also *sound*scape—our perceptual relationships to place are defined just as much by the ear as they are by the eye. Notably, McLuhan and Carpenter argue that soundscape "has no point of favoured focus": whereas the eyes can only see 180 degrees, being "bounded, directed, and limited to considerably less than half the visible world at any given moment," the ears are "all encompassing, constantly alert to any sound originating in their boundless sphere" (68–69). This explains, for example, why emergency vehicles use aural alerts: visual cues can only be consumed at the correct distance and angle.

McLuhan and Carpenter (1960, 68–69) further suggest that sound-space is dynamic: it "creates its own dimensions moment by moment." The soundscape is "a sphere without fixed boundaries; space made by the thing itself, not space containing the thing" (68–69). In other words, whereas the spectator's visual environment is defined by the eye's perceptual limits, acoustic space generates its own shape and scope; its (hypothetically limitless) reaches are dictated by each noise's volume. Even if defensive barriers, patriotic bunting, and sectarian murals mark the visual limits of single-identity neighborhoods in the North, policing residential segregation and telling locals that they do not belong, acoustic space is often *shared* space. Sound-signals readily slip across even the most imposing of "Peace Walls" and reach even the most militantly oppositional of ears. Sound therefore defines community differently than does sight, and this book argues that many Northern Irish poets interested in peacebuilding tap into its unifying potential.

Jean-Luc Nancy's book on sound-space, *A L'écoute* (*Listening*), adds to McLuhan and Carpenter's insights an examination of acoustic space's fundamental temporality—its ongoing *becoming*. The auditory field is always in flux, and whereas "visual presence is already there, available, before I see it," sonorous presence "*arrives* . . . and propagates throughout the entire body something of its effects." Listening is therefore a mode of perception by which time becomes space: sound is constantly "opening,"

---

textures. In response to this research, McLuhan and Carpenter began to take the idea of sound-space seriously, theorizing its impact on our daily lives.

"spreading," and "expand[ing]" as it becomes sound*scape* (Nancy 2007, 14).[10] Building on these observations in light of Carson, Mahon, and Muldoon's "Troubled" soundscapes, I suggest that whereas the eye expects enduring landmarks lining well-worn routes, the ear is more instinctively attuned to fleeting auditory cues. Sound can therefore be a tonic to conflict's visual disorientations, and it can trace the city's contours when architectural spaces—the "[p]izza parlours, massage parlours, night-clubs, drinking-clubs, antique shops, designer studios" that "momentarily populate the wilderness and the blitz sites" (Carson 1989, "Question Time" 57)—vanish in the blink of an eye, confounding pedestrian passersby.

The forthcoming chapters argue that Carson, Mahon, and Muldoon all source a sense of place from aural cues, promoting sound as a register in which belonging and community-building might be productively reimagined. Carson (1989), for example, suggests that violence severs seeing from believing, leaving the cityscape a motley patchwork of "holes knocked into holes" ("Question Time" 61). He responds to this defamiliarization by remapping place in acoustic space, sketching a semiotics of sound with which Belfast natives navigate an otherwise slippery city. This acoustic scaffolding helps locals to move safely through place; even when the city is uncannily illegible, it is not yet entirely inaudible. The

10. Nancy makes this point by citing a scene from *Parsifal*, Wagner's 1882 opera based on the Arthurian knight Parzival's quest for the Holy Grail. During the course of the opera, the forest of Montsalvat gradually transforms into the Hall of the Grail, where the ritual of the Eucharist is to be performed. As the knight Gurnemanz and the young Parzival walk to the hall, Parzival observes that he has barely moved, and yet seems to have traveled so far. In response, Gurnemanz replies, "You see, my son, here time becomes space" ("Du siehst, mein Sohn, zum Raum wird hier die Ziet," a line that many have taken as a reflection on the opera's desire to be set in an "ideal" space, one irreducible to particular place, to achieve a kind of timelessness. Tellingly, though, once Gurnemanz sings his enigmatic line, an orchestral interlude introduces and accompanies the opera's gradual shift in scenery, allowing *sound*'s time to fill the stage's space and to suggest how space can contain constant movement and transformation. As musicologist Viktor Zuckerkandl puts it, "Far from taking us out of space . . . music discloses to us a mode of being of spatiality that, except through music, is accessible only with difficulty and indirectly" (quoted in Plantenga 2001, 78).

"vacillating roulette trickle" of Carson's signature "trundling" tin can, a "vatic . . . ghost . . . heard tripping down the gutter, but never seen, any time there might be trouble in the offing" (Carson 1997, 124), serves as an acoustic alert for civilians on both sides of Belfast's Shankill/Falls Road divide. It is a community Morse code, a "centripetal sound" (Schafer 1977, 54) unifying "thousands" of local ears, and a pedestrian's guide to the city's "unravelled" streetscapes (Carson 1989, "Hamlet" lines 16, 42).

Analyzing these three poets through the lens of sound studies can also redirect critical conversations about contemporary Ulster writing. The refrains so often rehearsed about these poets—Muldoon's supposed slipperiness, Mahon's restless melancholia, and Carson's grim meditations on violence and waste, all anxious reactions to dislocation and loss—must chime alongside acknowledgments of the ways in which these writers try to reclaim place (however partially and provisionally). Their poetry is not only preoccupied with "suspense" and "uncertainty" (Allison 1995, 89), but it is also a rejoinder to this anxiety: an effort to reconnect with place in the face of longstanding division and disorientation. Carson, Mahon, and Muldoon all move beyond mourning long-lost landscapes by bearing ear-witness to local soundscapes and using poetry to exercise political agency.

Moreover, whereas Irish writing is often accused of being mired in nostalgia, these poets are responsive to both the old and the new. Their shared turn to sound does invoke elements of traditional oral culture, but it does not simply reveal a wistful desire to return to that culture; the work also responds to new media technologies like radio and recorded music. Muldoon's poetry, for example, draws equally on his education in bardic story and song and on his love of rock 'n' roll. In his writing, he considers how best to reconcile past and present. Consequently, I suggest that we must turn our ears to Northern literature's "tuning of the world" (Schafer 1977, 1); its strains are often politically productive and can serve as a potential counter to the country's constitutive geographical violence.

Poetic Soundscapes

Although these writers frequently thematize the relationship between sound and place, identifying and investigating important earmarks, their work also mines sound's formal possibilities. Sometimes the poetry echoes environmental sound, as with Carson's efforts to infuse his long-line verse with the cadences of Irish traditional music (particularly the eight-bar reel) and the meandering lines of Belfast pub talk, all of which contribute to his poetry echoing the city of his birth. Elsewhere, poetic sound effects become sources of second-degree sense, provocatively layering latent meanings over a text's manifest themes.

Some critics hold the poetic "phonotext" (G. Stewart 1990, 28) to be an irrationally emotive phenomenon, suggesting that because acoustic devices like rhythm and rhyme move the body (i.e., we spontaneously tap our toes in time with an upbeat tempo), they have much more to do with how we feel than what we think. In *Yeats, the Master of Sound*, for example, Brian Devine (2006, 8) considers Yeats' acoustic poetics to be "an oral art-form rather than a philosophical tract, and an art-form which seeks its denouement in the reader's heart rather than in his mind." This treatment of the heart and mind as distant, disparate entities is blindly (or, rather, deafly) reductive: besides the obvious objection that Yeats is no empty balladeer, sound isn't simply precognitive, and emotion isn't necessarily irrational.[11] In fact, sound is actively meaning-making; sound-signals structure our encounters with the world, and affective responses provide guiding schemas for these encounters.[12] Although poetry rife with sound

11. Robert Frost's notion of the "sound of sense" is instructive here, particularly because Frost has been cited as a major influence on both Paul Muldoon and Derek Mahon. Frost believed that poetry could capture the tones of "living speech" and that its cadences and inflections could in and of themselves convey meaning. In a 1913 letter to his friend John Bartlett, Frost explained, "The best place to get the abstract sound of sense is from voices behind a door that cuts off the words" (quoted in Parini 1999, 134), suggesting that rhythm and sound-pattern are far from semantically subordinate to poetry's lexical content.

12. On this point, see neuroscientist Antonio Damasio's groundbreaking works, *The Feeling of What Happens: Body and Emotion in the Making of Consciousness* (1999) and *Descartes' Error: Emotion, Reason, and the Human Brain* ([1994] 2005). Damasio argues that emotions are brain representations of body states, and that they point our minds in moments of crisis toward ways in which we can re-establish homeostasis. According to Damasio (1999, 39–41), emotions are essential and meaningful; we cannot, he contends, make rational decisions without them.

effects can prompt the critical fear that "the poet is happy to lose some part of agency to the random potentialities of language as sound" (Patke 2008, 282), I argue that this response relies on a false dichotomy between sound and sense. In addition, I propose that poetic sound can be *politically* meaningful; rhythm's associative energies and rhyme's connective force often make worlds collide in surprising and suggestive ways. Muldoon's collections, for instance, use recurring leitmotifs to make connections between far-flung people and places; rhymes that chime from poem to poem (and even from volume to volume) suggest links between disparate contexts even when those links aren't thematically explicit. This strategy resonates throughout Muldoon's work, and it suggests that he too relies on sound to cross borders and build communities.

Although sound, as I have argued, is a temporal phenomenon, and so the acoustic connections developed in poetry are perhaps fleeting, they are nevertheless recursive: poetry haunts our minds precisely *because* of its sounds—because of the mnemonic value of rhythm and rhyme. As Susan Stewart (2002, 104) describes it, "the sound of poetry is heard in the way a promise is heard": as "an action made in speech, in the sense not of something scripted or repeatable but of something that 'happens,' that 'occurs' as an event and can be continually called on, called to mind, in the unfolding present." If poetry's "promise" stems from its repeated returns to its listener, then the relationships it voices linger long after first reading and retain, at least in echoes, their political weight.

Cross-Cultural Counterpoints

Carson, Mahon, and Muldoon are far from the first poets to develop a "sound of sense"; nearly all poetry relies on sound play in some way. However, in this book I investigate what makes the (post-)colonial acoustic of contemporary Northern Irish poets unique.[13] I suggest that Carson, Mahon, and Muldoon's perceptual turn—Carson's "sounding the city,"

13. I am using the term "(post-)colonial" to indicate the vexed political status of Northern Ireland: a largely self-governing British colony that cooperates on some policy areas with the Irish Republic and that is still the scene of vehement nationalist protest.

Mahon's "bearing earwitness," and Muldoon's "becoming opera"—is part of a shared post-partisan politics: a common conviction that poetry can contribute, however modestly, to Northern Ireland's peacebuilding process. This contribution relies on poetry's capacity to tap into forms of community that go beyond physical proximity. In Jahan Ramazani's (2009) words, poetry as a genre can uniquely engineer "rhythmic and sonic coordinations of [geographical] distances" (14); verse can travel on "caravans of sound" (54–55) by compressing "discrepant idioms and soundscapes" (41).

As I have suggested, the fact that sound-signals can cross visual boundaries in a deeply divided Ulster is especially significant. While barricades and "Peace Walls" continue to sever Catholic from Protestant communities, reinforcing tribal belongings, sound's breadth can occasion surprising connections, suggesting that acoustic space may be a breeding ground for unexpected, perhaps even unwelcome, cross-border affinities and affiliations.[14] Community, then, might emerge from common earwitnessing, a possibility that complicates the North's competing cultural exclusivisms. Although sound is sometimes reflective of sectarian tension in the region, particularly during parade season when flutes and lambeg drums commandeer local airwaves, it also transcends this tension in surprising ways, suggesting that communities with precious few connections have common means of relating to place. Shared sound-space makes for a shared sense of homeplace—a sentiment that goes against the grain of the country's mutually exclusive visual cues.

The poets discussed here are invested in highlighting Ulster's characteristic sense-impressions: Carson with his urban sound-signals, Mahon

14. This is not to equate seeing with lack and hearing with plenitude; human beings, after all, have a normative auditory range, and we can sometimes drown out or muffle unpleasant noise. It is, however, to suggest that acoustic space has a qualitatively different scale and scope than visual space, and to wonder what perceptual and emotional possibilities these (undertheorized) differences might provide. See Chapter 7 for a discussion of loanwords that have crossed unbidden between Irish and English, suggesting that the cross-culturalities forged in acoustic space might work against the visual segregation of Catholic and Protestant communities in the North.

and his marine rhythms, and the textures of Muldoon's Moy. However, these local intimacies are supplemented in each poet's work by transnational affiliations, such that community is structured by sympathies both smaller and larger than the nation-state. As Mahon himself once put it, "surrounded as [they are] by . . . what Ferlinghetti called 'the hollering monsters of the imagination of disaster' . . . [Ulster poets must find] voice[s] which, while remaining true to [local] intonations, ha[ve] something to say beyond the shores of Ireland" (quoted in Clark 2006, 154). Indeed, the development of both local communities (e.g., fostering a shared Belfast identity) and "global intimacies" (Brydon 2007, 991) is especially important in Northern Ireland because it suggests the possibility of belonging beyond rival nationalisms (allegiances to the United Kingdom or a united Ireland) and represents a potential step toward lasting peace in the region.

In contemporary Northern Ireland, almost twenty years after the peace process, there has been a resurgence of paramilitary attacks on security and commercial targets as well as increased violence during parades and flag protests. It is therefore crucial to foreground comparatist currents in Irish poetry, a genre sometimes still critiqued as excessively self-regarding.[15] However, it is also important for Northern poets to avoid disengaging from local intonations altogether because the ongoing demands of reconciliation in the region require literature's imaginative input.[16] As Brendan Kennelly (2000, 1105) describes it, "[t]he important thing for Irish poetry now is to be open to all kinds of influences from cultures all over the world. . . . Insularity . . . can lead to the most inflated view of one's self and the most distorted views of others. . . . But an intelligent, vigilant, outward-looking insularity, not obsessed with self-protection, learning from contrast . . . developing the sense of proportion, eager to experience

15. For an elaboration of this critique, see Brendan Kennelly (2000), "Irish Poetry Since Yeats," in David Pierce's *Irish Writing in the Twentieth Century*.

16. See Richard Rankin Russell's (2010) *Poetry and Peace* for an assessment of poetry's potential role in peacebuilding and reconciliation processes in the North. With particular reference to Michael Longley and Seamus Heaney, Rankin Russell carefully evaluates the possible contributions and the necessary limitations of art's place in Northern Irish politics.

difference in whatever shape or form, can be a healthy, productive state for a poet." The poets under study in this book take up Kennelly's posture of "outward-looking insularity," both in their engagement of particular places—the Shankill/Falls Road divide, Antrim's Glengormley, the townlands of Collegeland—and in their search for common ground beyond their country's bounds.

As an example, Carson writes other wars into dialogue with the Troubles: a mention of Belfast's Balaclava Street occasions a meditation on Crimea's Battle of Balaclava. Similarly, Muldoon's local histories often collide with those of indigenous America by way of a mutual *Meeting the British* (the title of his 1987 collection). Ramazani (2009, 58) refers to this phenomenon as "translocation," a concept connoting the relationship between local affinities and global solidarities. "Translocal" poetry, Ramazani argues, involves imaginative travel that enables close relationships between "discrepant topographies" (58). Ramazani uses Muldoon's poetry as one of his literary case studies, suggesting that Muldoon works across boundaries of place, tribe, and ethnicity and takes advantage of poetry's "remarkable freedom of movement and affiliative connection" (40–41): its ability to juxtapose "discrepant idioms and soundscapes, tropes and subgenres" (63) and to suggest how "cross-cultural vectors" can "fuse . . . jangle . . . [or] counterpoint one another" (4). These "counterpoints" might be called communities-in-sympathy: groups in political or emotional proximity even if at a physical distance. As Ramazani's rhetoric suggests ("soundscapes," "jangle," "counterpoint"), although sound serves as a local tie that binds, it is also the basis of these long-distance relationships. After all, as McLuhan and Carpenter (1960, 69) remind us, "[t]he universe is the potential map of auditory space"; global intimacies demand the soundscape's potentially "boundless" shape and scope. Acoustic space, in other words, can accommodate belongings far beyond those the eye can see.

As I argue in Chapters 2 and 3, for Ciaran Carson, close listening enables a fresh approach to a "Troubled" Belfast: an approach that allows him to rekindle belonging in the face of violence's visual violations. After documenting the conflict's "demolitions"—landmarks that are there one day, gone the next, "a fresh breeze sweep[ing] through the gap" (Carson

1989, "Question Time" 57)—Carson develops in their stead a detailed Belfast soundscape. This strategy suggests that when the eye is no longer a reliable guide to place, the ear may become a kind of compass. Carson's aural cues, including the recurring clatter of his cautionary tin can, often transcend community divides, making an illegible Belfast audible to Protestant and Catholic civilians alike and reshaping sectarian space as a mutually immersive auditory field. Moreover, having expressed interest in how the tempi of local tales and tunes can move people together in time—the experience, as Carson (1986a, 3) puts it, of "[a] room puls[ing] like a diaphragm," "punters . . . nodding joyfully into their pints"—he experiments with how this hospitality might take poetic form. His signature long line, for instance, is indebted to the rhythms of the eight-bar reel and is shaped by the accentuated, articulated playing common to traditional tunes rather than by regular poetic meter. This style lends his verse an irresistibly kinetic vigor.[17] Carson's (1986a, 4) lines leave "whole rooms jumping"; they become acoustic gathering places for Belfast locals—civilians on both sides of the political divide—and for his own literary earwitnesses. Carson is himself a sort of Belfast *seanchaí*: a yarn-spinner who borrows the time signatures of song and story as community-building tools.

Similarly, Derek Mahon combats Ulster's geographical violence by turning to the ear. Like Carson, he develops an acoustic phenomenology, but as I argue in Chapters 4 and 5, Mahon aims specifically at an *ecological* intimacy. As a non-Unionist Protestant growing up in a restive Belfast, Mahon (2002, 109) considered himself a political outsider on home turf and adopted a "'plague on both your houses' attitude" to the conflict. Thus feeling that he is beyond the bounds of human community, Mahon explores the possibility of connecting with place in a more fundamental way: the embodied relationship of the subject to the so-called "object world." In particular, Mahon adopts a poetic posture that Adrienne Janus (2007, 183) calls a "liminality of listening," leaving most of his speakers visually marginal yet within critical earshot of local scenes. This posture allows the poet

17. See the conversations with Carson documented in Neil Corcoran's (1992, 217) "One Step Forward, Two Steps Back."

to bear earwitness to the island's otherwise "mute phenomena" (the title of one of his early poems). His collections variously overhear and resound "the sob story / of a stone in the road" in County Mayo (Mahon 2011, "The Mayo Tao" lines 13–14) and the cries of mushrooms in a derelict Wexford shed. More restless than the firmly urban Carson, Mahon's soundscapes range both Northern Ireland and the Irish Republic; his poems name a series of specific spaces (Derry, Donegal, Portrush) to which his speakers commit their senses. Ultimately, this approach lends itself to an ecocritical politics, with the poet protesting the ways in which both the "white noise of sectarian hate" (Mahon 2011, "Northern Star" line 22) and the "noisy knowledge" (Mahon 1997b, XIX line 40) of global capitalism mute the sounds of local landscapes. Mahon (2002, 119) is therefore a committed acoustic ecologist: he investigates how surround sound provides us with a sense of place and uses his own bardic music to advocate on behalf of sustainable soundscapes.

Of the three poets I discuss in this book, Paul Muldoon has the widest range; his work is the most persistently global in scope. Perhaps taking a cue from McLuhan and Carpenter (1960, 69), who theorize the soundscape as a sphere "without fixed boundaries," Muldoon reimagines community in acoustic space, charting connections that transcend the territory—connections that begin in Belfast and end at the Rio Grande.[18] In other words, Muldoon advances "translocalism" against local tribalism. Although critics have typically neglected Muldoon's four opera libretti and have largely dismissed his songwriting as a diversionary hobby, Chapters 6 and 7 examine these works in detail, proposing Muldoon's musical engagements as pedagogical primers for his poetry. The operas and songs literally sound out cross-cultural connections, allowing hybridity's harmonies and dissonances to chime loud and clear, and the poems follow suit on the page. Muldoon treats his volumes as elaborate echo-chambers, borrowing musical devices like recurring leitmotifs and textured vocals and deploying them as poetic tactics. For instance, just as opera's so-called "reminiscence

18. See "The More a Man Has the More a Man Wants" from Muldoon's 1983 collection *Quoof.*

motifs" or "melody memories" resonate throughout a score and gradually accrue associative force, so too do Muldoon's collections carry forward whispers of poems past. These ringings and re-ringings occasion unexpected connections: characters who seem far from intuitively linked (such as the native Irishman and the visiting Apache in "The More a Man Has the More a Man Wants," Muldoon 1983) often prove to be intimately in tune. Apropos of Elmer Kennedy-Andrews' (2008, 2) assertion that "[t]he history of Northern Ireland is bloody testimony to the trouble that arises when discourses of 'home,' 'belonging' and 'nation' are linked to territory and bounded place," Muldoon's sound effects work against sectarianism by forging communities-in-sympathy, often based on proximate colonial histories, in sound-space's potentially boundless sphere. Like the libretti and the lyrics, the poems work to chime together distant people and places, gradually building global intimacies.

Coda

After acknowledging the value of poetic post-partisanship, this argument's optimism must be curtailed; literary gestures toward reconciliation, although culturally vital, cannot defuse flag protests or resolve Stormont stalemates. Carson, Mahon, and Muldoon's poetry is marked by this recognition: their work is palliative, but far from utopian. As Elmer Kennedy-Andrews (2005a, 116) says of Muldoon, his concept of community is "a balancing act on the border between rootedness and disintegration," and this applies equally to Carson and Mahon, who similarly mark the limits of their self-made solidarities. In each case, these limits are sounded out, such that skips, scratches, and static check the poetry's acoustic conviviality.

The poetic soundscape—both the tenor and the vehicle of the writers' political sentiments—is at once a sphere of possibility and the place where possibility's limits are made audible. Carson's occasional lapses from long-line lyricism into a staccato stutter, for example, register the ongoing effects of cultural trauma. Poetry alone, these lapses suggest, cannot counter essentialism and exclusivism, and the fear and loathing prompted by riots and attacks are always in danger of being co-opted by oppositional identity politics.

Muldoon (1987b) is similarly modest about what poetry can achieve in the face of violent conflict; his "7, Middagh Street," from *Meeting the British*, proclaims that "history's a twisted root / with art its small, translucent fruit / and never the other way round" (lines 78–79). This perhaps explains why each of his operas approaches harmonious cross-cultural community before swerving into dissonance and division. For example, the band of misfits in Muldoon and Hagen's (2003) *Vera of Las Vegas*—a pair of reformed paramilitaries on the run alongside an assortment of America's "others," including an African American transvestite and a chorus of costumed Pequod Native Americans—sings its way toward the comforts of a common "auditory topography" (Carter 2001) but cannot remain immune to conflict's political pressures. Taco, one of the paramilitaries, backs out of his wedding to Vera at the eleventh hour and is returned to Northern Ireland, where he is once again subjected to the conflict's rigidly binary terms: Protestant and Catholic, us and them, perpetrator and victim. The return to conflict is signified by sound: the curtain falls on the jarring tones of torture, including the ominous ticking of an MI-5 parcel bomb, Vera's far-away "wail[s]," and "the judder of blood in [Taco's] ears" brought on by his interrogators' repeated "slaps" (Muldoon and Hagen 2003).

Ultimately, Mahon, Muldoon, and Carson all mediate between the current realities of identity conflict and the possibilities of future community; they use sound as both a salve for and a symptom of trauma. In this book I eavesdrop on the poetry's political efforts and tune into its desires for stable peace in the still-divided North.

2

CIARAN CARSON

Sounding the City

Prelude: From Sight to Sound

The 1989 prose poem "Question Time" suggests perhaps *the* animating impulse of Ciaran Carson's work: violence as it conditions the city or, rather, violence as it conditions locals' experiences of the city. The poem, like much of Carson's writing, is insistently phenomenological; it elevates the speculative perceptions of the pedestrian while advising us not to trust the map's would-be panoptical power. This perspective seems particularly well suited to Carson's "Troubled" (and "post-Troubled," if there is such a thing) Belfast, as sectarian conflict, the grim progeny of colonial conquest, continually unmakes and defamiliarizes the cityscape, causing its spaces to be "sucked back into nothingness by the rewind button" ("Question Time" 58).[1] As "Question Time" suggests, Belfast's landmarks—from the now-demolished Grand Central Hotel, once a favorite paramilitary target, to the pizza parlors and nightclubs that fleetingly populate the city's streets—are contingent, potentially temporary, and alarmingly open to

1. Carson, a lifelong Belfast resident, has written extensively (almost obsessively) about the Troubles in Northern Ireland throughout most of his early volumes and addresses the subject more circuitously in his recent work. In an interview with Elmer Kennedy-Andrews, Carson (2009a, 17) comments that "[the country's] fractured history keeps impinging on what I write. *For All We Know*, for example, began as some kind of fictional love story, an attempt to put the war behind me, but before long elements of various conflicts, including our local row, found their way into the poems. It seems inescapable."

being "swallowed in the maw of time and trouble" (63). Violence, according to Carson, turns homeplace into an uncanny shape-shifter. One moment Gass' Bicycle Shop is there, intact, a familiar street-side scene, and in the blink of an eye it is gone, "a fresh breeze sweep[ing] through the gap" (63). The pattern of palliation and interruption in "Question Time" also points to this perceptual uncertainty. The sense of promise extended by its italicized passages—George Benn's sketch of a thriving Victorian city, the easy familiarity with place suggested by the speaker's comforting clichés—is immediately curtailed by doubt: even if "*I know this place like the back of my hand*," the probability of future "wounds, sutures, and excisions" hinders present efforts to keep the cityscape neatly in view (63). This is precisely, Carson writes, why conflict forecloses cartography; maps simply cannot keep pace with Belfast's additions and deletions, with newly minted roadblocks and freshly shorn blitz sites.

As "Question Time" progresses, Carson becomes more and more frustrated with maps' apparent presumptuousness and their claims to "contain" the city, and his figurative language slides into the frank pronouncement that "[m]aps and street directories are suspect" (58). This sentiment, one of the volume's leitmotifs, is later refigured as a tautological tagline: "[only t]he city," Carson (1989, 69) quips in "Revised Version," "[can be] a map of the city." Belfast, in other words, is insistently conditional, and this insecurity makes a mockery of the map's indicative mood.

Several critics have recognized Carson's efforts to deconstruct official city blueprints and have highlighted his conviction that "maps . . . avoid the moment" (Carson 1989, "Question Time" 58) and his counsel that "everything will be revised" (57). Neal Alexander (2010, 62), for instance, argues that Carson's approach to the cityscape is uniquely rhizomatic; Belfast's built environment "metamorphos[es] in response to bombings and demolition, decay and redevelopment," and Carson's poetry suggests that the map's aerial perspective ignores the movements of life at street level.[2]

2. On this point, see also Jonathan Allison (1995, 93), whose "'Everything Provisional'" approaches Carson's (1989) *Belfast Confetti* linguistically, suggesting that Carson's repeated use of the modal auxiliary evokes the city's conditionality (its "violent,

However, most responses to Carson's work claim his poetry as a map of another kind—the city seen, as it were, through the eyes of the flâneur. In "A City of the Mind" Giulio Bonacci (2001, 5) casts Carson as a furtive rewriter of city plans, going so far as to suggest that "the one image that best represents Carson's poetry . . . [is] the map, but a map which . . . more closely resembles a labyrinth than a street-plan." I would argue, to the contrary, that this kind of analysis problematically oversimplifies the poetry and that Carson's peculiar affection for the temporal and the experiential points to something far more profound about sensation and lived space. In fact, Carson's work makes the rather radical point that conflict severs seeing from believing. As Carson (1989) observes in "Question Time," when the cityscape amounts to "holes knocked into holes," and its staple visual spaces—"ramps, barricades, diversions, Peace Lines"—are liminal at best, the "little piggy" navigating homeplace inevitably feels lost (61). It is, therefore, not only the map that cannot be trusted—the eye itself is likewise suspect.

Eric Falci (2012) refers to this phenomenon as Carson's "splintering visuals" (123), explaining that the poetry toggles between "the overhead view of a map and the situated view of a set of eyes" (127) to deconstruct the stability of both perspectives. However, I argue that even though Carson's poetry overturns visual orientation, it offers another means (albeit partial and provisional) of understanding space: sound. In other words, when one cannot quite believe one's eyes, the ear's possibilities might be extended; Carson accordingly deconstructs the "street directory" and bears earwitness to the city in its stead. Throughout his volumes, he takes pains to evoke a Belfast soundscape: a semiotics of sound with which locals navigate the otherwise unstable city. These efforts suggest that he thinks of place in acoustic space and of being *in* place as a sonic state.[3]

---

unknowable, ever-changing, self-destructive but also self-regenerating [capacity]"), and John Goodby (2009, 69), who describes Carson as heir to the "loco-descriptive" poetic tradition: a phenomenologically engaged literary model that "exploits the links between the rhythms of walking, thinking, and writing."

3. Although the concept of sound-space is so central to Carson's poetry, it has gone surprisingly unnoticed in relevant scholarship. However, a handful of critics do deserve

More Than Meets the Eye: Belfast as "Demolition City"

During the Troubles, much of Belfast was carved up into sectarian outposts: enclaves marked as "no-go zones" for the "other side." These enclaves were (and are still) typically signaled by insistent sectarian symbols: flags, political murals, paramilitary graffiti, painted curbstones, and so on. Even today, the sheer amount of spray paint on Belfast's walls, both in the form of elaborate political murals (makeshift war memorials, renderings of community martyrs, or calls to arms) and more cryptic paramilitary acronyms and slogans (RIRA, PIRA, INLA, UYM, UDF, UFF[4]), is perhaps the city's most striking feature. The graffiti serves as a strident visual schematic of the conflict, and it manages to militarize otherwise benign architectural spaces; even neighborhood trash bins are habitually claimed in the Queen's name.

In an effort to defuse violence in some of Belfast's interface areas, so-called "Peace Walls" were erected throughout the city, most of which remain intact today (BIP 2011). These walls amount to massive, menacing barriers, some climbing as high as thirteen meters, that sever shared spaces (including a public park) and curtail former pedestrian travel

credit for ably initiating the kind of exploration I am undertaking. In his contribution to Nicholas Allen and Aaron Kelly's *The Cities of Belfast*, for instance, Alan Gillis (2003) comments on the ways in which Carson complicates seeing (according to Gillis, it's impossible to "see what's before your eyes" in Carson's work because it "turbinates with the relativity and contradictions of multi-perspectivism" [183]). In *Writing Home*, Elmer Kennedy-Andrews (2008, 218) identifies Carson's complementary interest in the "heard world"—a treatment of Belfast, as Eamonn Hughes (2009, 103) describes it, as a "clamorous place." Similarly, Kathleen McCracken (1995, 365) briefly argues in "Ciaran Carson: Unravelling the Conditional, Mapping the Provisional" that Carson's poetry develops a sort of "aural sign system": his "haunting sounds and gestures, the innuendo of pub talk" and "the 'punctuation' of machine gun fire, interrogations, conversation."

4. These acronyms stand for, respectively, the Real Irish Republican Army, the Provisional IRA, the Irish National Liberation Army (all Republican paramilitary groups), the Ulster Young Militants, the Ulster Defense Force, and the Ulster Freedom Fighters (three of their Loyalist counterparts). By 2015, most of these organizations had agreed to either a ceasefire or complete disarmament, although several splinter groups have refused decommissioning and some, including RIRA, are still fully operative.

patterns (Boal 2002, 693). Similarly, during the Troubles, many Belfast through-streets were turned into cul-de-sacs so as to avoid potentially violent cross-community contact. This strategy disturbed pedestrian life, feeding walkers back into their own neighborhoods (and their own political, ideological, and religious milieux) rather than allowing for the unregulated wanderings and chance encounters typically thought to define city life. Belfast's urban planners even decided to build the M1 motorway as a de facto buffer zone between rival communities—and although "[a] wall, in time, can be dismantled . . . how in the world do you overcome six lanes of traffic?" (Patterson 2006, 63).

Edna Longley (1994) adopts this view of the city as a "tribal map" (90) in her survey of modern Belfast writing. She links the city's visual stratification to pervasive literary representations of its "inhospitality" (88). Longley assembles a litany of adjectives from the likes of Michael McLaverty, Louis MacNeice, John Hewitt, Derek Mahon, and John Montague to suggest the seeming ubiquity of this sentiment—"the force of [the writer and the city's] mutual rejection" (88). This force points, in turn, to the lived impact of the cityscape's geographical sectarianism: Belfast's factional outposts, stamped with paramilitary trademarks, betray comfortable visual belonging. As heir to the literary tradition that Longley describes, Carson takes the optics of his city's unhomeliness very much to heart. His poetry remarks repeatedly on conflict's visual markers. Walls scrawled with tags, sometimes whitewashed but ever rewritten anew, appear throughout his work: "[L]ike the menu, everything's chalked up, and every now and then, wiped clean" (Carson 1989, "Barfly" line 7). In "Queen's Gambit," from *Belfast Confetti*, Carson (1989) argues that these sectarian symbols leave the city irreparably stratified and sometimes entirely inscrutable. The poem's Belfast is an urban palimpsest; it is written and rewritten until unreadable. "Like the names on a school desk," Belfast's graffiticized messages are "carved into one another till they're indecipherable" (Carson 1989, "Queen's Gambit" line 34). Indeed, "Queen's Gambit" is centrally concerned with failures of representation, including the city's own—a chord first struck by the narrator's ironic misrecollection of the classic Bing Crosby lyric, "It's Easy to Remember (And So Hard to Forget)." The converse, "it's so hard to remember, and so easy to forget" (line 33) the conflict's casualties, seems coldly counterintuitive, but when so many people require memorializing, new epitaphs overwrite the old into obscurity, coloring the city's walls a uniform grey. The city's would-be commemorators, in other words, face "that frottage effect again" (line 35): their competing narratives of the conflict write the city into virtual illegibility.

Carson's seemingly cavalier comparison of graffiti artists to schoolboys defacing their desks highlights a desensitization to conflict—the perception that violence has become as routine as the rote childhood mornings described in his "Slate Street School"[5]—and a conviction that the cityscape itself is a casualty of war: it is "carved [up]" (Carson 1989, "Queen's Gambit" line 34) until "whole segments of the map . . . fall off" (line 38). This gruesome "carving" is also suggested by the poem's often startling enjambment. Its lines are wrenched forcefully from their syntactical pairs: "grained / And blackened" (lines 35–36); "jittering / With numerals and flak" (lines 37–38).

Belfast's visual impenetrability in "Queen's Gambit" is echoed in the volume's subsequent "Schoolboys and Idlers of Pompeii." As Carson (1989, 52) writes in "Schoolboys," "At times, it seems that every inch of Belfast has been written-on, erased, and written-on again: messages, curses, political imperatives, but mostly names, or nicknames—Robbo, Mackers, Scoot, Fra—sometimes litanized obsessively on every brick of a gable wall . . . cancelling each other out in their bid to be remembered." Again, here, competing claims to the city's spaces cancel one another out, producing a textual excess that leaves the city visually indecipherable and repels any sense of belonging for the pedestrian passerby. These passages reveal Carson's misgivings about things seen; treating Belfast as a text ripe for the reading produces only disorientation and disappointment. Carson ultimately suggests in his poetry that forms of feeling at home based on comforting visual familiarity are simply unavailable to the denizens of a "Troubled" city.

5. "Slate Street School," from Carson's (1987) *The Irish for No*, begins, "Back again. Day One. Fingers blue with cold. I joined the lengthening queue. / Roll call. Then inside: chalk dust and iced milk, the smell of watered ink" (lines 1–2).

"Queen's Gambit" also reminds us of Carson's (1989) fascination with the foibles of the map; the line "[w]ith so many foldings and unfoldings, whole segments of the map have fallen off" (line 38) undermines the document's "bird's eye view" pretences to authoritative representation. Carson's work often concerns itself with the *history* of cartography in Ireland, linking the practice to British imperial intervention and thereby justifying his antipathy to the blueprint's will-to-power over place. His volumes often treat colonial cartography as a kind of foundational trauma, with maps circulating as disciplinary documents and measures of an empire's would-be mastery of subaltern space.[6]

In "Revised Version," Carson (1989) stages cartography as a show of imperial force: "Improve, wipe out, begin again, imagine, change: the map appended to the Parliamentary Report of 1859 *shows very clearly the improvements effected by the making of Victoria Street and Corporation Street, which are laid down on the map over the old lanes and small streets, as follows*; so we follow the ghosts of Forest Lane, Weigh-House Lane, Back Lane, Elbow Lane, Blue Bell Entry, Stone Cutter's Entry, Quay Lane, Ireland's Entry, names that seem to spring up from an invented past" (68). Citing parliamentary records, Carson casts official cartography as a kind of calculated blindness—a bid to sever past from present. New roads with resonantly imperial names like "Victoria Street" and "Corporation Street" are superimposed on the city's "old lanes and small streets." Belfast's streets under erasure, victims of symbolic violence, are today but ghosts; the likes of "Weigh-House Lane," "Elbow Lane," and "Stone Cutter's Entry" remain ellipses, long excised from national narratives.

Also in "Revised Version," Carson (1989) mentions documents from 1680, 1685, 1823, 1851, 1859, and 1875: dates that suggest William Petty's 1655–56 Down Survey and the nineteenth-century Ordnance Survey as the poem's historical points of reference.[7] The Down Survey, which followed

6. This is a common conceit in the Irish canon, thematized perhaps most famously by Brian Friel's (1981) play *Translations*.

7. See J. H. Andrews' (2002) *A Paper Landscape* for a very thorough history of both ordnance surveys, and see Sir Charles Close's ([1926] 1969) *The Early Years of the Ordnance Survey* for details of the nineteenth-century project.

Cromwell's conquest of Ireland, charted lands forcibly confiscated from Irish Catholic holders and redistributed to English and Scottish Protestant settlers: a quite literal effort to "unhome" colonial subjects. One hundred fifty years later, the Liverpool-mandated Ordnance Survey, a long-term project spearheaded for its first twenty-six years by Major General Thomas Colby, moved through local territory, with British surveyors redrawing borders and de-Gaelicizing Irish place names. This project literally shifted the ground between locals' feet, strategically alienating natives from once-familiar visual spaces. In fact, Colby explicitly framed the survey as a cartographic expression of the newly minted United Kingdom: a geographical enactment of the 1800 Act of Union and the revocation of Irish Home Rule.[8] Contemporary maps of Northern Ireland, Carson points out, are similarly coercive. Jails, for instance, are intentionally excluded from city blueprints; they are left as ominous "blank zones" in service of state security (Carson 1989, "Intelligence" 81). Although many critics read poems like "Revised Version" as calls to subaltern street-level *re*-mapping, asserting that "maps function for Carson paradoxically both as forms of imposition to be resisted and as the means by which such resistance can be effected" (Alexander 2010, 61), I argue instead that these poems demand a clean perceptual break. In other words, the cartographic trauma that "Revised Version" mourns and memorializes requires a complete sensory reorientation; its treatment of sight sets the stage for Carson's turn to sound.

Above all else, it is contemporary sectarian conflict—the violent legacy of imperial intervention—that most clearly heralds the epistemological

8. The extent to which the survey willfully undertook strategies of anglicization has been a matter of critical controversy. In *A Paper Landscape*, Andrews (2002) suggests that the survey's officers sought primarily to standardize place names. This observation led Edna Longley (1985) to accuse Brian Friel of over-editorializing historical events in an effort to postcolonialize Ireland's past. Friel, firing back at Longley, criticized her for an overreliance on the objectivity of history, arguing instead for the coexistence of multiple interpretive histories (Friel, Andrews, and Barry 1983, 118). Ultimately, the survey's political aims likely fell somewhere between standardization and de-Gaelicization. Intentionality aside, many Gaelic place names either disappeared or were actively suppressed during the course of British imperial intervention in Ireland (see Smyth 2001, 51).

exhaustion of the visual and compels Carson's compensatory earwitnessing. In many of his poems, Carson counters the axiom "seeing is believing" by arguing that there is always potentially more (or less) to the city than meets the eye. In "Gate," also from *Belfast Confetti*, Carson (1989) offers a literal example of the city's illegibility: he holds wayward flak responsible for *Terminus* Boutique's sign appearing as "*e minus*" when the poet-speaker passes by the shop (lines 1–2). Likewise, the *Belfast Telegraph* building's clock has been stopped in its tracks by "last week's . . . explosion" (line 7), and it now marks only the time of its own malfunction. Once again, conflict wrenches a formerly reliable signifier from its signified and unsettles the cityscape's visual cues. The poem's formal economy also repeats this dissociative logic. Word pairs that might otherwise make neat couplets are pulled apart and distance-rhymed, such that "flak" and "askew" very nearly fade from memory before chiming with "track" and "through." These pairs also point *semantically* to the "contingency and provisionality" of place (Carson 1989, "Revised Version" 67):[9] "track" and "through," which read as declarative directives (paths to pursue, ways to get from A to B), are qualified by the evasive maneuvers demanded by wayward "flak" and security gates hanging ominously "askew." The speaker in "Gate" also admits that it is difficult to keep track of paramilitary attacks; his concession suggests the banality of the decades-long conflict. At the heart of the poem, then, is the absolute immanence of violence: the city can (and does) change in the blink of an eye. Its streetscapes are frequently left awry by roadside explosions. This uncertainty in turn collapses optic (and the map's panoptic) logic; even the watchful eye, it seems, is foiled by the city's self-consumption. As Carson (1989) puts it elsewhere, "Belfast . . .

9. Notably, Carson's use of the word "provisional," beyond suggesting Belfast's perpetual demolition and (sometimes) reconstruction, also conjures the specter of the Provisional IRA (the "Provos"), one of the more active Republican paramilitary splinter groups. Carson (1989) makes this point outright in "The Mouth" with his use of violently halting syntax to herald a dismembered body and to emphasize provisionality's ominous double meaning: "There was this head had this mouth he kept shooting off. Unfortunately. / It could have been worse for us than it was for him. Provisionally" (lines 1–2).

swallow[s itself] up . . . in its intestine war" ("Brick" 75), and the spectator comes "[i]n waking life [to] expect streets which are not there" ("Revised Version" 66).

"Gate" is not the only poem in which Carson makes this point; conflict's unnerving power over the shape-shifting city is one of his most insistent themes. He perpetually keeps violence in view in his poetry, staging scene after violent scene—army checkpoints, car bombs, pubs blown to bits—and relentlessly writing wasteland over former cityscape. The cumulative weight of these moments normalizes violence, and in a piece of sinister shorthand, Carson (1989) christens Belfast a "demolition city" ("Schoolboys and Idlers of Pompeii" 54, "Intelligence" 82). This repetition also enforces for the reader a suspicion of the seen, as one comes to expect the almost immediate deconstruction (or simply destruction) of any sight described. Carson's (2001) *Selected Poems*, in which many of these "war poems" are collected, seems to be structured according to this pattern of consolation and disruption. The anthologized excerpts from 1987's *The Irish for No*, for instance, juxtapose the unusually lyric passage concluding "Whatever Sleep It Is" with the stark reminder of Belfast's self-destructiveness in "Belfast Confetti":

> And the milkman looks up, momentarily
> Amazed at curtains, wings, gusting from the attic window . . .
>
> . . . .
>
> Tomorrow yawns ahead
> With routine promises; tomorrow, after all, he will be free. (Carson 1987, "Whatever Sleep It Is" lines 47–50)
>
> **Belfast Confetti**
> Suddenly as the riot squad moved in, it was raining exclamation marks,
> Nuts, bolts, nails, car-keys. A fount of broken type. (Carson 1989, "Belfast Confetti" lines 1–2)

The "suddenly" that begins "Belfast Confetti" is sudden indeed; we are thrown into a raid *in medias res*, which is a hard left turn from the previous poem's meditative mood. The promise extended by the line "tomorrow, after all, he will be free" is quickly curtailed by the trappings of conflict:

explosions, machine-gun fire, and the poem's eponymous "Belfast confetti"—the "nuts, bolts, and nails" lacing paramilitary bombs as makeshift shrapnel. The opening stanza of "Belfast Confetti" obliterates the possibility of reading the city. The milkman rubs his bleary eyes and boom! Typeface litters the smouldering streets. This suggests violence's capacity to make strange once-familiar sights; Crimea Street, for instance, which the poet-speaker knows to be a throughway, here ominously turns out to be a dead end. The passage's own punctuation reinforces this theme: Carson's constant cataloguing—"Nuts, bolts, nails, car-keys" and "Balaclava, Raglan, Inkerman, Odessa"—makes for a telegraphic, breathless sense of his speaker's frenetic back and forth, and the "burst of rapid fire," which appears on the page as an interruptive ellipsis, leaves the reader hanging while the speaker dodges gunshots. The only nameable objects in "Belfast Confetti" and the only referents that don't slip from the speaker's grasp after the city becomes illegible are the war's ubiquitous commercial trappings: brand names that become all-too-familiar facts of Belfast life (e.g., Saracen tanks and Makrolon face shields [line 8]).

Notably, the poem's self-referentiality—its troping of orthography as weaponry—seems to suggest its lineation as a sort of schematic city grid. If a hyphenated line, for instance, stands in for a firing riot squad, then the phrase "I know this labyrinth so well—Balaclava, Raglan, Inkerman, Odessa Street" (Carson 1989, "Belfast Confetti" line 6) finds the speaker cornered by advancing forces between Balaclava and Odessa. If a full stop represents a roadblock, the speaker's efforts to escape to safety are twice rerouted in the poem's second line.

However, this legend, which acts as a kind of cipher for the passage's and the city's decryption, does eventually fall short. Once the poem draws attention to itself as a graphic object, the reader begins to monitor its symbols almost paranoically, obsessing over what to make, for instance, of the dash between "car" and "keys." This red herring allows "Belfast Confetti" to tacitly repeat the injunction of "Question Time"—"No, don't trust maps"—by calling even its own efforts at cartographic orientation into question. The poem, in other words, draws attention to its methods of manipulation and its modes of surveillance, eventually leaving the reader suspiciously self-conscious of these tactics. This enforced scepticism dashes readers' hopes that Carson will re-map the city. Despite critics' libidinal investments in the contrary, he is no kindly Virgil or guiding geographical buffer against Belfast's chaos.

In her reading of "Belfast Confetti," to take just one example of such an investment, Fran Brearton (2001, 385) suggests that "[t]he city is mapped symbolically through hyphens, thus . . . restoring the depth to the inked line. . . . This is the map of Belfast . . . as shorthand or symbols . . . as a symbolic map of the landscape which is also a map of poetry itself." Contrary to this analysis, I argue that the poem extends the possibility of the map only to withdraw this possibility; it leaves the reader, alongside its speaker, facing a "fusillade of question marks" (Carson 1989, "Belfast Confetti" line 9). This is not to say that the poet-speaker has no desire to read the city. In fact, if the poem is considered symptomatically, the failure of visual orientation—"I know this labyrinth so well . . . Why can't I escape?"—is a source of frustration and even devastation. Carson's matter-of-fact pronouncements that "maps don't *mean*" are haunted by the hope that they might.

Ultimately, Carson's city is fundamentally illegible: it is constantly "revised" by violence and, for the long-time local, visually compromised by what once was. In a space so often destroyed and rebuilt, the remembrance of things past makes of the city a *trompe d'oeil* where what is seen can never quite be believed. For Carson's speakers, Belfast is a place where the past haunts the present and where streets and shops are the stuff of memory. His poems repeatedly trope his own childhood landscape as a sort of hallucinatory phantom limb: "I know this place like the back of my hand, except / My hand is cut off at the wrist" (Carson 1987, "33333" lines 8–9).[10] In "Question Time" (Carson 1989) he points to this haunting

10. This trope also alludes to the Red Hand of Ulster, an image that still adorns the region's flag. The Red Hand is a symbol of claim to Ulster province: it is based on the myth that Ulster's kingship was decided by a boat race in which victory went to the first hand to touch shore. One potential king, seeing that he was close to losing the race, cut off his hand and threw it to shore. His sacrifice and triumph supposedly reflected his true love of Ulster. The Red Hand, then, is the bloodied hand of embattled victory. Carson's (1999b) "Nine Hostages" explicitly references the Red Hand ("I cut my hand off at the wrist and

when the narrator takes a disorienting "spin" down once-familiar streets: "Where I remember rows of houses, factories, there is recent wasteland, broken bricks, chickweed, chain-link fencing. Eventually I find a new road I never knew existed—or is it an old street deprived of all its landmarks?—which leads into the Springfield Road. Familiar territory now, well, almost, for going down the Kashmir Road into Bombay Street—burned out in '68, some new houses there—I come to the other side of the Peace Line, which now backs on to St Gall's School—still there, graffiticized, wire mesh on the windows, but still the same, almost" (60–61). The repeated "almost" in the passage marks a traumatic break from what once was, and yet former landmarks hover spectrally over the scene. Its speaker turns down a road that could either be newly built or, uncannily, an "old street deprived of all its landmarks."

It is important to note that "Question Time" takes place where the primarily Protestant Shankill meets the Catholic Falls Road: one of Belfast's most hotly contested interface spaces. As Carson (1989) describes it elsewhere in the poem, these two roads "joined together as unhappy Siamese twins, one sporadically and mechanically beating the other round the head" (59)—a beating to which Carson bore witness as a youngster from his nearby childhood home. The volatility of this joining, which is suggested by the area's provocatively named Kashmir Street (analogizing Belfast to another long-disputed territory), is marked by the rapidity with which the community's landmarks are overturned; the poem's "recent wasteland, broken bricks" testify to the neighborhood's latest clashes.

Although the theme of defamiliarization in "Question Time" conveys the city's profound insecurity, with any recognizable markers immediately qualified by a shaky "almost," it also takes a crucial (and heretofore critically unremarked) second step: it deconstructs eyewitnessing as a framework for objectively apprehending the world. The city at war—a

threw it at the shore" [line 1]), as does his "Bloody Hand" ("Was it the left hand / Hacked off at the wrist and thrown to the shores of Ulster?" [Carson 1989, lines 6–7]). Carson's frequent allusions to the Red Hand bring its mythology to bear on current claims to contested territory; Ulster is still subject to political tugs of war between Unionists and Nationalists and between the United Kingdom and the Republic of Ireland.

space of absolute contingency—demands a break from equations of sight with moments of insight; Carson suggests in his poetry that seeing can no longer mean transparently understanding space.

A Phenomenology of Sound: Carson's "Ragged Chorus"

Because Carson is less concerned with the status of the city itself than with the experience of being *in* the city and the effects of this interaction with place, he is keen to advocate a perceptual turn in light of the eye's failings. When alienated from lived geography, Carson seeks another means of feeling at home and therefore proposes a phenomenological alternative: encountering the environment by way of the ear. Carson's poems are carefully attuned to their sonic surroundings; when deprived of visual cues, his speakers often apprehend place in acoustic space. Jean-Luc Nancy's (2007, trans. from 2002) sense of sound's *becoming*—his argument that "visual presence is already there, available, before I see it, whereas sonorous presence *arrives* . . . and propagates throughout the entire body something of its effects" (14)—is especially relevant to Carson's work. Although the poet-speaker's eye expects enduring landmarks and is disoriented by their destruction and decay, his ear has long been attuned to fleeting auditory cues. In other words, the soundscape is always already in motion, so it is poised to accommodate the "demolition city's" kinesis.

James Joyce's work, especially in *Ulysses* and *Finnegans Wake*, is an important literary precursor to Carson's urban "placelore." Joyce's characters very often navigate a shape-shifting Dublin by way of sonic signals, especially street sounds, advertising jingles, and barroom buzz. The famous "Sirens" episode in *Ulysses*, for example, is an aural pastiche of ballads, synecdochic sounds (e.g., money jingling, boots creaking) standing in for various characters, and snippets of conversation, and it treats sound as a crucial conduit between Bloom and his surroundings. Carson (2009a, 20) has himself highlighted Joyce's influence on his poetry, suggesting in an interview that he borrows the strategy of "sounding the city" from *Ulysses*: "Joyce has always interested me, as much for his rendering of the music of the city—sounds of traffic, printing shops, cutlery in restaurants, songs, fragments of speech—as for any overarching narrative, more *Ulysses*, perhaps, than *Dubliners*. I love his delight in the particular, and

I'm sure it lies behind many of my own attempts to render the actuality of things. . . . I just saw myself as describing what was there. The multifarious sounds . . . of the city impressed themselves on me as a kind of instant onomatopoeia. Not so much about Belfast, as *of* Belfast."

In Carson's war-torn Belfast, Joyce's tactics take on even more urgency. If a "Troubled" city repels visual belonging, then efforts to re-establish a sense of place and to reimagine community by way of sound are perhaps affective imperatives. Carson is well aware that Belfast's soundscape is symptomatic of the conflict and that its rattle and hum cannot always be hospitable. Nevertheless, his work suggests that even when sound signifies insecurity, it still provides an important means of navigating the inscrutable city. Familiar earmarks—sounds of symbolic significance in a particular space—allow locals to move through place, and when the city becomes illegible, one might orient oneself by way of audible directives.

Carson's *The Star Factory* (1997), which is half memoir, half whimsical Belfast meditation cast in melodic prose, sets the stage for his poetry's soundings. Most significantly, it reflects on a local earmark that serves as one of his oeuvre's "keynote sounds": a unique signal or crucial acoustic anchor that echoes throughout his collections. This sound is the "vacillating roulette trickle" of a tin can trundling down the Lower Falls: the "vatic . . . ghost . . . heard tripping down the gutter, but never seen, any time there might be trouble in the offing" (124). The can's clatter, in other words, contributes to the city's auditory texture and serves as a sort of subterranean alarm or aural alert for civilians on both sides of the Shankill/Falls divide. Just as policemen blare their car sirens to take advantage of acoustic space's expansive scope, the sound issuing a warning long before the cruiser's blinking light meets the eye, Belfast's informal bush telegraph does the same. The can's resonant rhythmic clacks serve as a community Morse code, allowing pedestrians to re-route and clear out before an imminent attack.

In *The Star Factory* Carson (1997) explains that the "tripping" tin was first heard in the early 1920s when a policeman was killed on the corner of Balaclava Street during the Anglo-Irish War's sectarian clashes, and he latterly situates the sound as a feature of his own childhood's heard world: "[A]s Glandore blurs into Balaclava, the can resound[s] off the street in fits and starts—melismatic, rallentando phrases, broken by lulls and false denouements—till at last it ticks to a stop" (124). Even in Carson's prose, there exists a remarkable unity of form and content; the can "hails" neighborhood hearers, and this passage vicariously immerses its reader/auditor in the local soundscape it describes. The attacks of the plosive /t/ sounds in "fits" and "starts" are a jolt to the ear after the calming blends of "*Gl*andore" and "Bala*cl*ava"—a shock appropriate to the can resoundingly raising its alarm. The passage continues with the multisyllabic drawing-out of "melismatic" and "rallentando": terms that typically direct the protracted pace of a musical line, meaning "singing several notes to a single syllable of text" and "gradually slowing," respectively. This slackening pace coincides with the calming double "l" of "rallentando" and "lulls": an orderly internal rhyme that trips lightly off the tip of the tongue. Again, here, Carson's soundscape echoes his semantic content, with his prose mimicking the "false denouements" of the can's acoustic journey as it wends its way out of earshot. As the tin finally rolls to a halt at the end of the laneway, Carson turns to his own monosyllabic clatter: the passage's final eight words are short and sharp ("till at last it ticks to a stop"), slowing the phrase's tempo and summoning the can's last staccato gasps.

The cautionary tin can in *The Star Factory* resounds throughout Carson's work, serving as a poetic leitmotif. In fact, Carson (1989) uses the can in "Hamlet" as phonic scaffolding for one of his clearest statements of his work's perceptual goals: the poem foregrounds auditory attunement, treating sonic signals as navigational guides to place. "Hamlet" is set in Belfast's now-demolished Clock Bar, itself a type of echo-chamber. Its punters are collectively immersed in the conversational, interruptive cadences of barroom banter and are attuned to the featured voice of a good yarn-spinner. The *seanchaí* in "Hamlet," a latter-day bard of sorts, recounts with dramatic flourish his story of the 1922 killing of a policeman outside Belfast's National Bank. He listens to "some wag's" (line 8) rambling interjections before returning to his performance and embellishing his tale with noir clichés: "*At any rate, / This sergeant's number came up; not a winning one. The bullet had his name on it*" (lines 12–13). The narrator has a penchant for onomatopoeic sound effects (he embroiders his stories with evocative expressions like "skittered," "hisses," and "clanking") and for the paronomasic sound puns that emerge as he slips deftly between languages ("*fál*" becomes "Falls" when transliterated and translates as both "hedge" and "boundary, frontier"). These techniques suggest that he is a raconteur of sorts—one of those semiprofessional tale-tellers whom Carson so often stations in his Belfast pubs.

The tale being told in "Hamlet" bears earwitness to the city; the *seanchaí* explains that the "trundling" tin can first announced itself on the night of the policeman's murder, and that the "thousands" of people within earshot were moved together to safety by its aural alerts. As these observations suggest, within both the framing narrative and the story itself, the ear replaces the eye as a mediator of place. Carson provides next to no visual description of the pub, so the Clock Bar's dimensions are simply the reaches of its patrons' voices, and the tin can serves as a community earmark: something that "thousands heard, and no one ever / Saw" (Carson 1989, "Hamlet" lines 16–17).[11] The poem frames the crescendos and diminuendos of the can's onomatopoeic "skittering" as guiding imperatives heard against a backdrop of visual insecurity.[12]

Also in "Hamlet," Carson's (1989) mention of the National Bank conjures the specter of bank bombings (including that of Bloody Friday), and this reference suggests the troubling impermanence of Belfast's landmarks. Apropos of this subject, the poem's first section concludes with a nod to a "mercury tilt device": a type of homemade fuse often used by paramilitary groups to trigger bombs. The fuse "only connects" (E. M.

11. In "Schoolboys and Idlers of Pompeii" Carson (1989, 53) also thematizes the infamous tin can, repeating his descriptions of the phenomenon in "Hamlet" almost to a word: "the tin can which was heard that night rolling down Balaklava Street into Raglan Street, and which was heard again for years after, whenever there was trouble in the offing; thousands heard it, no one saw it."

12. The relationship of Carson's "Hamlet" to Shakespeare's *Hamlet* seems to rest largely on the theme of spectral prophesy. Carson frames the "skittering" can as a "tin ghost" heralding a so-called "*strange eruption to our state*" (a line used by Shakespeare's Horatio to describe Hamlet's foretold threats to Denmark). By Carson's pen, however, Shakespeare's figurative language becomes bluntly literal: the "*eruption*" that the can's "roulette trickle" predicts is that of a homemade bomb set to destroy the cityscape.

Forster's [2000] famous humanist credo is jarringly recycled here as a harbinger of calamity) to destroy conventional readings of the cityscape (Carson 1989, "Hamlet" lines 24–25).

Carson shrugs off linear narrative in favor of free associative movement in "Hamlet," instead using sound effects like alliteration ("*f*ew," "*f*ast," "*f*iction"; "*a*rchaic *a*narchists' *a*larm-clock") and same-word rhyme to assemble aural coherence. Although "Hamlet" has no conventional rhyme scheme, when Carson *does* use rhyme, he does so to play on names of places: "clock" and "Clock" in line 1, "Pound" and "*pound*" in line 8, "falls" and "*fál*" in line 9 (also linked by way of internal rhyme to "wall," "all," and "call" in lines 12 and 14). These names are repeatedly highlighted because the geographical spaces to which they refer have either been obscured or have slipped entirely from view. The Clock Bar, once at the corner of Clonard Street and the Falls Road, no longer exists; the Pound Loney, an area used in the nineteenth century as an enclosure for cattle on their way to market, became Divis Flats Housing Estate in the 1960s (a complex since largely demolished);[13] and the Falls Road, as Carson's (1989) "Question Time" reminds us, has been uncannily defamiliarized with the passing of time ("Where I remember rows of houses, factories, there is recent wasteland, broken bricks, chickweed, chain-link fencing" [60]). Carson therefore builds sonic structure out of geographical illegibility; his same-word rhymes are a way for the audience, the poem's own acoustic community, to navigate his lines. This "echolocation" is the poem's formal parallel to the tin can it thematizes: it makes a visually volatile space meaningfully audible.

Carson again emphasizes this perceptual arc later on in "Hamlet." The poem's third section figures the city as a dismembered body: a pastiche of gruesomely severed pieces. Raglan Street, for instance, is an "unravelled . . . sleeve," and the poem uses brusque enjambment to stress that

13. Divis Flats was a significant Troubles-era flashpoint: Patrick Rooney, the first child victim of the conflict, was killed in Divis Tower when the Royal Ulster Constabulary fired a machine gun into the building. The British Army later occupied the top floors of the building as an observation post and sniper's nest.

Balaklava Street's "helmet" has been "torn away from [its] mouth" (lines 42–43). Nevertheless, the road remains hauntingly hearable thanks to the tin can's prophetic "roulette trickle." The poem therefore reiterates the can's role as a navigational aid, its sound laden with semiotic weight (it seems to say "Danger! Trouble is around the corner").

The third section of the poem also situates the tin can in a broader neighborhood soundscape. When "[t]he dim glow of Garnet . . . go[es] out" (Carson 1989, "Hamlet" line 43), familiar noises still limn the community's limits. This passage's alliterative "g" evokes a guttering candle that heralds the blinding darkness; seeing, after all, requires external illumination, whereas hearing operates autonomously. Beyond marking place's dimensions, though, sound also seems able to condition feeling *in* place. The train's distant "shunting" (line 44) and the faint cries of children—the neighborhood's comforting white noise—serve as the keynote sounds to the can's strident foreground signals. These prosaic sounds, as the calming /ʃ/ in "shunting" suggests, soothe the speaker's jangled nerves. Carson therefore describes a community's "homing refrain" in "Hamlet," highlighting the calming domestic earmarks to which locals are together in tune and pointing to the possibility of negotiating belonging in acoustic space.

This refrain also sets the stage for the comparatively hushed concluding tones in "Hamlet." The poem ends by connecting sound to time; the pub's clock gestures toward both the evening's and the city's anxious impermanence (Carson 1989, "Hamlet" line 60). This passage, however, also makes a case for reconsidering place in acoustic space. The phrase "time / Is conversation" (lines 61–62) suggests that the soundscape can accommodate lived temporality and that it is open to momentary movement and change. Carson's lines ring of Nancy's (2007, 14) "sonorous present": sound *arrives*, and as "words blossom from . . . speakers' mouths" (Carson 1989, "Hamlet" line 63), they open "a space that is [their] own, the very spreading out of [their] resonance . . . and reverberation" (Nancy 2007, 16). Similarly, earlier in the poem Carson compares the tin can's acoustic "fits and starts" to a "wisp of smoke," a temporary plume that is here one moment, gone the next. Whereas visual change (like the bank bombing of Bloody Friday) reads as a disorienting "strange eruption to our state"

(Carson 1989, "Hamlet" line 38), sound-space advances, retreats, and redefines its own dimensions. Accordingly, the poem's last lines are insistently aural: the pub is again defined by its barkeep's fruitless "shouts of *time*" and tale-tellers' late-night rants rather than by yellowing Guinness adverts or dimly lit snugs. The final stanza's most resonant figure is the "hedge"—here likely meaning "evasion," given the game of wits that is the *seanchaí*'s circle—"that flits incessantly into the present" (line 62). In a single phrase, Carson links sound with time and recapitulates theme with form; the line's repeated unrounded /ɛ/ sounds ("h*e*dge," "inc*e*ssantly," "pr*e*sent") are "flitting" again and again into earshot. Ultimately, "Hamlet" compellingly rethinks space as soundscape's scope rather than as a visual field.

Music and Voice: The "Score" of Carson's Belfast

Carson's admonitory tin can, the community's vernacular warning system, initiates a broader exploration of sound as a GPS device: a navigational system for those trying to understand and negotiate place. His poetry indicates that the city's "score" can be meaningfully parsed for cultural cues, and it often performs this interpretive process. Following this ear-minded logic, in "Night Out" Carson (1989) treats the city symphonically; its speaker takes his body's and his community's bearings from local tempi. The pub in the poem is framed as an acoustic space dominated by a live band's raucous tunes. *Four Green Fields*, the band's refrain in the poem, is a popular Nationalist ballad and a fitting accompaniment to conflict's strident tones.[14] The song's lyrics allude to the British seizure of Irish provinces (the titular "four green fields") and cite W. B. Yeats' (1937) play "Cathleen Ní Houlihan" to urge a militant Republican response: "But my sons have sons as brave as were their fathers; / My fourth green field will bloom once again." The tune is also punctuated by a second rhythm

14. *Four Green Fields* was penned by folk musician Tommy Makem in 1967, just before the outbreak of the Troubles. When Makem himself performed the song, he often prefaced it with a recitation of Seamus Heaney's (1998) "Requiem for the Croppies," which suggests a give and take between music and poetry on the subject of Irish Nationalist politics.

in "Night Out" when the song's verse is answered by a machine gun's "ragged chorus." This volley of shots, reinforced by the near-onomatopoeic "b—b—b—b" of the stanza's second line and the staccato syntax of its third, echoes "beyond the breeze-block walls" (Carson 1989, "Night Out" line 7) but penetrates the pub's inner sanctum.

The speaker's sense of aural geography suggests that sound gives shape to the city's spaces; he stays put at the pub because the shots remain at a relatively safe distance (their cracks are resounding in a nearby alley). The night that Carson (1989) describes in "Night Out" seems to be a syncopated interval; the polyrhythm of its "rounds of drink, of bullets, of applause" (line 9) points to the overlapping cadences—the conflict's competing earmarks—clamoring for the speaker's attention. The poem's analysis of its local soundscape frames these "rounds" as a *musical* round, with different voices contrapuntally circulating a single melodic fragment. The call to arms in *Four Green Fields* and the "broken rhythm / Of machine-gun fire" (lines 7–8) march to the beat of the same ideological drum, similarly policing sectarian divides. Carson therefore suggests in the poem that bearing earwitness to the city amounts to taking its political temperature and to moving more securely through place.

Militant music in Belfast—one of the city's signature earmarks (the aural cues that Carson's poet-speakers analyze to make sense of the city's climate)—is closely tied to the partisan cacophony of parade season. Parades in Northern Ireland are particularly contentious political flashpoints because they represent competing claims to local territory. Their long and checkered history dates back to William of Orange's victory in the 1690 Battle of the Boyne, which solidified the political dominance of local Protestants. Celebratory Protestant parades began commemorating the conflict approximately one hundred years later after the founding of the Loyal Orange Order, and these parades are still staged annually by Orangemen on the twelfth of July (often simply called "the Twelfth"). Rival Catholic parades eventually sprung up; for example, the Ancient Order of Hibernians (a Nationalist fraternity) began publicly marking occasions such as Lady Day (the Feast of the Annunciation of the Virgin Mary) and St. Patrick's Day. However, after partition in 1921, the British government restricted Catholic demonstrations in the North and often expressly prohibited them: an imbalance that explains why parading is now considered a primarily Protestant tradition. Nevertheless, subterranean processions continued, and throughout the twentieth century the number of parades in Northern Ireland multiplied exponentially as both Republican and Unionist groups memorialized significant victories and defeats. Local chapters of the Loyalist Apprentice Boys, for instance, continue to commemorate the 1689 Siege of Derry/Londonderry, whereas Nationalists mark the 1916 Easter Rising and the 1981 Republican hunger strikes. After the Belfast Agreement in 1998, officials created a Parades Commission to monitor and regulate local processions, and although some groups have refused to report to the commission, it counted a remarkable 4364 parades in the North in 2012 alone.[15] This suggests the lingering political currency of parading traditions, and given marching's rather incendiary role during the Troubles (many processions devolved into riots and fights and yielded scores of local casualties), it is no surprise that they feature prominently in Carson's poetry.

Although Northern Ireland's parades naturally involve visual spectacle, which has long been theorized as a crucial means of holding political sway,[16] they rely even more heavily on aural assertions of power. The Orange Walks on the Twelfth, for instance, which remain parade season's political centerpieces, feature the resonant tones of lambeg drums. Lambegs are large, loud instruments; they can reach up to 120 decibels (louder than a power saw or a sandblaster and very near the threshold of physical pain [125 decibels]) and are thought by many to have arrived in Ulster with William of Orange's troops. In *Ethnicity, Identity and Music*, an ethnomusicological study of the contemporary North, Martin Stokes (1994) argues that the lambeg drums assert a militaristic claim to sound-space. Given that the parades are more widely heard than seen, the lambegs also force an acoustic recognition of the political polarization of place: "The

15. See the Parades Commission's official website at http://www.paradescommission.org/.

16. Guy Debord ([1967] 1983) offers a particularly nuanced analysis of the relationship of visual display to political power.

space patrolled in these marches consists of more than a route which could be traced on a map, but the wide area in the city from which the sounds of the lambeg drums can be heard" (Stokes 1994, 9). Although a parade, in other words, pays but a passing visual visit to the streets on its route, its sounds can almost fascistically monopolize a city's airwaves. Stokes suggests that these "assault[s] on the ears" are more than just disruptive noise—they are carefully engineered semiotic statements: "The 12 July parades by Protestant Orangemen work to define city space in Belfast as the domain of Ulster Protestants and British rule" (8). Stokes' descriptions reveal the North's parades and their performative efforts to lay political claim to territory as examples of acoustic ecologist R. Murray Schafer's (1977) theory of "sound imperialism." Attempts to dominate other peoples and value systems, Schafer suggests, are often crucially underpinned by "subjugation by Noise" (77). If certain sounds can interrupt and dominate other acoustic activities, then they can assert very real power over place, especially if they manage to drown out the comparatively hushed tones of dissenting voices. Carson's work advances precisely this argument; in his poetry he listens in on Protestant parades and rival Catholic responses, and he points to their efforts to make militant claims on the city's pulse.

"Twelfth Day," from Carson's 1999 collection, *The Twelfth of Never*, explicitly stages this sentiment.[17] The title refers, of course, to the Twelfth's annual Orange parades, and the poem suggests the impossibility of evading their clamorous grasp. Its poet-speaker is, like so many of Carson's narrators, a careful listener, and the poem's early lines are preoccupied with the sounds of his pastoral reverie. Having absented himself from the city's parade route, hoping to avoid the Twelfth's customary violence, he seeks refuge in a summer meadow and is soothed by the soporific

17. "The Twelfth of Never" is an idiom meaning "a future date that will never come to pass." In the famous 1957 Johnny Mathis song by the same name, the singer tells his beloved that he will love her until the twelfth of never, meaning that his affections will never wane. In the context of Carson's collection, which is preoccupied with deconstructing and dismantling would-be utopias, the phrase indicts the Orange marches on the Twelfth: neither Unionists nor Nationalists, Carson suggests, will ever achieve the political aims they seek, and so their parades are but bombastic testaments to the conflict's futility.

"volume of the field" (line 5). His sleepy ears alight on the comforting hum of "insect decibel" (line 4) and he frames the field as a transistor radio broadcasting its four-legged denizens' merry "chitterings" (line 6). The poem's octave, which playfully combines Petrarchan (abba) with Shakespearian (cdcd) stanza form, and the first half of its concluding sestet suggest the ear's potential consolations: sprawled out, eyes closed, far from the city's industrial roar, the speaker treats the meadow's sounds as an acoustic tonic of sorts—a heady cocktail of natural rhythms moving together in harmony (line 11). The sonnet's volta, however, comes in its last three lines: harmony suddenly gives way to cacophony, and the speaker is shaken abruptly awake as the field starts "pulsing like an Orange drum" (line 14)—an acoustic prelude to the parade's approaching violence.

In this way, Carson (1999b) demonstrates in "Twelfth Day" that locals are at the mercy of the lambeg's clarion call; even a conscientious objector's calm can be compromised by "someone turn[ing] the volume up in Portadown" (line 13). This reference is far from incidental: since the early 1970s, Portadown (a town in County Armagh) has been the site of a particularly contentious parade dispute known as the "Drumcree conflict." The conflict's most recent incarnation erupted in the mid-1990s when local residents contested the Orange Order's march on the Twelfth down the largely Catholic Garvaghy Road. The conflict resulted in violent riots with hundreds of injuries and arrests and several deaths, including three young children from a mixed-religion family whose home was firebombed by Loyalist militants.[18] These events hover over the poem's final lines, and Carson's choice of words suggests that the Orange Walk's stridency turns everything topsy-turvy: someone turns the volume *up* in Porta*down*—a movement reminiscent of the dizzying "border bomb" described by Carson's (1989) poem "Yes":

18. At the Quinn brothers' funeral mass, Bishop Patrick Walsh announced from the pulpit, "For all too long the airwaves and the printed page have been saturated with noises—strident, harsh, discordant noises—carrying words of hatred, of incitement, of recrimination, words not found in the vocabulary of Christianity. . . . But the time for words is over. It's now time for silence, a silence in which we will hear the voice of God" (quoted in Greg Harkin's article in the *Examiner*, July 15, 1998).

> I'm about to quote from Basho's *The Narrow Road to the Deep North*
> . . . .
> When it goes off and . . .
> everything reverses South. (lines 6–9)

The parade also throws the poem itself off kilter. Carson (1999b) wrote "Twelfth Day" in a near-perfect pattern of alexandrines, but its lilting rhythm gives way to an iambic militancy in its fourteen-syllable final line, mimicking the march's measured pace: "And then I heard the whole field pulsing like an Orange drum" (line 14). Likewise, the poem's sound patterns take a turn for the sinister as its final sestet approaches. Whereas the opening line of "Twelfth Day" dances alliteratively between alternating /d/ and /b/ sounds, the harsh consonance of the final stanza ("twixt," "index") suggests the parade's severe sectarian soundscape. These seemingly sudden disruptions are subtly plotted before the final tercet: Carson's insects march in formation down the field, colonizing its flowers' stalks, and these phrases in the poem conjure a parade's regimented movements and the specter of its sound imperialism. The prophetic scene makes a point about sound's ability to foreshadow based on the ear's wide-ranging perceptual reaches. Perhaps the poem's aural alerts (the field's "pulsing," like the tin can before it) are, after all, propitious, as they offer forewarning before violence meets the eye. Once again, Carson ties hearing to meaning-making and models his signature phenomenology of sound.

Although "Twelfth Day" faults a Protestant parade for hijacking local frequencies, the very next poem in Carson's (1999b) collection, "The Ay O'Haitch" (a transliteration of "The A O'H," shorthand for "The Ancient Order of Hibernians"), equally takes a Catholic march to task.[19] It is no accident that the two poems are uncomfortably juxtaposed; parade season is a process of clamorous one-upmanship. Carson's poetry indicts

19. In an interview in the *Guardian* (January 16, 2009), Carson claimed that although he grew up in an interface area, he was 12 years old before he met anyone from the "other side" (the Protestant Shankill Road). His first cross-community friendship foundered during marching season, he said, and his parade poems certainly speak to the deeper entrenchment of community divides during such times.

this partisan noise pollution, which he describes in "The Ay O'Haitch" as a cacophonous combination of accordions and "borrowed" lambeg drums (lines 9–10).[20] Carson suggests in this poem that the North's parades are competing claims to *community*. Rhythm can discipline bodies, moving hearts and minds together in time, and the marches' martial measures serve precisely this purpose.[21] Written largely in iambic hexameter, "The Ay O'Haitch" echoes the parade's militancy by way of its regular, even regulative, rhythms, and the poem emphasizes the procession's efforts to marshal pedestrians by linking these rhythms to civilian recruitment: "Will you, Sir, join our Union of Hibernians?" (line 14). The poem is similarly regimented by a very turgid rhyme scheme; few words manage to escape its insistently associative patterns. Carson constantly makes connections via assonance ("bl*ow*," "g*oa*tskins," "n*o*ble"), perfect end-rhyme ("drums"/"sums," "Hibernians"/"Hibernians," "pedestrians"/ "equestrians"), and sprung rhyme ("accordions"/"drums"/"Hibernians"/ "equestrians"/"sums"), and some words even find two or three rhyming pairs. This obsessive connectivity is itself a symbol of the parade's coercive community formation. In "The Ay O'Haitch" the Hibernians' "borrowed" (line 10) lambegs ring resoundingly back to the Orange Walk in "Twelfth Day" in an effort to move locals (literally) to their cause.

As disruptive as parade season can be, when these two poems are read together, they still seem to suggest the parades' sounds as a kind of litmus test for the city's political climate. Even the distant listener can tell whether

20. Although lambeg drums are typically associated with Protestant marches, the instrument is of cultural and historical significance to both groups and is used widely throughout the parade season.

21. As Carson indicates in "Twelfth Day" and "The Ay O'Haitch," two rhythms can be nearly identical even while representing different political affiliations. This suggests that sound patterns operate on various levels: they can have immediate physiological effects (muscles tense to the screeching of nails on a chalkboard), but they can also operate as aesthetic or cultural codes (the tin can only means "trouble" to the initiated listener). As I argue in chapter 3, Carson manipulates sound for both visceral and semiological purposes, and these competing if not incompatible theories are sometimes a source of tension in his poetry.

a march is more music (as in "The Ay O'Haitch") or riot (as "Twelfth Day" seems to predict for Portadown), and locals can use these aural cues to decide whether to clear out or stay put as a parade approaches. Parade season in Belfast remains tense, but although Carson frames the "demolition city" as visually unreadable, its sounds can yet be parsed for sense. In "Twelfth Day" he traces this perceptual arc: the poem offers next to no visual evidence of its surroundings, and its speaker instead encounters his environment entirely by way of the ear.

In using sound to navigate place and place's volatile politics, Carson's speakers rely on the ways in which conflict is *voiced*. Speech in Northern Ireland registers supposed political sympathies: the letter "H," for instance—as the title of "The Ay O'Haitch" suggests—is a type of tribal shibboleth, and it is taught as such in segregated schools. The Catholic pronunciation is "haitch," considered standard in Hiberno-English, and the Protestant pronunciation, as in most English variants, is "aitch." In his poem "H," from the "Letters from the Alphabet" sequence in *Opera Et Cetera*, Carson (1996) plays on this distinction, pointing out the ways in which sound is saturated with social meaning. The poem ventriloquizes an inmate in Long Kesh, the infamous prison just outside Belfast where paramilitary prisoners were incarcerated during the Troubles. The prison is nicknamed "the Maze" because of the electoral district in which it is located, and its name also befits a building that is cropped from maps and obscured to the passerby by blank concrete walls, leaving the area a visual puzzle to the pedestrian. The prison is best known for its "H-Blocks," the buildings where so-called "terrorists" were held after the British government revoked their Special Category Status, and which became the staging ground of the Republicans' subsequent dirty protests and hunger strikes.[22] Although Republican and Loyalist groups were segregated in the

22. Special Category Status essentially meant that paramilitary prisoners were treated as prisoners of war and therefore granted certain political protections under the Geneva Convention: they were allowed to wear their own clothes, to consort freely with other members of their paramilitary faction, and to have access to extra food parcels and family visits. The British government decided to reclassify these prisoners as "terrorists" in 1976, which precipitated several years of Republican prisoner protests. These protests

jail blocks, Long Kesh was often the scene of proxy conflict, with rival prisoners plotting ambushes and attacks. In 1997, for instance, Loyalist Volunteer Force leader Billy Wright was killed in Long Kesh by armed INLA inmates.

As Carson points out in "H," pronunciation in Northern Ireland encodes a particularly loaded politics, and the letter "H" polices sectarian divides. Whether "the H in H-Block is *aitch* or *haitch*" (Carson 1996, "H" lines 7–8) can literally be a matter of life and death. Carson emphasizes this volatility by juxtaposing this line with competing paramilitary slogans: the Loyalist catchphrases "What we have we hold" and "Not an inch" chafe ominously against the Republicans' proverbial "Our day will come" (lines 7–8). The question "Does it matter?" is a rhetorical one, answered vehemently in the poem's following line: "Everything is in the ways / You say them" (lines 9–10). This concluding credo, which reflects Carson's entire oeuvre, suggests that the content of speech sometimes matters less than its phonetic packaging. When local locution is laden with ideological weight, its *what* can be easily superseded by its *how*. In surveying Belfast's semiotics of sound, Carson's poetry must therefore carefully plot the politics of voice; in a space so thoroughly polarized, intonation can often mean partisan interpellation.[23]

Although this interpellation means that speech can be vexingly politicized given an errant lilt, it also means that one can try to strategize where

culminated in the hunger strikes of 1981, during which ten Republican prisoners died including Bobby Sands, who was elected to Parliament while in prison. After the strikes ended, four of the prisoners' five demands were met by then-Secretary of State James Prior.

23. Beyond the "aitch"/"haitch" divide, Carson also repeatedly alights on the distinction between Bel*fast*—the accent "[o]n the *fast*, as if the name was Irish, which it was (or is)" (Carson 1989, "Jawbox" line 7)—and *Bel*fast, the so-called "educated" pronunciation, conditioned by BBC influence (Carson 1997, 45). In "Jawbox" Carson highlights the dangerous distance between these two inflections while making a point about the (would-be, should-be) proximity of Catholic and Protestant: the poem compares crossing the Hiberno-English/Received Pronunciation border to riding the oft-bombed railway line between Dundalk and Newry, "[o]r / Newry and Dundalk, depending / Where you're coming from: like the difference between Cambodia and Kampuchea" (lines 25–26).

to speak up, where to pass via careful ventriloquy, and where to stay silent. Like the cautionary tin can or the resonant tones of parade routes, the wagging of local tongues produces an important perceptual guide to the visually indecipherable cityscape. Carson presents familiar earmarks in his poetry, parses their symbolic significance, and orients his speakers by way of these audible directives. Even when sound symptomatizes the conflict, therefore, it still serves as an important means of navigating the illegible city.

3

CIARAN CARSON

From Song to Stutter

Yarn-Spinning: Carson as Belfast *Seanchaí*

Although Ciaran Carson takes pains to explain how the ear reveals insecurity in his "Troubled" city, he nonetheless asserts that sound can be a profound source of comfort and even of conciliatory community. Carson often shapes his volumes' soundscapes as sources of conviviality, channeling the cadences of local *seanchaithe* (tale-tellers) with the energies of traditional music sessions. Carson (2002, 145) has himself experienced these phenomena as potent means of community-building, and so he seeks, as he puts it, to "get [them] into the poetry": "[s]peech and slabber" and song serve his work as both subject matter and poetic sound effects.

Carson swore off poetry entirely between 1978 and 1987 because he felt it couldn't achieve music's immediacy, but he subsequently returned to the genre to infuse it with orality's vibrancy:

> I was going around Cork, Galway, Sligo, [playing music] and thought that a poem, in comparison, wasn't right—it was twee, you know? Poetry seemed like airy-fairy nonsense. Whereas if you're in a room, and you hear the music, and you're playing it here and now—it's of now, and it's not a thing that you're on your own with. . . . When I did come back to writing it was through trying to accommodate bar-talk . . . [which] can be entirely odd and strange if you hear it right, or maybe I mean wrong. Sitting in a pub, you can tune into some ostensibly ordinary

> conversation, and it can become weird and wonderful. I wanted to get that into the poetry.[1] (Carson 2002, 145)

As Paul Muldoon said in an article in *The Guardian* about Carson (January 17, 2009), "the territorial aspect of his achievement . . . [is his] tak[ing] in the rubble and rumpus and riddling of day-to-day life in Belfast." Muldoon's statement suggests that Carson manages to reterritorialize a visually deterritorialized Belfast by way of sound. In reshaping the city as an auditory field, Carson (1986a, 3) is especially interested in how the tempi of local song and story can move people together in time—the experience, as he puts it, of "[a] room puls[ing] like a diaphragm," "punters . . . nodding joyfully into their pints"—and so he experiments with how this hospitality might take poetic form.

In this chapter, I examine both Carson's musical "long line" and his occasional lapses from lyricism into a staccato stutter, the latter being most abundantly audible in his 2003 volume *Breaking News*. I diagnose this stutter as a sign that sites of trauma can never quite be contained: the poetry, almost despite itself, vocalizes an anxious excess. All the same, if a "Troubled" city repels visual belonging, then efforts to reimagine community via the ear are crucial means of restoring a more positive politics of place.

One of Carson's signature poetic devices is his oft-remarked long line. The vast majority of the poems in each of Carson's eleven original volumes, with the exception of his first collection, *The New Estate* (1976),

1. As this statement suggests, although Carson structures his poetic soundscapes around aural cues, his work remains well aware of its own textuality. For Carson, orality and literature are intimately connected, and his attempts to "get [sound] into the poetry" are evident on the page. Kinesis and breath (rather than meter) are his work's driving forces, and spacing and punctuation serve as his "stave": a means of transcribing intended breaths and breaks so that readers might become auditors, directed through a poem by the ear. David Wheatley (2009, 47–48) argues that Carson pays a "[Charles] Olson-like attention to breath, breathing, and its connections to speech," suggesting that poetry's "respiratory system" is centrally regulated by line breaks and typography. Therefore, a careful reader of Carson's work must also lend an ear to his poetry's animating voice with its bouncing cadences and mediating breaths.

Breaking News (2003), and his two most recent efforts, *On the Night Watch* (2009b) and *Until Before After* (2010), rely centrally on this technique. The line, which varies syllabically but is typically at least sentence-length (it often carries over into a second line when typeset) and makes for prose-y, enjambed stanzas, poaches rhythmically from both Irish traditional music and the tempi of local pub talk. Indeed, Carson's style has been variously termed an "old-timer's voice" (Hufstader 1999, 219), "the . . . voice of the good 'seanchaí'" (Ní Dhomhnaill 1988, 117), and "a personality of place in language" (McCracken 1995, 359).[2] Carson himself credits the cadences of barroom storytelling—the abrupt rhythms of the Belfast idiom, the meandering, self-corrective line of the tale, the playful, ironic disposition[3]—with inspiring his turn to poetry. As he explained it in an interview with Aida Edemariam (*The Guardian*, January 17, 2009), "[I met a storyteller called John Campbell from Armagh, who would] tell yarns, in a very deliberate sort of rhythm, and you gradually realised that what seemed to be offhand was actually words put forward as a statement of style, and it occurred to me that I could do poems that were of that understanding of the world—the long line thing. And the songs—Da-a da da da diddly da da—the idea that you could write a line which had a tie with song as well. And that you could apply that to stuff about the violence." Inasmuch, then, as poems like "H" (Carson 1996) and "Jawbox" (Carson 1989) suggest that pronunciation can divide, Carson's work also locates a common energy and vitality in Belfast speech. His poetry seems to take up Tom Paulin's (2003b) suggestion that "[i]t ought to be possible . . . to found a national literature on [Belfast's] scutching vernacular" (239), its "great, marvelous, clattery tenderness" (233). There is something of (nonsectarian) collectivity in these shared sounds, and Carson channels the

2. On Ní Dhomhnaill's point, Carson, a native Irish speaker (an unusual phenomenon in Belfast, even sixty years ago), has also claimed the language as an influence. In an interview with John Brown, Carson (2002, 145) suggests that some of his poetry tries to rewrite (or resound) English "through the medium of . . . older Irish," with its "assonantal, alliterative structures" and its "tremendous witty energy."

3. I am borrowing here from Edna Longley (1994, 98), who suggests bathos, irony, and wit as characteristic of Belfast speech.

"clattery" rhythms and wry wit of the Belfast *seanchaí* to participate in Paulin's grassroots community-building.[4]

Carson's notion of the comforts of a common cadence, however, is not quite the straightforward post-partisan hope of Seamus Heaney's (1972) "Broagh," in which he points out that "strangers [find] / difficult to manage" the last "-gh" in "Broagh" (lines 13–14) and therefore suggests that speech sounds can provide a kind of insular unity in the North. In fact, Carson's stories still refer compulsively to the conflict, so even his most concerted efforts to sound the way toward cross-community sympathies are marked by this shared sense of civilian loss (see my discussion later in this chapter of Carson's notion of trauma's unincorporability and the ways in which this is reflected in symptomatic stuttering sound patterns). Nevertheless, as Edna Longley (1994, 59) argues (and I with her), Carson's poems serve as "elegies and replacements for the communal narratives that a seanachie [sic] could once command," and they therefore "interpret the way in which more contingent and fluid relations [can] breach . . . local, familial, clannish and theocentric horizons."

Carson's (1987) "Dresden" in *The Irish for No* is one of his earliest and most commonly cited forays into tale-telling territory. With this poem, Carson began "telling it slant" (Hufstader 1999, 222); his poetic long line parallels his wandering city itineraries in moving against the bluntness of violence (219). "Dresden" is incredibly digressive and is full of distinctive verbal tics: the phrase "or rather" seems to be this particular storyteller's

4. Eric Falci (2012) argues that Carson's work after *Belfast Confetti* (1989), particularly in *First Language* (1993) and *Opera Et Cetera* (1996), breaks with the tale-telling tenor of the earlier volumes. Falci suggests that the narrative success of the long line "is warped by the imposition of rhymes" (135) in these mid-career collections, "resulting in a move away from an aestheticized orality and toward something much more baroque, even mannered" (135). Although these poems do rely more on line-final rhyme than does Carson's earlier work, their expansive line lengths still allow for the teller's looping rhythms and associative narrative logic. Moreover, because Carson's previous collections make ample use of internal rhyme, a move toward line-final rhyme seems an organizational rather than a conceptual shift (particularly given Carson's continued use of enjambment, which means that the poems in *Opera Et Cetera* sound virtually identical to those in *Belfast Confetti* when read aloud).

crutch. These patterns, maintained throughout the five-page poem, are initiated by its elliptical opening lines: "Horse Boyle was called Horse Boyle because of his brother Mule; / Though why Mule was called Mule is anybody's guess. I stayed there once, / Or rather, I nearly stayed there once. But that's another story" (Carson 1987, "Dresden" lines 1–3). As this passage suggests, the poem nimbly manages stories within stories within stories, all with the lively tenor of the consummate yarn-spinner. Its free associative narrative wendings, for instance, capture the conversational spontaneity of a *seanchaí*: "I stayed there once, / Or rather, I nearly stayed there once. But that's another story." Carson also largely avoids end-rhyme; in fact, the entire poem steers clear of traditional formalism to open itself to story's generic cross-fertilizations. Only the concluding couplet (lines 89–90) chimes in "Dresden," and even that simply serves to signal the story's dramatic dénouement as a sort of bardic flourish.

Today's professional *seanchaithe*, like Carson's mentor John Campbell, are often considered stylistic heirs to the Gaelic bardic tradition. Although the tales themselves, conditioned by centuries of conflict and cultural erasure, are perhaps a far cry from medieval bards' authoritative chronicles, the framing voices in the tales still draw on early mnemonic techniques. Alliteration, for instance, is in many oral cultures an important means of encoding story. Its repeated sounds act as cognitive retrieval cues and allow tale-tellers to recite at length, and Carson borrows this strategy to lend "Dresden" poetic shape. The name "Mule," for instance, repeated three times in the opening two lines of "Dresden," sets the stage for a pattern of recurring "em-words" that subsequently structure the poem (Carson 1987, "Dresden" lines 46–47). Assonance is another important mode of bardic sound-play and it lends "Dresden" its internal logic: repeated /eɪ/ and /oʊ/ diphthongs seem to signal descriptions of local landscape. This pattern is established in the opening stanza with the connections chimed among "baroque," "encroached," "ochre," and "over," as well as "rate" and "baked": sound schemes that later connect with such vowel-heavy passages as "To this d*a*y he could hear the gr*a*te / And scr*a*pe as the sp*a*de struck h*o*me, for it reminded him of br*o*ken b*o*nes" (lines 39–42).

Carson's formal attention to speech sounds and to story-telling strategies in "Dresden" matches his thematic concern with orality and aurality.

As do so many of his poems, "Dresden" highlights sound's symbolic value and the heard world's potential to herald the seen. Horse and Mule stack empty tins in front of their caravan that, when toppled, serve as "watchdogs" announcing a visitor's approach (Carson 1987, "Dresden" lines 4–7). The poem reflects on its own efforts to build a circle of listeners—an intimate auditory sphere—by thematizing the role of "tellers" within the community. Horse is both the subject of the framing voice's yarn and himself a yarn-spinner; he keeps his "ears to the ground" and every day makes the rounds of the townland to share the latest news (line 21). To emphasize Horse's place as local *seanchaí*, the unnamed narrator shares one of Horse's stories and ably ventriloquizes his subject via subtle shifts in vocabulary and tone.[5] The tale-within-a-tale is that of "young Flynn," a new paramilitary recruit ordered to bring explosives across the border into Derry. When a policeman steps onto the bus, eager to get home for tea, Flynn thinks he is there to apprehend him and confesses to his crime. Flynn is thereafter jailed for seven years, during which he "learn[s] to speak / The best of Irish" (lines 34–35). This yarn indicates that Horse's tale-telling is an all-important local source of news—a type of informal bush telegraph.

Indeed, Horse's anecdotes do act as community primers on current affairs; they initiate a subterranean hum that buzzes with rumor and gossip. Carson here makes the point that underground hearsay, a uniquely oral phenomenon, often beats official channels to the reportorial punch. The role of the *seanchaí* in facilitating the viral spread of word-of-mouth sound bites is significant given the framing context that some of Carson's other poems provide. "Queen's Gambit" (Carson 1989), for example, argues that just as the state censors maps for "security purposes," so too does it mute inflammatory local news stories, leaving oral tale-telling to provide relief from the press' evasive hedging. The poem makes this point by casting a newspaper report of a paramilitary attack as *literally* illegible,

5. These shifts suggest Horse's attunement to the community-building value of regional sound: his reliance on idiosyncratic slang ("peeler") and idiomatic phrases ("in my young day," "for all the world like x") frame his stories themselves as communal acoustic spaces.

blurred by a spilled cup of tea, then juxtaposing this hazy image with a fully fleshed-out oral rendition of the same story delivered by the narrator's barber:

> *But now hear this:*
> *This Post Office van bombs out from Tomb Street loading bay, its side door open*
> *And they've got this effing Gatling gun or something going full blast*
> *Dot, dot, dot, dot—and the Brits are all shot up*[.] (Carson 1989, "Queen's Gambit" lines 88–91)

The colorful tale-teller in "Queen's Gambit" regales everyone who sits in his chair with his latest round of rumors, embellishing his stories with innuendo and embroidering them with elaborate sound effects, while Horse daily "[c]ome dusk set[s] off on his rounds" (Carson 1987, "Dresden" line 23) to share his "breaking news." The internal rhyme scheme in "Dresden" ("ground," "round," "town") highlights this pattern of hearing and re-telling—a rumor sprouts, Horse sows its seeds, and soon the whole town is harvesting fruit—ultimately suggesting that the *seanchaí* is a crucial source of grassroots intelligence and a sonic catalyst of community.

Carson's (1987) take on sound in "Dresden" is not unequivocally positive. Whereas alliteration can trigger the tale-teller's memory and help him to wax poetic in performance, sound's associative capacity can also make past trauma uncomfortably present. As Neil Corcoran (1992, 220–21) describes it, "Dresden" theorizes noise's ability to "set . . . the memory on edge." Indeed, the ear's vulnerability, given that it hears in surround sound and cannot simply be closed in the face of unwelcome stimuli, permits unpredictable passage to the heart. Aural cues—sounds echoing those that first accompanied traumatic events—can re-invoke the moment of trauma, summoning past suffering and disturbing present affect. There are two particular passages in "Dresden" that highlight this phenomenon. First, the "grate / And scrape" (lines 41–42) of the newly paroled young Flynn's spade as he tries to turn the miserable Carrick ground spontaneously recall the "Troubling" sounds of his time as an IRA initiate. These sounds "set . . . [his] teeth on edge" because they are wedded by his subconscious to paramilitary grave digging ("remind[ing] him of broken bones") and perhaps also to prison work camps (lines 41–43). Acoustic triggers, in other words, force a remembrance of unnerving things past. Similarly, Horse himself is troubled by his years as a rear-gunner in the Royal Air Force. As Carson describes in the poem, Horse participated in the infamous fire-bombing of Dresden during World War II and suggests that the sounds of the attack remain today his "haunting melody":[6]

> As he remembered it, long afterwards, he could hear, or almost hear
> Between the rapid desultory thunderclaps, a thousand tinkling echoes—
> All across the map of Dresden, store-rooms full of china shivered,
> teetered
> And collapsed, an avalanche of porcelain, slushing and cascading[.]
> (Carson 1987, "Dresden" lines 74–76)

In this, too, we see the part that sound plays in post-traumatic stress disorder. For Horse, the sensory impact of a traumatic event (the attack on Dresden) has been internalized, even somatized, and the past has taken up permanent residence in his body. Carson writes in "Dresden" that, even years later, Horse can still hear the "rapid desultory thunderclaps" of bombs and the (real or imagined) "tinkling" destruction of Dresden porcelain.[7] Inasmuch, then, as the invasive tones of external soundscape can produce trauma, so too can aural memories, which make lasting perceptual imprints on our bodies. However, the signature circumlocutions and sing-song bardic techniques are maintained in "Dresden" even throughout these harrowing episodes, allowing the poem to continue moving against violence's concussive immediacy. Carson therefore suggests that even when sound does injury, it can also be a therapeutic tonic. Ultimately, "Dresden" harnesses sound's associative function as a yarn-spinner's

6. I borrow this evocative phrase from *The Haunting Melody: Psychoanalytic Experiences in Life and Music* by Theodor Reik (1953), who reads the leitmotifs by which we are haunted—the songs or sounds stuck in one's head—as symptoms of repressed drives and concealed feelings.

7. "Dresden porcelain" refers to the prized neo-rococo chinaware manufactured throughout the city in the nineteenth century, which was famously marked with a blue crown stamp.

mnemonic, positing a story's wending aural pathways as acoustic gathering places for local community: crucial alternatives to visual topographies in Carson's violently unhomely city.

The "Good Tune": Song and Sonic Community

Beyond the hospitable sounds of local *seanchaithe*, Carson also draws acoustic influence from Irish traditional music. Carson spent more than twenty years as the traditional arts officer with the Arts Council of Northern Ireland; he is also an accomplished session flautist and has written two books on the subject of traditional music. Consequently, it is hardly surprising to hear him claim, for example, the eight-bar reel as a formative influence on the poetic long line (see N. Corcoran 1992, 217). Carson charts this cross-fertilization in *Last Night's Fun* (1986a), a whimsical prose volume that intellectually combines music and poetry. Although Carson's Belfast poetry doesn't allow for visual continuity, *Last Night's Fun* does gesture toward a type of sonic genealogy for the city. The book treats the traditional tune—the soundtrack of the city's pubs and kitchen *céilidhe*—as cultural mnemonic: "You can hear as if you were some ghost from the future, floating in on the sound waves that connect the present here-and-now to the present then" (3). Carson titled the book after one such tune, the words of which have been "worn into shape by many ears and mouths" (116) and to which "many feet have moved . . . in different times" (198). In pointing to his city's musical pedigree, Carson seems to argue for the imbrication of sound with (collective) memory: "As we apprehend the tune, we enter in and out of time, and mark its various times. . . . The ghosts of voices circulate in grooves of dust" (198). For Carson, sound lingers, however spectrally, in the present, and it tells us something about the history of place. The tune, he says, "is not a story, but stories cling to it; it is a rolling stone that gathers moss" (197).

This phrase reflects Carson's sense of the contemporary currency of traditional cultural modes. Music has long been bound up with Irish identity, and its performance is often cast as a ritual of sorts: a rite that might make present the past from whence it came. Many people still feel that traditional music carries with it a sense of authenticity, allowing even present-day Irish to feel connected to cultural legacies and to the history of place. As Geoff Wallis and Sue Wilson (2005, 5) describe it in *The Rough Guide to Irish Music*, traditional tunes provide "[a] continuous link between present and past." However, there are others, perhaps most famously poet Thomas Kinsella, who dispute this continuity, arguing that the ruptures of colonization and anglicization have irreparably distanced contemporary Ireland, especially the still-contested North, from this history. These foundational traumas, Kinsella (1970) says, have enforced a kind of cultural amnesia, and today even speaking the Irish language or playing traditional music cannot establish living contact with ancient traditions: "[The past] is mine, but only at two enormous removes—across a century's silence, and through an exchange of worlds. . . . I stand on one side of a great rift, and can feel the discontinuity in myself" (59). Carson, on the other hand, clearly considers traditional music a bearer of cultural value and historical gravity, but this consideration rests on a redefinition of tradition consistent with the features of the music itself. Edna Longley (1994, 60) offers precisely this sort of reading of Carson's work: "[B]eing an exponent and interpreter of Irish traditional music," she suggests, "Carson views 'tradition' as always contemporary, always improvised in the present on a unique occasion, yet transmitted down long, multiple, intricate chains from the past." Longley's argument emerges organically from the genre's particulars; after all, song is never static. Traditional tunes are perpetually inflected by modern influences and styles, adapted from their original key signatures, and variously interpreted and ornamented by different players. However, there often exists a base "thread of connection" (Ní Uallacháin 2003, 34) running through these tunes that, even if fragile, taps into the past of "people and place" (16). These claims suggest why the tune, as Carson (1986a, 197) says, "is not a story": it doesn't transparently represent a pre-colonial cultural world or reintroduce ancestral tales strategically erased from the Irish repertoire. All the same, though, "stories cling to it" (Carson 1986a, 197): it is a living, breathing, ever-changing repository of things past—an aural calculus of gains and losses.[8]

8. Carson (2009a, 19) has argued explicitly for the receptive flexibility of tradition: "I consider myself Irish, if Irish means to welcome other influences and other cultures,

In *Last Night's Fun* Carson (1986a) points to how and why poetry can be so readily infused with traditional music's patterns: poetry, like music, changes in the ears and mouths of its readers, and the soundscape of the poem is slightly different every time it is read (and even mis-read). Carson's work, which tends toward digressive, looping narratives, is peculiarly decentered and is always ready to "open up under new management" (Carson 1986a, 120). Carson tells us that the notion of "correctness" is anathema to traditional tunes: music is subject to individual improvisation and is always prepared to take "another handling" (120). Therefore, it is a genre well suited to literary poaching.

In *The Given Note* Seán Crosson (2008, 3) charts such borrowings, suggesting that "traditional music offers, through the rituals of its performance, a . . . sense of community which Irish poets have attempted to recreate for the reception of their own work." Carson (2009a, 15) is undoubtedly one such cross-disciplinarian; as he himself explains it, "some of my own work has been called 'genre-defying': maybe I learned that from the music, since every tune recalls other circumstances in which it has been played; and the conversation and anecdotes sparked off by the tunes are essential to a good session. . . . The tunes themselves are ostensibly simple, but capable of infinite variation. The music is always renewable in the light of the now." Moreover, in *Last Night's Fun* Carson (1986a, 90) suggests why he *wants* to infuse his poetry with music: even if the traditional tune is constantly changing and evolving, it nonetheless "becomes a family tree . . . a way of renegotiating lost time. Our knowledge of the past is changed each time we hear it; our present time, imbued with yesterday, comes out with bent dimensions." Musicians can take comfort in knowing that the tunes they play have been shaped, however incomprehensibly, by generations of local "brains and hands" (90) and that their performances recapitulate these historical gestures and take their places in a long acoustic lineage.

---

and recognizing one's obligation to them. I am indebted to the English language, for one thing. And I've suggested elsewhere that Irish traditional music, historically, has always assimilated other kinds of music—Scottish, English, and European, among others. They are made Irish by an Irish style of playing."

As Carson (1986a, 90) describes it, the tune's "wider circle" is something "we can only dimly comprehend": its "congregation is uncountable . . . unknowable." Nevertheless, "the tune has been passed to us by a series of invisible and visible presences, and we like to think of the man who made it or purloined it or dreamed it up" (90). These comments suggest music's potential as a community-building tool—a means of homemaking in acoustic space—and explain why Carson wants to harness its capacity for conviviality and why he wants to make his poetic line sing.

Carson also explains that traditional tunes can organize *cross*-border community rather than simply underscoring sectarian divides. He has suggested in his work, after all, that music can be mobilized factionally in Belfast, especially during parade season, to police political boundaries. In *Last Night's Fun* (1986a) and the comprehensive *Pocket Guide to Irish Traditional Music* (1986b), Carson openly critiques the willful ideologizing of traditional music. He denounces the ways in which dance music has been framed as the province of Catholic musicians since the mid-century revival, and he works to excavate the history of tunes' shared heritage (1986b, 47). Carson points out, in particular, that session players are most often driven by the "good tune," and that Protestants play songs coded as Catholic and vice versa. He also tries to debunk the myth of the "party tune," noting the uncanny resemblances between so-called "Orange" and "Green" songs. In his *Pocket Guide to Irish Traditional Music* Carson (1986b, 47) cites Hugh Shields' comment that "party songs are culturally complementary: while expressing different allegiances they use similar themes, forms, styles and melodies," and in *Last Night's Fun* Carson (1986a, 185) concludes that "what constitutes a 'party' tune depends on verbal labels and the perception of the hearer," rather than on anything intrinsic to the song itself.

Fintan Vallely (2008) largely substantiates Carson's claims in *Tuned Out: Traditional Music and Identity in Northern Ireland*. Vallely argues that views of traditional music as "Fenian" are simply "superficial and misinformed" (4) given the long history of Protestant contributions to the genre. He also refutes the tired maxim that "Catholics dance and Protestants march": "Orange marching bands are making an unambiguous political statement that commandeers open public space. Orangemen wish and need to have political space tonally defined. It is perhaps simple and convenient for them to mis-assign Traditional music to nationalism. With Traditional music, though, both actors and spectators at a session *may* be experiencing an occasion politically, but if this is done, it is usually done privately" (140). Ultimately, this suggests that music's galvanizing force can be broadly communal and can act as a potential catalyst to sociality: "The music is concerned with conversation, crack, diversion, passing the time. It is about being in one place at one time, and remembering all the other times" (Carson 1986b, 8).[9]

Carson's faith in the tune's capacity to move people together—to get "the place . . . jumping" (Carson 1986a, 4)—inflects his writing in several specific ways. First, "to get . . . into the poetry" (Carson 2002, 145) something of what he's experienced in traditional music sessions, Carson uses the traditional dance form known as the reel as the long line's rhythmic precedent: "[T]he line and rhythm of a reel is always in my ear, the way you extend notes beyond ostensible bar lines, or cut them short: going against the form all the time, but observing it. . . . It's supposed to tease the reader a little, or to keep him on the edge of the seat" (quoted in N. Corcoran 1992, 217).[10] This "teasing" effort to curtail or extend a poem's beat is evidenced by Carson's fondness for startling enjambment; he often sets up the line as a sentence-level unit and then frustrates the audience's expec-

9. "Crack" is the anglicized spelling of *craic*, an Irish word that refers generally to entertainment, conviviality, and good conversation. It is often invoked in the context of pub culture and traditional music sessions. According to Guinn Batten (1995, 537), *craic* is more than chat; it "broaches genres, spawning music and song, poems and stories, other performances of pleasure that may defy definition." Given Carson's attempt to act as a "tape-recorder . . . [a]n ear overhearing things in bars" (Carson 2002, 148), and to capture not only music but the "sophisticated gabble" (Carson 2009a, 19) surrounding it, *craic* is perhaps his work's defining tenor.

10. Carson's compositional process is suggestive in this regard; when Nuala Ní Dhomhnaill once asked him how he wrote his distinctive long lines, he replied, "[M]usic comes into [my] head, a line from a jig or a reel that is in [my] head as [I am] writing the line of poetry, and . . . the words . . . eventually come" (quoted in Crosson 2008, 250).

tation. For example, Carson (1996) primarily wrote "S" in neat couplets, and although the poem typically maps grammar onto meter, aligning line breaks with breaths, it occasionally breaks mid-sentence, even mid-word, in service of rhyme. Here idiosyncratic surprises move against phrasal regularity, which is a formal device that Carson borrows from the reel. "Prox- / Opera" (Carson 1996, "S" lines 5–6), for instance, is a startling cut, although it does work on the poem's behalf by enabling "Prox-" to suggest proxy, an actor playing a role, and by alluding to Benedict Kiely's (1979) novel, *Proxopera*, about a man forced to choose between driving an IRA bomb into town or seeing his family slain.[11] "Parox- / Ysms" (lines 7–8) is an even more unexpected break, this time coming halfway through a word. On the level of the line, this "pull[s the reader] up short" (Carson 1990, 82–83), but if one considers the couplet as a unit, it mimes an unanticipated tie: a note held across a bar line that creates suspense resolved in the following measure. Despite this unusual flourish, the poem still carries its thematic tune: "Parox" suggests Paroxetine, an antidepressant (trade name Paxil), which is appropriate to the passage's affect, and "ysms" as a suffix means "a practice or condition of," making semantic sense of "Ysms of grief." Like the reel, then, the poem maintains a balance between formal fixity—it tells a coherent tale and upholds its pattern of rhyming couplets throughout—and creative means of moving from one metrical unit to the next.

In "S" Carson (1996) also suggests a second way in which his poetry taps into traditional forms: tunes' circularity and cyclicality. Seán Ó Riada (quoted in Crosson 2004, 104)[12] captured the cyclical nature of traditional music in his memorable treatment of the ouroboros as an emblem of the genre. Carson demonstrates this circularity in "S" via recurring direct address to Miranda. He offsets her name in each instance by framing

11. This sleight of hand equates paramilitary performances with opera's histrionics, suggesting that both stage spectacle to garner sympathy.

12. Ó Riada was one of the most important composers and players in Irish traditional music's mid-century renaissance. His work influenced several contemporary Irish poets, most notably Thomas Kinsella, with whom he collaborated, and who elegized him fondly in *A Selected Life* (1972).

breaths: "you were Carmen, Miranda, you were Madama Butterfly"[13] (line 5); "I was there, Miranda, in the empty theatre" (line 9). As Seán Crosson (2008, 241–42) explains, traditional tunes are often structured around a "sense of returning," with repeated figures serving as "remembering[s] of points previously left," and Carson's Miranda is one such leitmotif. In his *Pocket Guide to Irish Traditional Music* Carson (1986b) tweaks this sense of the genre's iterability by identifying the principle of "repetition with variation" (7) as one of the genre's signature devices and paying tribute to the contained improvisation of the traditional performer: "The musician does what he is doing . . . and then he does it again, only differently" (9). Carson very often extends these premises to his poetry: "S," for example, ends almost where it began, with the poem's very first line being "remembered," "only differently," by its last. Both of these lines pay careful attention to the sounds of the poem's titular letter (an aspirated versus a voiceless /s/). They also maintain, thanks to their punctuation, a similar meter ("I see you now, Miranda," "Where were you, Miranda?"), and the lines keep their subject in view (glimpsed as the poem opens, Miranda has vanished by the time it concludes). Like the ouroboros, therefore, the tail of "S" is in its mouth, and the poem manages to capture the meeting of formal stability and casual variation that characterizes a traditional music session.

Seán Crosson (2004, 107) also suggests that Carson's penchant for "trisyllabic substitution in essentially disyllabic lines" makes his poetry ring of traditional music's rhythms, and metrical analysis proves Crosson's car true.[14] A triplet (sometimes called a "treble" by players) is one of traditional music's most common ornaments; it involves playing three notes in quick succession in the place of one quarter or two eighths. If songs are written down, trebles aren't typically notated because they come at the discretion of the individual player and are used idiosyncratically to emphasize

13. In this case, the line's structure also enables a double meaning: although the poem's Miranda is Bizet's Carmen, there is also a reference here to Carmen Miranda, the iconic 1940s Brazilian-Portuguese singer and actress.

14. Lucy Collins (2006) wrote a somewhat less specific article on the subject of Carson's efforts to get music into his poetry, which also suggests the force of this generic overlap.

particular components of the tune. Carson borrows this rhythmic shift for poetic embellishment: "S," for instance, is largely iambic, but triplets occasionally interrupt its metrical regularity. These disruptions come most often in service of Miranda's name, which is itself an amphibrachic foot. This pattern is established in the poem's very first line, which scans iambically, admitting only a single dactylic foot ("with a sigh") before landing on "Miranda," its concluding amphibrach. The poem circles around its addressee, repeating her name almost compulsively throughout—and given Miranda's position as the poem's anchor and centripetal center, it is perhaps only appropriate that she also direct and redirect its rhythmic flow. Traditional music's forms therefore marshal Carson's tempi, and they also work to expand and contract the poetic line for thematic emphasis.

Finally, as Carson (1986b, 10) notes in his *Pocket Guide*, when executed with technical prowess, Irish traditional music is much more deliberately accentuated than its classical counterpart. On this point, Carson singles out flautist John McKenna's 1920s tune recordings for praise, saying that McKenna's emphatic breathing "can [itself] suggest a whole world of . . . melodic possibility" (Carson 1986b, 27). This sentiment seems to carry over into Carson's own collections; one can feel in his poetry's lines the "pulsing" energy of a session, where "what matters is . . . the beat . . . [its] forceful logic" (Carson 1986a, 3). This is true of much of Carson's long line verse, particularly where its rhythms are irregular; perhaps stronger footfalls and internal rhyme are necessary to regulate the run-on lines. In "John Ruskin in Belfast," for example, Carson (1989) writes measured gems like "As the wrack resolves itself in skeins and hanks, in terraces and sinks and troughs" (line 14) and "The dung of horses, dogs and rats and men; the knitted, knotted streets" (line 17). Even "S" (Carson 1996), which is generally quite lyrical, includes moments of driving rhythmic force. The poem's fourth stanza, with its "parox- / Ysms of grief! Those swooning cadences! Those rolling eyes and Rs!" (lines 7–8) has an emphatic beat appropriate to its exclamatory affect. This emphasis is facilitated by the strategic line break that allows "Ysms" to assume unexpected rhythmic authority.

Insofar as traditional music is concerned, rhythmic vigor works to move bodies and to move them *together* in time. In *Last Night's Fun*

Carson (1986a, 3–4) accordingly frames the traditional session as a collectively kinetic experience: "[T]he place is jumping: whoops and gulders, clicking bottles, tapping feet. The whole room pulses like a diaphragm. . . . Joe is in full flight on 'The Ships are Sailing,' soaring above the cacophonous drums and the hum and buzz and clatter of the dance floor." The fact that Carson's writing captures this verve allows his poetry to approximate the same; his rhythmic emphases seem to demand a tapping toe or a bobbing head, making of his audience a circle of lilting literary listeners. This poetic strategy suggests that Carson's work consistently experiments with sound's capacity to shape community. Given his conviction that the "Troubled" city repels visuospatial belonging, this experiment becomes an emotional and political imperative of a kind: Carson's (2002, 147–48) efforts to "act as a . . . [barroom] tape-recorder," capturing the cadences of the "old boy playing in a corner . . . [to whom all] are drawn to listen," seek to provide sensory relief from Belfast's otherwise unhomely moment. Shared sound impressions mark acoustic gathering places for Belfast locals (civilians on both sides of the political divide) and for Carson's literary earwitnesses.

When Carson gives public readings, the exchange between music and poetry and the sense of a room's shared rhythm are palpable. When read aloud, the acoustics that Carson plots on the page are amplified, and when recited alongside traditional tunes, the poetry more audibly veers into melody. Carson very often orchestrates his appearances so as to chart these genre-crossings: for example, his hour-long contribution to Boston University's "Irish Voices" performance series in 2013 begins with a tune (Carson plays flute while his wife Deirdre plays fiddle), moves into a translation of Seán Ó Ríordáin, returns to a set of two hornpipes, proceeds into selections from Carson's (1996) *Opera Et Cetera* collection, segues into a march, which Carson uses to mediate "some stuff about war," and concludes with a handful of Rimbaud translations from his recent volume, *In the Light Of* (2012).[15] These seamless shifts from playing to reading

15. The event can be viewed in full on YouTube at http://www.youtube.com/watch?v=oOtJe7jgdcs.

highlight the proximities between the two; for example, when Carson introduces his "As I Roved Out," a take on Rimbaud's "Aube," he indicates that his translations are "based on Irish songs" and sings a few bars from the tune to demonstrate how the rhythms of Irish music can accommodate French alexandrines. Similarly, when Carson reads "O" and "K" from *Opera Et Cetera* (1996), the poems' lively rhythms and cyclical returns to the same sounds and motifs reveal them as kin to the dance tunes that precede them in the evening's performance. Carson's readings of his own poems are also emphatically accentuated; his vocal style is measured but energetic, lingering on stressed beats then driving into the next bar. As I have suggested, it is these deliberate footfalls that give traditional music sessions both their rhythmic vitality and their feeling of communal verve, and the same applies to Carson's poetry in performance. Although the audience is cropped from the video, one imagines Carson's auditors swaying together in time. Tellingly, Carson concludes the evening by explicitly linking music and verse, noting that "[a]t the back of all I do in writing . . . there's an absolute sense that there has to be . . . a melody to it . . . [a sense] that there's a song in back there somewhere, that it's haunting me." Everyone in the room at Boston University—and beyond, given the clip's circulation on the web—moves to this haunting melody; Carson's performance capitalizes on "the dynamic pulse" (Carson 1986a, 11) of shared sound.

He Stuttered: Carson's Acoustic Remains

Despite all of this aural conviviality, there remains an unincorporable residue in Carson's poetry. Although the city is more audible than legible, and although Carson ably marshals acoustic community, life in a conflict zone, it seems, can never quite be neatly contained. It is sound itself that here reveals its own untidy excesses: the stutter, an aural signal of suffering, intermittently irrupts on the level of both form and theme, forcing the poetry to sound the limits of its project. This strategy emerges from Carson's interest in investigating conflict's psychic impact, which is an especially pressing concern in the "Troubled" North. Since the signing of the Belfast Agreement in 1998, nationwide studies have shown that as much as 30 percent of the population meets the diagnostic criteria for post-traumatic stress disorder (Fey et al. 1999, 11). Carson's work concerns itself with this widespread cultural trauma. He repeatedly returns, for instance, to motifs of dismemberment and mutilation, and he remains preoccupied with the gruesome phantom limb. The stuttering line goes a step further and symptomatizes this pathology: it suggests that Carson takes seriously what it might mean to "interioriz[e] . . . the violence of history" (Wheatley 2009, 64).

This strategy has been recognized by several critics, including Jonathan Hufstader, Elmer Kennedy-Andrews, and Michael McAteer. Hufstader (1999, 219), for instance, suggests that "social violence . . . impedes direct speech," spurring either hesitation or circumlocution in the work. McAteer (2009) goes so far as to argue that the defining cadence of Carson's poetry is the "cultivated stammer," saying that his verse's "staccato quality" suggests the uncertainty of present or recently past conflict ("one," after all, "never know[s] what's around the corner") and likewise ensures that readers are never forewarned about "what might spill onto the page" (125–26). Carson himself has commented outright on this tactic; he does in fact stutter when he speaks, and this impediment carries over, he suggests, into his creative process: "My enormous hand was writing on the wall. The words began to stutter / As the quill ran out" (Carson 1996, "Graecum Est: Non Legitur" lines 8–9); "I was trying to complete a sentence in my head, but it kept stuttering" (Carson 1987, "Belfast Confetti," line 4). These lines point to Carson's self-professed "gargled doggerel" (Carson 1996, "Zulu" line 10) as a response to cultural rupture. Inasmuch, then, as Carson is interested in community-building and in the soundscape's potential inclusivity, his poetry also heralds violence's reverberations. In other words, there exists a productive tension in Carson's work between the stutter and his otherwise musical line. Sound is both a consolatory effort to contain trauma and, perhaps despite itself, a symptom *of* this trauma.

This struggle is nowhere more audible than in "Asylum" (Carson 1987). A jittery Belfast vignette, "Asylum" opens with an introduction to the speaker's Uncle John and a sketching of a series of family connections. The passage also reads ominously as a litany of severed body parts—John "had / His father's eyes, his mother's nose; and I myself . . . / Had his mouth" (lines 3–4)—and recalls the grisly remains of a paramilitary attack. This hovering violence emphatically hits home when Uncle John is subsequently said to have "A second cousin's hands, or a cousin's twice removed" (line 6), a line that is a disturbing double entendre and that highlights the conflict's domestic impact. The poem connects these images to Uncle John's various compulsions (e.g., his "jigging and clicking" [line 1] the door latch, which comes alongside his anxiously "[q]uickening pulse" [line 16]), suggesting that Carson holds local violence responsible for his phobic remembering and repeating (but never quite working through). Uncle John is also hypersensitive to sounds, and his ears prick throughout the poem to the "yelps of children" (line 14) and the "melancholic parp[s] of . . . car-horn[s]" (line 28). He is particularly discomfited by tin cans clattering and cars backfiring, markers of Belfast violence long etched into memory. His (over-)reactions to these noises are coded not just as signs of his madness, but as a generalizable sensitivity to local sound-signals. His apprehensive attentions seem sane enough when illuminated by the "Troubled" tones of street-level Belfast that Carson elaborates elsewhere: the ominous clacking of a spring-loaded Ford Sierra and the "whirring and ticking" of the "Remote Handling Equipment (Tracked) Explosive Ordnance Disposal unit" used to disarm its bomb (Carson 1989, "Queen's Gambit" lines 1–3). Although aural cues can lend navigability to a chameleonic city, turning an ear to violence and insecurity is hardly an easy task. Uncle John's suffering is invasively recalled by sensory triggers, such that his present is repeatedly repossessed by his past.

As "Asylum" progresses, Carson (1987) allows sound to operate as not only disease but symptom; we later learn that Uncle John's tics include a pronounced stutter (line 58). His "babbling, stammering" (line 59) is associated with his bearing witness to a difficult birth, although the passage also conjures the specter of sexual violence ("they said to shut her mouth"; "more, they said" [lines 61, 63]) and therefore refers at least obliquely to the conflict. Carson's ventriloquizing of Uncle John, especially the frenetic repetition of "she pushed," highlights John's stutter, and this allows the passage to frame traumatic experience as a foil to direct speech. Curiously, this excerpt comes on the heels of, and in stark contrast to, the lyrical fluidity of Uncle John's singing voice: "Or he might sing a song: perhaps *I'm going down the town / And I know who's going with me.*

I have a wee boy of my own, and his name is—/ Here he'd mention my name" (lines 39–41). This juxtaposition stages Carson's poetic struggle between sound's comforts and its shortfalls in an especially explicit way: musical conviviality, although consolatory, can sometimes give way to stammering hesitancy in the face of extreme violence.[16] Even Carson's own line is sometimes forced to stutter, with his "[g]etting nearer, nearer" mirroring the compulsive reiterability of Uncle John's syntax: an inheritance foreshadowed early in "Asylum" when the poet-speaker concedes that he "ha[s] his [uncle's] mouth" (line 4). The poem's structure writ large also enacts a type of stutter. Nearly every stanza ends by returning to one of Uncle John's central sensory triggers: "An electric / Yellow bakery van hummed by; he sniffed the air. A car backfired" (line 18); "A yellow bakery van hums by. There is a lull, and then a car backfires" (line 34); and "A yellow bakery van went by; he sniffed the ozone. A car backfired" (line 48). Therefore, the poetry *itself* exhibits signs of trauma; its neurotic recapitulation of its central tropes mirrors the psyche's spontaneous returns to originary ruptures. Carson even offers an explicit account of this phenomenon in "Asylum," explaining that post-traumatic stress disorder makes permeable temporal barriers and allows the past to encroach menacingly on the present: "You can tell that this was all some time ago, although it does repeat itself" (line 49).

Breaking News, Carson's 2003 collection, is perhaps the most sustained test of the poet's stuttering line. Its poems are consistently minimalist and almost telegraphic. The page serves as a stave on which fear's shallow breaths are inscribed: the poems are punctuated throughout by abrupt line breaks—cuts that capture harried, halting, almost hysterical rhythms that represent the gasps and wheezes of tales of terror retold. Although Carson's placelore has since returned to a longer, looser cadence (see *For All We Know* [2008], which is in part about Belfast's "local row" [Carson 2009a, 17]), some reviewers have received the pared-back poetics

16. This struggle has an autobiographical basis: although Carson stutters when he speaks, the impediment vanishes when he sings or plays the flute.

of *Breaking News* as an effort to evoke the fragility and tension of the post-ceasefire city.[17] Although it departs from the long line, the collection is nonetheless similarly inspired by Belfast earmarks.[18] When asked by Elmer Kennedy-Andrews in an interview about the volume, Carson cast the sounds of heightened urban surveillance as its muse: "[A]s it happened, the first poems that emerged in the short line were conceived when a helicopter used to come and perch above my house night after night. I could hear some kind of minimalist staccato beat going on throughout that unceasing din" (Carson 2009a, 21). The poem "Spin cycle" (Carson 2003), for example, is explicitly conditioned by this "beat," with both its theme and form hinging on the convulsive rotations of a hovering helicopter's propeller. The onomatopoeic "thug-thug" (line 7) of the chopper, the speaker's keynote sound, rhymed with his prophylactic "ear-plugs" (line 11), is recapitulated here by the poem's own rhythm. Everything, as it were, goes "centrifugal" (line 13); the poem pulls away from its axis, leaving hiccupping, halting fragments—the short line as syntactical shrapnel. Carson delivers the poem in one- or two-word "staccato bursts and arrests" (Kennedy-Andrews 2008, 207); its line breaks structure a splintering, stammering sound-scheme ("I couldn't / hear / myself / speak" [lines 3–6]). Carson creates form and content together in "Spin cycle": the poem's limping gait links instruments of state surveillance to civilian trauma. The disconcerting feeling of being scrutinized, even targeted, produces the poem's anxious energies, and the short line's "twitching" fits and starts operate as the very sound of (post-)conflict pathology.

17. See Ross Moore's (2008) "We Don't Know the Half of It," a review of *For All We Know* in *Culture Northern Ireland*.

18. Carson's most recent collections, *On the Night Watch* (2009b) and *Until Before After* (2010), are also for the most part minimalist and monosyllabic. Prompted by Carson's wife's serious illness, these collections meditate much more concertedly on personal than on collective trauma, taking the hospital room more than the city as a space of mourning. Given that I am primarily interested in Carson's urban placelore, I bracket the volumes here, following the poet's own recognition that these books are "somewhat of a departure" from the oeuvre (see Aida Edemariam's "A Life in Poetry: Ciaran Carson," *The Guardian*, January 17, 2009).

This connection is broadly characteristic of the volume as a whole; the chopper's strident tones later give way to the "dotty Morse" and "atmospheric static" (Carson 1997, 172) of short-wave radio, another tool of clandestine reconnaissance (official and otherwise).[19] In the poem "Trap" Carson (2003) narrates one such exchange between policemen or paramilitaries (the two were proximate enough during the Troubles, when the Police Service of Northern Ireland was still the largely Protestant Royal Ulster Constabulary) on their radios as they are interrupted by intervening static:

> I don't
> read you
> what the
> over[.] (Carson 2003, "Trap" lines 7–10)

These latter line breaks read as the radio's white noise, suggesting a sentry or "tail" reporting back to his superiors at headquarters. They also encode the narrator's nervous tic, a stammering hesitancy warranted both by the ubiquity of watching and being watched in the "Troubled" city and the explosive image of the tail's "cocked . . . rifle" (lines 6, 4). An example of Carson's self-proclaimed "ragged chorus" (1989, "Night Out" line 8), "Trap" again connects surveillance to acute trauma and channels this trauma into its stuttering line. Its line breaks suspend the poem's flow and sound the anxiously skipped beats of its speaker's heart. Like so many

19. In a beautiful and very sound-bound passage from *The Star Factory*, Carson (1997, 172) confesses to eavesdropping via short-wave radio: "In the small hours, at the height of the Troubles . . . I used to listen to the short-wave police radio, from which I learned the alphabet of *Alpha, Bravo, Charlie, Delta* [the military shorthand that Carson also uses to subtitle the poems in *Opera Et Cetera* (1996)]. . . . So convincing was the aural landscape, that I sometimes believed the police could overhear me, or at least know that I was listening to their stillicides of window-wiper swash, as they crawled through West Belfast in unmarked cars. Such paranoia was common then, and perhaps necessary, given the proliferation of bugs and other, increasingly sophisticated surveillance devices (one of which can pick up the vibrations of a window-pane at some incredible distance, and translate their shivers into conversation, the glass acting as a tympanum)."

of Carson's poems, "Trap" conveys a sense of paranoia: a neurosis conditioned by the inescapable immanence of violence. Carson's narrators are habituated to conflict, and yet there remains something fundamentally unincorporable about this habituation. It becomes a psychic strain that prompts the poem's sonic stumbling: the stutter as the exhumed remains of the poet's lilting long line. Ultimately, despite Carson's continued efforts to build acoustic community and conviviality, the site of trauma cannot always be neatly contained, and in *Breaking News* he seems to vocalize this symptomatic overflow. The struggle between these two strategies—the consolatory cadences of a *seanchaí*'s circle or the *craic* of a *céilidh* and the foreshortened stuttering line—is the rhythmic center around which Carson's work revolves. Sound is both a salve for and a symptom of trauma.

Sound and/as Sense in Carson's Poetry

The tension around sound's possible relationship to a "politics of good feeling" is bound up with a second struggle under which Carson's poetry strains. His collections are caught between two competing theories of sound: first, the notion of sound as pure phenomenon, producing visceral and immediately embodied effects; and second, the notion of sounds as signifiers (signs in elaborate systems of signs that accrue meaning only in cultural or aesthetic contexts). Carson's conviction, for instance, that rhythm forces bodies to move and can create communities of bodies moving together, or his notion that sound-signals can reflexively recall traumatic events and transmit immediate affective charges, suggests that acoustic causes and effects are biologically linked. Conversely, sounds like Belfast's cautionary tin can are semanticized; they are material effects to which meaning can be adhered by particular sets of circumstances. Carson considers sound to be both universal and particular and both biological and cultural. He believes that the tones of tale-telling and tune-playing can naturally soothe and that they can serve as sources of instinctive collectivity. Nevertheless Carson must parse out the tin can's psychic and political effects for those beyond the Shankill/Falls divide, explaining to outsiders how the community's sounds are recalibrated by conflict. When he argues that sound is a navigational tool, an affective trigger, a kinetic stimulus that can (quite literally) move bodies, or a means of apprehending and negotiating place, his poetry writhes under these structuring tensions.

Although Carson's theories of sound may be in competition, they are far from mutually exclusive. Poetic soundscapes are always capable of playing simultaneously with autonomic sound effects and strategic sound engineering. Rhythm, for instance, can and does regulate heart rate, and can be employed as a metronome of sorts to produce predictable effects on its reader-auditors. Several studies have corroborated this connection, including Bettermann et al.'s compelling 2002 test of art therapy's physiological efficacy. The study, published in the *International Journal of Cardiology*, finds that "the artistic creation of rhythmic patterns in time or space . . . [does indeed] affect physiological time signatures in man" (78). By monitoring subjects' heart rates during a series of poetry exercises, the researchers substantiated the restorative relationship between art therapy and cardiac, respiratory, and psychosomatic disorders.

Conversely, other poetic sounds are entirely context-specific; the same /u:/ ("oo") that soothes the ear when echoed successively becomes a menacing stutter when repeated haltingly or wrenched apart by sudden line breaks. The phoneme, in other words, gains its meaning in the aesthetic context of the poem or the stanza. Carson's work moves freely between these two takes on sound, and he appears to be interested in their collision: his poetry explores the ways in which the phenomenal world conditions perception, but it also investigates the freedom this world gives us to remake its meanings (and the place of poetry in this remaking). This friction is the very source of Carson's signature perceptual arc. He can hardly avoid the sensations of war, but he *can* reassemble the "pulsing[s] . . . [of] Orange drum[s]" (Carson 1999b, "Twelfth Day" line 14) and "broken rhythm[s] / Of machine-gun fire" (Carson 1989, "Night Out" lines 7–8) forcibly impressed on him as an acoustic code of sorts: a semiotics of sound guiding city travel. The night's "ragged chorus" ("Night Out" line 8), even while heralding insecurity, can yet make sense of the "demolition city" and can reorient the careful auditor.

At times in his poetry, Carson even argues that sound might offer a means (however tentative) of feeling at home, or of putting a broken place back together, as when "the noise of children playing . . . the whip-whop of a skipping rope, singing" (Carson 1987, "Patchwork" lines 47–48) maps the streets, suggesting a violence slightly abated. However, as Carson points out, although sound can make the otherwise slippery city navigable, turning an ear to conflict is far from easy. In "Night Out," for instance, Carson (1989) describes blasts beyond the breeze-block walls as aural alerts: signs that disrupt a session's songs and rounds of applause. Carson's soundscapes therefore remain ambivalent; voices are as often discordant in them as they are harmonious. Ultimately, whether or not eavesdropping on the city is difficult, the following point remains: Carson champions a revisionary phenomenology and offers a radical statement about our sensory understanding of the world. When seeing is severed from believing, he re-maps place in sound-space, casting Belfast's auditory texture as the pedestrian's most reliable guide. These observations mark Carson's poetry as theory, and they stand as his work's most important contribution.

4

DEREK MAHON

Bearing Earwitness

Mahon as Acoustic Ecologist

Derek Mahon is typically cast by critics as a poet of "place and displacement" (Haughton 1992, 87) and as a writer whose vexed relationship to his home country constantly, even compulsively, guides his pen. Admittedly, quite unlike Ciaran Carson, Mahon feels keenly his own unhomeliness in the North. Born and raised in Belfast as a non-Unionist Protestant, he can neither lay claim to the comforts of a common Celticism nor take refuge in Loyalist patriotism. Indeed, Mahon has long professed to feel stifled by the city's seeming claustrophobia and the calcified positions of its conflict. "For a large part of my life," he concedes, "I've been *terrified* of home" (Mahon 2002, 109). Peter Ercegovac (1999) calls this calcification the "ethno-genesis" of group identity: the North's post-partition cycles of mutual demonization that defined Catholic against Protestant (and vice versa) in ever more essentialist terms. Moreover, as debates about the "national question" (Northern Ireland's continued union with the United Kingdom versus its annexation by the Irish Free State) intensified mid-century, and as Catholics' concerns grew about civil rights violations at the hands of the Protestant majority, religious differences were superimposed on militantly oppositional politics. As this logic rigidified, it left little room for the likes of young Mahon, who had once fancied himself an anti-establishmentarian and a Protestant "all-Irelander" patterned after

Unless otherwise indicated, the versions of the poems referenced in this chapter are drawn from Mahon's (2011) *New Collected Poems*.

Yeats and his fellow Anglo-Irish Revivalists. This posture proved unsustainable as conflict brewed in the North and Unionism and Republicanism became increasingly absolutist, demanding that Northerners' subject positions dictate their political sympathies.

When the Troubles erupted, making overt violence of latent acrimony, Mahon was caught between Ulster's two worlds and peppered by their frenetic crossfire. "Marching for civil rights was terrific," he explains, "but bombs and killing people? I never put a name to my own position and I still can't, which suits me fine. From time to time you get a kick from some critic for not being sufficiently political, or for being a closet unionist or a closet republican. . . . But there is all this ambiguity. That is poetry" (see Nicholas Wroe's interview with Mahon in *The Guardian*, July 22, 2006). In light of this discomfiting "ambiguity," an anxiety that animates Mahon's work even today, the budding poet left Belfast for Trinity College Dublin in 1960 and never substantively returned. As the Troubles reached fever pitch, Mahon's guilt and distaste became next to unbearable, driving him into exile overseas: "I couldn't deal with it. I could only develop a kind of contempt for what I felt was the barbarism, on both sides. But I *knew* the Protestant side; I knew them inside out. I was one of them, and perhaps I couldn't bear to look at my own face among them. So I adopted a 'plague on both your houses' attitude" (Mahon 2002, 116).

Although Mahon has been wandering and writing outside of Belfast for the better part of fifty years, he has yet to find a suitable surrogate home. He has moved throughout the United Kingdom, Europe, Canada, the United States, and more, but his poetry remains on perpetual pilgrimage to Ireland, hovering at the margins of both the North and the Republic. As the screeds of critical material on the subject suggest, questions of place, and of feeling *in* place, remain among Mahon's major themes.[1] The introduction to Hugh Haughton's definitive 2007 study of Mahon's

1. See, for example, Eamonn Hughes' (2002) "'Weird / Haecceity': Place in Derek Mahon's Poetry," Richard Tillinghast's (2008) "Derek Mahon: Exile and Stranger," Hugh Haughton's (1992) "Place and Displacement in Derek Mahon," and Kathleen Shields' (1994) "Derek Mahon's Poetry of Belonging."

oeuvre, for instance, is tellingly titled "The Poetics of Home." Curiously, though, much of the existing criticism tries either to claim Mahon as a comfortably cosmopolitan global nomad (Zamorano Llena 2007, 103) and a writer who revisits the cloying North only to cast it off and become a citizen of the world, or to dismiss him as a misanthropic exile whose takes on home turf are disaffected and almost painfully bleak.[2] In my view, both of these perspectives miss the mark: the former strands Mahon in a sea of near-meaningless fluidity whereas the latter charges him with a stubborn hermetism, and neither acknowledges his poetry's obsessive purchase on the particulars of place. Far from melancholically withdrawing into cerebral abstraction in the face of unbelonging, Mahon's poetry is insistently perceptual; it turns to local landscapes and intimately apprehends their phenomenal worlds. His poems' titles, for instance, often name specific spaces—Belfast, Derry, Dublin, Donegal, Glengormley, Aran, Portrush, and so on—to which his poet-speakers then commit their senses, and his body of work gradually builds a phenomenological relationship to homeplace in the face of political alienation. Although he may be absent from the island's human community, Mahon explores the possibility of connecting to place in a more fundamental way: the embodied relationship of the subject to the so-called "object world."

Social ecologist Murray Bookchin (2005, 466–67) calls this kind of relationship "mutualism" or "complementarity." Allowing nature to open itself to us, he suggests, enables an *ecological* community, one of "organic interdependencies" (466) and "fecund, supportive interrelationships" (464) between human beings and the biosphere. A long tradition of this kind of community formation exists in Irish literature: centuries of nature poets, dating back to Amergin and the early proto-Celts, invested in a pastoral reverence for homeplace—a fixation on local geography that Eamonn Hughes (2002, 98) terms "topomania." This proximity to place became particularly important during the colonial period when natives' physical claims to territory were severed and different relationships to

2. Tom Paulin (1984, 18) has called Mahon "an intransigent aesthete who rejects life almost completely."

local landscapes—existential, even spiritual connections—developed in their stead. As Oona Frawley (2005, 5) argues, the (post-)colonial "Irish pastoral" is amplified by nostalgia or "homesickness," and so the mode, poetically descriptive but rooted in particular landscapes and place-names (79), becomes a means of "memorializing—and so reviving" (58) something lost. In some ways, Mahon, albeit a Protestant, backhandedly inherits this tradition: unhomed by local conflict, he tries to renegotiate belonging by way of the natural world.

But Mahon is not simply an immersive nature poet in the canonical mold. His self-professed liminality, which in his poem "The Sea in Winter" he calls "working on the circumference" (line 50) or "living on the edge of space" (line 68), means that his relationship to place must remain ever so slightly remote. Mahon at once relishes and regrets his solitude, finding it both personally troubling and politically enabling. Indeed, marginalization can afford the writer an independent intellectual agency, and it can perhaps even become an *ethos*—both an ethics and its own accustomed place. Although Mahon clearly cannot comfortably belong in the North, he can still keenly observe his home turf.

Stan Smith (2005) is one of very few critics to recognize Mahon's commitment to this kind of peculiarly distanced perception; he identifies Mahon's "phenomenological" posture and finally suggests "voyeurism" as the poetry's very "ontological condition" (171). Although Smith usefully elaborates Mahon's careful attunement to lived space, I think that Mahon is far more eavesdropper than voyeur. His work is insistently auditory and is perpetually bearing earwitness to the world. Moreover, Mahon uses the ear as a framing device precisely *because* of his marginality. Denied direct belonging—a disenfranchisement that manifests itself in the poetry as visual estrangement (as speakers "lying low" or lurking just around the corner from street-side scenes ["Courtyards in Delft" line 29])—Mahon remains out of the community's line of sight yet within critical earshot.[3] Appropriately, Adrienne Janus (2007) has called Mahon's poetic posture

3. For examples of the sequestered poet-speaker "listening out," see "Sunday Morning," "Consolations of Philosophy," "Rock Music," *The Yellow Book* (Mahon 1997b, retitled

a "liminality of listening" (183), suggesting that the ear is Mahon's primary "mode of poetic attention" (181) and mediator of place. Ultimately, Mahon's poetry offers a uniquely *acoustic* phenomenology: a thoughtful attention to the flux of its auditory field.

Mahon uses this "liminality of listening" to advance an ecocritical agenda. His solicitude for the natural world suggests that the "global village" crucially includes our lived and liv*ing* environment, and his work therefore listens in on and gives voice to otherwise "mute phenomena."[4] As Kathleen Mullaney (1989, 45) describes, Mahon's verse is "a respectful, patient, and self-effacing effort to 'let speak'" and to "listen to the poetry that surrounds us." However, to act as "clairauditor" or "clear hearer" for these mute phenomena (Schafer 1977, 4) and to overhear, say, "the sob story / of a stone in the road" in County Mayo (Mahon 1975, "The Mayo Tao" lines 13–14) or the cries of mushrooms in a derelict Wexford shed, Mahon must also try to muffle the often dissonant din of the anthropological world.[5] His poetry therefore takes human noise pollution to task, charging both the stridency of local conflict—the "white noise of sectarian hate" ("Northern Star" line 22)—and the "noisy knowledge" of global capitalism (Mahon 1997b, XIX line 40) with invasive cacophony and with indiscriminately silencing the sounds of natural phenomena.

In light of this agenda, Mahon's work might be recuperated to advance the aims of acoustic ecology, which is a field devoted to studying the ways in which sound mediates relationships between living beings and their

---

"Decadence" in Mahon's 2011 *New Collected Poems*) VI ("To Eugene Lambe in Heaven") and XV ("Smoke"), and the recent "Roman Script."

4. "The Mute Phenomena" is the title of one of Mahon's (1975) more canonical poems, which originally appeared in *The Snow Party*.

5. On this point, see "Derek Mahon: History, Mute Phenomena and Beyond," in which Jerzy Jarniewicz (2002) argues that Mahon figures the human world, "the aftermath of the Fall," as a world of noise (its landscape, Jarniewicz suggests, is the city, which is often metonymically described by the poetry as noise) (91–92). See also Edna Longley's (2002, 33) "Looking Back from *The Yellow Book*": "There is a sense of the poet, like John Cage, orchestrating faint echoes, flutters, bangs and ripples. In Mahon, sounds that just break silence figure poetry; a louder 'roar' figures history."

environments. Founded in the late 1960s by R. Murray Schafer, acoustic ecology thinks of place in acoustic space—not just as a constellation of things seen, but also as a soundscape or a surround-sound sphere. Acoustic ecologists bear immersive earwitness to these soundscapes. They treat the world as a "macrocosmic musical composition" (Schafer 1977, 5), and they investigate how cities might best undertake acoustic design in service of both ecological preservation and "clean hearing." The first such large-scale undertaking, pursued by Schafer and his World Soundscape Project team of composers and academics, was the 1973 Vancouver Soundscape audio release. This project involved locational sound recordings designed to raise listener consciousness of the city's sonic environment and to interrogate how our soundscapes provide us with a sense of place and how we might design sustainable soundscapes in urban spaces.[6] (The 1973 recording was followed by a second compact disc release in 1997, which charted the city's *changing* soundscape.) As Schafer (1997) suggests during "On Acoustic Design," a recorded lecture included on the compact disc, he keeps ecocritical activism at the heart of his work and is motivated by the onslaught of so-called "sound imperialism." This term also appears in Schafer's (1977) foundational manifesto, *The Tuning of the World*, in which he argues that the efforts of Europe and North America to dominate other peoples and value systems have been crucially underpinned by sonic subjugation. Schafer (1977, 77) compares overbearing "acoustic profiles" to an empire's violent incursions: "A man with a jackhammer is imperialistic because he has the power to interrupt and dominate other acoustic activities in the vicinity."

Acoustic ecocriticism therefore appears to be a natural offshoot of postcolonial theory; a discipline already invested in protesting exclusivist definitions of "the human" is well placed to accommodate the lives of the phenomenal world. It is no surprise, then, that Mahon's work cleaves to acoustic ecology: he is awkwardly positioned at the "Troubled" nexus of colonizer and colonized—a sense of being between worlds that has

6. See Barry Truax's promotional site for the project at http://www.sfu.ca/~truax/vanpromo.html.

long shaped his writing. In protesting noise pollution, Mahon objects to both the unhomely effects of conflict's cacophony on the North's non-combatant ears and to the perceptual violence wreaked by this manmade clamor on the keynote sounds of the natural world: the archetypal tones of landscape and climate (water, wind, birds, insects, etc.) that serve as acoustic backdrops for our lives (Schafer 1977, 9). Mahon's investment in "auditory geographies" (Rodaway 1994, 89) therefore resonates both personally and politically: it reflects his ecological intimacy and his efforts to negotiate Bookchin's (2005, 466) "complementarity" when otherwise denied community, and it performs a kind of poetic activism on behalf of hi-fi soundscapes that enable clean hearing.[7] His poetry parallels Schafer's work, demonstrating a solicitude for the natural world and a wariness of anthropocentrism, and it ought to be considered (at least in part) as an acoustic ecological intervention.

Amplifying the "Mute Phenomena"

Paul Muldoon's (2000) *To Ireland, I*, a transcribed collection of Muldoon's 1998 Clarendon Lectures, identifies "liminality" and "narthecality" as concepts "central to the Irish experience" (9). Drawing particularly on Beckett, Muldoon suggests that a "terminal narthecality"—a term that Muldoon derives from "narthex," the passageway between the entrance and nave of a church—characterizes much of Irish literature (24), and he speculates that this feeling of being in between is a peculiarly postcolonial predicament: "[S]uccessive invasions of the country le[ft] a sense for many so-called native Irish people of their own invisibility" (9). As the voices of Gaelic culture waned and the influence of colonial Englishness remained ideologically fraught, many Irish writers felt as if, in poet Thomas Kinsella's (1970, 59) words, they were inhabiting "a great rift."

For Mahon, this sense of being sidelined is further exacerbated by the shame of minding the gap between perpetrator and victim: the curious

7. Schafer (1977) defines hi-fi soundscapes as acoustic spaces with a favorable signal to ambient noise ratio, and he sets them against lo-fi soundscapes, which are spaces suffering from the "sound congestion" (43) that abbreviates distant hearing.

place of a (lapsed) Protestant United Irishman in the "Troubled" North. Mahon's unbelonging, his unwillingness to claim his British birthright despite (or perhaps because of) having anti-Catholic B-Specials in the family, and his inability to furnish a consolatory second home in Irish cultural nationalism[8] conditioned even his earliest poetry. From his first full-length collection (*Night-Crossing*, 1968) on, his writing hovers above home turf but can never quite manage submersion in its scenes. In other words, Mahon's work is characterized by a *poetic* narthecality: his speakers stand removed and typically unseen; they are around the bend and perhaps beyond the pale. Because Mahon's speakers are often out of sight and estranged from local scenes, they tend to linger nearby and listen in.

"Aran" provides an important early diagnosis of Mahon's unhomeliness.[9] Its speaker is a visitor to the Aran Islands, an area that has especially intimate ties to Irish landscape and cultural tradition given its relative isolation and its preservation of Gaelic as the predominant vernacular.[10] Although any treatment of the Aran Islands as a time capsule of history and folklore is guilty of romantic mythmaking, given that tourism

8. The B-Specials, shorthand for the Ulster Special Constabulary, served as a reserve police force in Northern Ireland. An almost exclusively Unionist group, the USC was called on to bolster the Royal Ulster Constabulary whenever war measures were enacted in the North, including during partition and the IRA border campaign in the 1950s. The B-Specials were often accused of violently partisan policing, and they were finally disbanded by order of the Hunt Report in 1970.

9. The poem originally appeared as "In the Aran Islands" in Mahon's (1972b) *Lives*, and it was retitled "Aran" (with some minor changes) in Mahon's (1999) *Collected Poems*. Mahon is a notorious revisionist and is constantly reworking his old material, so many of his poems have been reincarnated more than once.

10. Even if Mahon indulges briefly in this sort of romanticization in "Aran," taking his place in a long line of urban Protestants imagining themselves on the islands (see also "Rathlin," about the eponymous island off the coast of Northern Ireland's County Antrim, for a similar story arc), he nonetheless disagrees with critics who equate "true Irishness" with life in the *Gaeltachtaí*, and he remains suspicious of the privileging of the Irish historical experience. In his introduction to *The Sphere Book of Modern Irish Poetry*, Mahon (1972a, 13–14) boldly asserts that "Whatever we mean by 'the Irish situation,' the shipyards of Belfast are no less a part of it than a country town in the Gaeltacht."

and technological change have indeed affected the region, the islands are nonetheless a far cry from the Belfast shipyards of Mahon's youth. Moreover, given the region's remoteness and inaccessibility, toward which severe coastal weather has long conspired, the islands have occasionally been sheltered from the mainland's cultural shifts and have managed to preserve a handful of pre-colonial practices. *Sean-nós* singing is one such practice: it is the original form of Irish traditional song, and it served in the early Middle Ages as a bardic record of local events and a bearer of collective memory.[11] The term *sean-nós*, meaning "in the old style," was applied to the genre retrospectively; it was first used in a 1904 competition to distinguish the native Irish tradition from the more popular English vibrato vocal style. Formally speaking, the *sean-nós* is an Irish-language genre that is performed unaccompanied, and it features a melismatic melodic line. The timbre of the *sean-nós* is typically quite nasal, and its rambling, run-on phrases and lack of dynamic shifts are sometimes described as "droning." In practice, droning often resembles an incantatory trance because its vocal register is meant to facilitate a kind of free associative singing from the soul. The social dynamics of the traditional *sean-nós* value this intimacy and circulate it via physical transference; a *sean-nós* performance is often accompanied by "hand-winding," which involves a sympathetic listener grasping and pumping the singer's hand to release the song in a moment of ecstatic musical communion. This tradition seems to have been sustained on the Aran Islands in a relatively organic way—a continuity that Tomás Ó Canainn (1979, 49) attributes to "the sean-nós . . . [being] at ease . . . in an Irish-speaking situation where the singer and his listener are in real communication."

Mahon's "Aran" begins with its speaker eavesdropping on a *sean-nós* singer from the narthex of a pub door. The performer sings as his hand is wound by "his girl," and our narrator turns an ear to the tune but remains

11. For more information on the *sean-nós*, see Mary McLaughlin's (2002) *Singing in Irish Gaelic*, Fintan Vallely's (1999) *Companion to Irish Traditional Music*, and Anthony McCann's 1998 article in *The Living Tradition Magazine*, "Sean-nós Singing: A Bluffers Guide."

painfully outside its inner circle. The singer is described as "earthed" (line 1): a sense of rootedness that seemingly stems from the song itself (the musical line can travel in time and can resound things long past). In addition, the performance requires community and even communion; the song is a collective endeavor as its "echoes" (line 12) are coaxed from the singer's throat by his lover's grasp. This partnership is signaled by the parallelism of the poem's opening lines: "He is earthed to his girl, one hand fastened / In hers" offers complementary phrases in anapestic dimeter, and their rhythms prove to be a perfect pairing. The poet-speaker, moved by the music and envious of the intimacy it generates, briefly fantasizes about sharing in this acoustic space. He admits "dream[ing him]self to th[eir] tradition" (line 15) and imagines himself being enveloped by song in the pub's echo-chamber. The poem's reverie passage suggests this daydream of belonging with its echoing rhymes' incantatory, almost liturgical quality (Clark 2006, 166–67). The second stanza's sudden burst of near-perfect end-rhyme, with the recursive resonance of "sand"/"land"/"hand" and "admiration"/"vibration"/"reverberation"/"imagination," similarly channels the sentiment of the poet-speaker's earlier outburst: "God, that was the way to do it, / Hand-clasping, echo-prolonging poet!" (lines 11–12).

The speaker does mark his distance from the island's indigenous inner circle by conceding his "fearful admiration" (line 13) of the performance, and his isolation is suggested spatially in the poem by his hovering beyond the session's view. He lingers for a while in the pub doorway and then absents himself from the scene altogether, slipping out for a solitary seaside walk. Although the tune exceeds the barroom's bounds and spills out onto the sand, it doesn't help the speaker feel in place; he remains, he admits, "[g]enerations off the land" (line 16). This sense of alienation is reinforced in the opening stanza by the poem's insistence on the word "out," which is repeated thrice for amplified effect between lines 5 and 8.

Furthermore, although the speaker briefly maintains what Carol Rumens (2007, 19) calls a "fantasy of incorporation," this fantasy is soon punctuated by the cracked caw of a gull. The gull's open-throated cries are mimicked in the poem's own soundscape by the persistent /ɵ/ and /oʊ/ sounds that conclude the first stanza ("*o*ver," "*o*cean," "h*oa*rse," "inchoate," "bone," "echo," "poet"). The caws dissipate the speaker's imaginary consolations and re-relegate him to the scene's margins. In fact, the gull becomes a figure of the speaker's isolation, symbolizing distance and aloofness and reminding him that he remains painfully out of synch with the *sean-nós*. It also serves as a type of mouthpiece for the poem's speaker; its "crack-voiced" caws ("Aran" line 24) seem to be the very sound of his "working on the circumference" ("The Sea in Winter" line 50). These liminal acoustics are reinforced formally by the final stanza of "Aran"; its last lines abruptly break the previous pattern of end-rhyme ("fierce," "either," and "waters" hardly chime) such that the final ring in one's ear is that of the poet-speaker's unbelonging. Moreover, although hyphenation seems to signal connection earlier in the poem (the dashes in "hand-clasping" and "echo-prolonging" act as bridges and suggest the proximity between the singer and his hand-winder), in this final stanza it takes on a distancing function with "crack-voiced rock-marauder" (line 24). These hyphens act more as rifts or graphic representations of Muldoon's narthecality, suggesting that Mahon's poet-speaker can at best haunt the margins of local community. The poem concludes, in other words, on a note of lingering anxiety, and it remains rather far from comfortable resolution.[12]

At the same time that it documents its speaker's dislocation, "Aran" suggests something more: although clearly distanced from cultural tradition, the narrative voice begins to develop a proximity to the natural world. Even if the island's shoreline is bleak and desolate, it becomes the scene of the speaker's would-be intimacy. While locals congregate in the pub, he alone bears earwitness to the "gull creak[ing] off from the tin roof" (line 7), to the ripples of the "forming waters" (line 26), and to the rustling of

12. "Aran" is a far cry from "Digging," a poem by Mahon's more famous Ulster contemporary, Seamus Heaney (1966). Heaney's poet-speaker watches his father "turning" the ground and envies his father's tactile intimacy with the land, but he eventually concludes that writing can provide a comparable cultural connection: "Between my finger and my thumb / The squat pen rests. / I'll dig with it" (lines 29–31). Mahon comes close to lampooning this too-neat denouement: "Aran" echoes with "hoarse inchoate / [s]creaming" (lines 9–10) and its sounds mark out the speaker's space as distanced critic.

the "nacreous sand" (line 14).[13] This relationship, if not compensatory, is at least a consolation because it allows the speaker to take (temporary) refuge in place. The line "No marsh-light holds a candle to this" (line 22) enables this reading; it refers to the night's enveloping darkness, but its idiomatic meaning also implies that Mahon's speaker finds sustenance in local landscapes. Although Mahon is neither marshaled by the beat of a lambeg drum nor lulled into meditation by the *sean-nós* (he is neither an Orangeman nor an "authentic" Irishman), his eavesdropping enables a perceptual relationship with homeplace to which nothing can "hold a candle."

Mahon's so-called "liminality of listening" (Janus 2007, 183) is therefore both a symptom of his alienation from human community and a step toward Murray Bookchin's (2005, 467) ecological "mutualism"—a kind of belonging in biodiversity. Bookchin (2005, 463) argues that ethical relationships with nature are essentially phenomenological because our bodies are implicated in the "interspecific support systems" and "planet-wide biogeochemical relationships" that ensure our very survival. In particular, Bookchin's rhetorical flourishes suggest that these rhizomatic relationships are mediated by the ear: "[A truly ecological sensibility] . . . will provide both humanity and nature with a common ethical *voice*. No longer would we have need of a Cartesian . . . dualism that leaves nature *mute* and mind isolated from the larger world of phenomena around it" (Bookchin 2005, 467, emphasis added).

Mahon's phonological posture, however, isn't simply a self-serving effort to tune in to ecological "complementarity," a term that Bookchin (2005, 466) uses to "affirm the role of community as a desideratum in nature and society"; it also operates as a critique of anthropocentrism. Mahon's earwitnessing aims to reveal the vitalism of the natural world. By amplifying the voices of ostensibly mute phenomena—voices often crowded out of earshot—Mahon argues that our lived environment is in fact liv*ing*.[14]

13. Although "nacreous" means "iridescent," the origin of the word is the Old Italian *naccara*, or "drum," which similarly suggests the poem's investment in things heard.

14. The best Mahon scholarship recognizes and responds to the poet's ecocritical pose. Elmer Kennedy-Andrews (2008, 173), for example, remarks that "[Mahon's] poetry emphasizes ecocentric values of close observation and appreciation of the miracle of the

In "A Poetics of Silence: Derek Mahon 'At One Remove,'" Kathleen Mullaney (1989) approximates this argument, linking Mahon's "deep respect for the world around him" (45) and "contempt for facile humanism" (47) to his poetry's commitment to sound. Mullaney claims that Mahon aims to self-silence, and that his poems serve as patient efforts to "listen to the poetry that surrounds us" (45) and to "let speak" (50) that which sounds in the absence of the human. Likewise, I suggest that Mahon's philosophy of listening casts the ecological world as a living organism. For Mahon, the ear momentarily quiets the tongue, which makes possible a humbling intimacy with other lives (human and otherwise). Mahon's "numinous materialism" (Haughton 2007, 343) is, in other words, an important ethical and political gesture. His poetry critiques "[man's] blithe . . . sense / of [his own] cosmic significance" (Mahon 1972b, "Beyond Howth Head" lines 65–66) and enters a plea on behalf of the lives laid waste by human rubbish.

This ear-minded effort to foreground ecological lives is precisely the pose of Mahon's "The Mayo Tao," which initially appeared in his 1975 collection *The Snow Party*. "The Mayo Tao" is an early poem that becomes a thematic touchstone for his later work. Mahon's anxiety about feeling (or failing to feel) at home saturates the volume, which returns compulsively to both Northern Ireland and the Irish Republic despite being written from temporary perches in London and Surrey. "Afterlives," for instance, fingers Troubles-era Belfast as a cacophony of "yap[ping] . . . orators" and "back street . . . gun[fire]" (lines 10–11), but the poet-speaker still wonders wistfully, "Perhaps if I'd stayed behind / And lived it bomb by bomb / I might have grown up at last / And learnt what is meant by home" (lines 45–48). "The Mayo Tao" is similarly shaped by the island's magnetic pull and is drawn almost despite itself to County Mayo on the Republic's northwestern coast. Here, the poet-speaker's sense of alienation from manmade

ordinary, collective ecological responsibility, and the claims of the natural world beyond ourselves." On the subject of Mahon's eco-poetics, see also Brendan Corcoran's (2008) "'Persisting for the Unborn': Derek Mahon's Elegaic Poetics," Hugh Haughton's (2002) "'The Bright Garbage on the Incoming Wave': Rubbish in the Poetry of Derek Mahon," and Haughton's (2007) *The Poetry of Derek Mahon* (the most exhaustive study of Mahon's work to date).

civilization distances him physically from other people; he takes refuge in a remote cottage that sits miles from its nearest neighbor. This visual estrangement, another iteration of Mahon's "lying low," compels the poet's characteristic turn to the ear, and the poem carefully develops his "liminal listening." In this case, Mahon's eavesdropping, having screened out the anthropological world's white noise, amplifies non-human voices and allows the poet to extend life's purview to the ecological world. Moreover, this so-called "geo-piety" (Haughton 2007, 172) enables a consolatory intimacy with non-human lives in the absence of human community and a phenomenological purchase on homeplace in the face of political alienation. As such, the poem works throughout to document its surrounding soundscape, which serves as a tonic to "unrelaxing / Scenes of sectarian strife" (Mahon 1975, "Autobiographies," lines 85–86).

Mahon (1975) opens "The Mayo Tao" by renouncing the trappings of the anthropological world, in which "dream kitchens" (line 1) connote conspicuous consumption—a desire that is all too human. This gesture of humility is also a conscious muting of human static that enables the poet-speaker to bear earwitness to subaltern frequencies. The subsequent line explicitly establishes an aural connection between the speaker and his environment: "a storm snores," Mahon trippingly intones, "on the desolate sea" (line 3). The line's pace is indebted to its surrounding soundscape: its rolling gait, shaped by the drawn-out speech sounds of its r-colored diphthongs (the repeated /ɔər/ in "storm" and "snores"), seems to be a kind of snore, mimicking the protracted rise and fall of a sleeper's breath. Once "The Mayo Tao" expressly immerses itself in its auditory field, the phenomenal world begins to clamor for its speaker's attentions: he spends his days "in conversation" (lines 8–10) with deer, blackbirds, fox, and badger. As the poem progresses, it animates even "a stone in the road" (line 14), locating vociferous life in what most would consider (as the expression "dumb as a rock" suggests) an insensible *thing*. For Mahon, though, keeping an ear to the ground means overhearing the voices of a landscape's supposedly mute phenomena, and his speaker is accordingly tasked with standing "for months listening to [the stone's] sob story" (line 13). This conversation dissolves subject/object distinctions—an important anti-anthropological move. As Adrienne Janus (2007, 181) describes it, Mahon's

"I" is "an ear . . . vibrating between mind and world," and his listening is therefore "a philosophical stance which moves beyond the subject/object divisions inherent to the 'specular' tradition in Western philosophy." Although sight sets a scene—a series of props and players assembled before a subject's eyes—binaural hearing's 360-degree range places the auditor *within* a world, casting the individual as a single broadband access node: a point in a wider acoustic field. The ear, then, enables an especially anti-Cartesian mode of being in the world, which phenomenologist Don Ihde (2007, 15) calls an "ontology of the auditory." It becomes difficult to elevate the human "I" over the geographical "it" when the biosphere's sounds are all-encompassing and the heard world "penetrates" the body in ways that things seen cannot (Ihde 2007, 81).

In "The Mayo Tao," Mahon (1975) builds the ostensible object world's search for a sympathetic ear into the poem's own sound-scheme: the speaker's lived landscapes whisper to him via an alliterative pattern of sibilant "esses." The fricative "s" shapes the passages about the speaker's surrounding sounds—the snoring storm, the stone's sob story, the confessions of "the stinking shore, the stars in the mud"—and this insistent hailing (psst!) drives him to speak on his environment's behalf (line 18). Thanks to its submersion in its soundscape, the poem finally arrives at an almost metaphysical relationship to place; it finds "an immanence in these things" (line 19)—a divinity in the material world. All the same, though, the poet-speaker feels "very far from home['s]" *human* community (Mahon 2002, 109), which is framed elsewhere in the volume as "fire-loving / People" who try to "Demand . . . that [he] inhabit, / Like them, a world of / Sirens, bin-lids / And bricked-up windows" (Mahon 1975, "The Last of the Fire Kings" lines 35–41). This ambivalence surrounding home-place is precisely what motivates Mahon's poetry, which explains why "The Mayo Tao" self-reflexively concludes with an act of writing (a poem within a poem): "I have been working for years / on a four-line poem / about the life of a leaf; / I think it might come out right this winter" (Mahon 1975, lines 25–28).

Despite Mahon's commitment to "mutualism" (Bookchin 2005, 467) in "The Mayo Tao," the conversations with otherwise mute phenomena in the poem remain somewhat precarious. Even when the reader tries to decenter the human as a point of ecological reference, the language itself remains fundamentally anthropocentric. As Matthias Jung (2001, 275) explains this position, "[i]f anthropocentrism is understood as naming from the human point of view, it has to be kept in mind that in an absolute sense language is always anthropocentric. Even 'ecological renaming' from the point of view of animals and plants . . . remains the expression of human projection, for how else could we reproduce the 'consciousness' of animals and plants? The naming from the point of view of other species logically would have to be 'caninocentric,' 'felidocentric,' 'bovidocentric,' etc. Their names again would not be 'objective' ecological designations, but would represent only other centrisms." That is to say, while trying to protest human beings' self-appointed pride of place in the biological world, Mahon's efforts to develop phytological and zoological points of view involve their own anthropocentric projections.

Imagining another species' consciousness, as Jung points out, requires analogizing the workings of the human mind. Whereas a poem like "Aran" simply foregrounds an attentive attunement to the natural world, suggesting birdsong's frequencies as phenomenological pathways to a deeper sense of place, "The Mayo Tao" claims to *speak* with passing "deer and blackbirds," necessarily generalizing human language and affect. However, as Derrida argues in his lecture on Francis Ponge (published in translation in 1984 as *Signéponge/Signsponge*), it is ethically possible for a poet to "give voice to things" ("*La parti pris des choses*"), as the title of Ponge's 1942 collection would have it, so long as he also works to "acquit" (14) himself for the necessary violence of his projections. Natural phenomena, Derrida suggests, are "impossible subjects" (15); Ponge is duty-bound to write on behalf of "things" even though they are irreducibly "other." That is, Ponge must speak for these "things" even though he will never manage transparent translation, and he must forever try to exonerate himself for his language's inevitable anthropomorphizing (Derrida 1984, 12–14). Mahon's work is similarly self-reflexive, and his desire for acquittal is revealed by the vexed qualifiers in "The Mayo Tao": the poet is driven by the "immanence in . . . things" *almost* to the point of speech, and he works perpetually on "a four-line poem / about the life of a leaf" that *might* eventually come out right (his "might" suggesting an infinitely deferred wish fulfillment). The documentation of cross-species conversations in "The Mayo Tao" is offset by the poem's concessions of epistemic violence; it acknowledges anthropomorphizing the animal and the vegetable as both necessity and disservice. However, despite the inadequacy of his language, Mahon cannot abandon the acoustic ecological project. He writes today with an even keener ear to the ground, seeking ever more ethical ways to speak in the name of a soundscape under erasure.

Against Sound Imperialism

To act as would-be clairauditor for the world's mute phenomena and to "listen to the poetry that surrounds us" (Mullaney 1989, 45), Mahon must try to muzzle the clamor of the anthropological world. Because "the contrast between the man-made world and the world of mute phenomena" in Mahon's poetry is uniquely auditory, "the human world" is often figured as "a world of noise" that endangers "the . . . order [of] natural phenomena" (Jarniewicz 2002, 92). In response to this threat, Mahon's work takes noise pollution to task, faulting both the stridency of local conflict and the cacophony of globalization for their invasive sound imperialism. Once again, here, Mahon has a firmly ecocritical aim in mind: he objects to noise that does perceptual violence to the keynote sounds of landscape and climate (Schafer 1977, 9). Two concerns seem to motivate this objection. First, Mahon suggests that sound congestion's abbreviation of considered hearing is also a symptom of human technology's destruction of the natural world. Mahon's investment in the world's auditory geography—a poetic activism on behalf of both hi-fi soundscapes and open ears—is therefore an effort to highlight "[t]he environmental crisis of the soundscape . . . the qualitative downward trend of the acoustic environment" (Westerkamp 2000, 3) and to protest the destruction of the Irish pastoral muse. Second, Mahon is attuned to the intimate relationship of sound and affect, in particular the sentiment of feeling at home.[15]

15. Steve Goodman (2009) calls this relationship "affective tone" (xiv), explaining that sound centrally modulates mood: "As film sound designers know only too well, certain frequencies can produce an affective tonality of fear in which the body is left poised

Because acoustic ecology is defined by the field's governing body, the World Forum for Acoustic Ecology, as "a way of knowing a place through sound,"[16] it is no surprise to hear one of Mahon's earliest poems proclaim that "One part of my mind must learn to know its place" ("Spring in Belfast" line 16), nor to see his later work pursue that "learning" via the ear. As Kendall Wrightson (2000, 11) explains in the inaugural issue of the World Forum for Acoustic Ecology's journal *Soundscape*, "the sound of a particular locality (its keynotes, sound signals and soundmarks) can—like local architecture, customs and dress—express a community's identity to the extent that settlements can be recognised and characterised by their soundscapes. . . . [Familiar sounds allow individuals to] maintain . . . relationship[s] with home." Therefore, without nature's sound signals, Mahon appears to have little purchase on homeplace. Wrightson (2000, 11) further suggests that "[i]n the lo-fi soundscape, meaningful sounds (and any associated acoustic colouration), can be masked to such an extent that an individual's 'aural space' is reduced. Where the effect is so pronounced that an individual can no longer hear the reflected sounds of his/her own movement or speech [common in many cities], aural space has effectively shrunk to enclose the individual, isolating the listener from the environment." It is precisely this kind of isolation to which Mahon objects. Given the poet's vexed (post-)colonial context (his position as a lapsed Protestant and his political narthecality), Mahon's perceptual relationships with place seem to be his only viable paths to rootedness and belonging. Mahon's landscape poetry serves as a tonic for his chronic unhomeliness—a homesickness that approaches home*less*ness (Frawley 2005, 5). His Irish pastoral turns to (eco-)protest, however, when his clairaudience is dampened by noise pollution. The din of the anthropological world masks meaningful sounds and threatens Mahon's efforts to negotiate belonging in biodiversity.

---

in anticipation, expectant of incoming events: every pore listens for the future. Just think of the *uneasy listening* of atonal or discordant sound, or the sense of dread induced by low-frequency drones" (189).

16. See WFAE's homepage at http://wfae.proscenia.net/.

This activist approach to Ireland's soundscapes—Mahon's response to the aural palettes of both the "Troubled" and post-"Troubled" North and the rapidly industrializing Republic—resonates loudly in the poem "Northern Star," which Mahon (1999) wrote for the release of his *Collected Poems*. Mahon penned "Northern Star" in memory of Stewart Parker, and he patterned it after a Parker play that dramatizes the life of Henry Joy McCracken and the eventual defeat at Antrim of the 1798 United Irish Rebellion. Parker (2000) wrote the play through the lens of a (political) history of Irish theater, and it moves through stylistic imitations of Wilde, Synge, Shaw, and so on.

In "Northern Star," Mahon (1999) references past Ulster violence to situate the current conflict as part of a long genealogical line, and the couplet "echoing down the continuous past / in the loved entries of Belfast" (lines 23–24) suggests this reiterative relationship. The poem slips almost undetected between the past and the present. It begins in phonological pose, immediately invoking the clamor of historical conflict. Mahon describes "ancestral voices" (line 1) that resonated in 1798 and that call even today from beyond the grave: the restless reverberations of colonial conquest still dominate Belfast's bandwidth. The poem's opening stanzas seem to lionize the United Irishmen as "inspired conspirators" (line 7) heeding history's calls and paying them forward: McCracken and Wolfe Tone pledge to fight for Ireland's independence at Mac Airt's Fort, their "trenchant resolutions / echoing in [Cave Hill's] whin-scented air" (lines 14–15). The rebels' demands for justice initially appear as an organic outgrowth of local landscape: the words of these so-called "children of nature" (line 13) are gently "adrift like thistledown everywhere" (line 16). However, as the historical record shows, the rebellion became a bloody civil war that descended into "'shite / and lunacy'" (lines 18–19). Despite the United Irishmen's avowed non-partisanship, sectarian cruelties were committed by both rebels and government forces. The especially violent Loyalist campaign at Wexford, for instance, involved the summary executions of many suspected United Irishmen, and retaliations during the desperate final battles at Vinegar Hill punitively equated Protestantism with Loyalism (several unarmed Protestant prisoners were piked to death).

Tellingly, this "white noise of sectarian hate" (Mahon 1999, "Northern Star" line 22), the legacy of would-be liberation that Mahon develops as a local soundtrack to be remixed by contemporary conflict, disrupts even the poem's own acoustic keel. When violence erupts thematically in the poem's third stanza, the poem's previous pattern of perfect end-rhyme ("ghosts"/"hosts," "down"/"Down," "thatch"/"catch," "Hill"/"still," etc.) is thrown suddenly off kilter ("incomplete"/"hate"). Moreover, the conflict's cacophony is anticipated acoustically by the poem's earlier verses, which allows sound to provide second-degree commentary on the poem's sense. At the level of content, "Northern Star" initially celebrates the rebels' valiant efforts to "make history" (line 8); however, the poem's form ominously qualifies its theme by same-word chiming the "echoing" (line 15) of the rebels' pledges with the "echoing" (line 23) of the sectarian strife described later on. Similarly, the double meaning of the lines, "their music above politics still / as starlight shines above a bog" (lines 10–11) allows the poem's "music" to serve as a prelude to its subsequent views of violence: "above politics" connotes aesthetic purity and ideological neutrality, but the simile suggests that "party tunes" can *reflect* partisan politics just as water does light. This passage also harkens back to Parker's play, which concludes with McCracken's hanging and the pulsing of an Orange drum "drowning out" (Parker 2000, 82) the play's ambient sound—a move that Hugh Haughton (2002, 327) calls "the play's final dissonance": an acoustic cue that reminds listeners of contemporary parade route hostilities.

Apropos of Parker's effort to excavate the history of present-day conflict, the final stanzas of "Northern Star" explicitly discuss the Troubles and frame the North's post-partition clashes as the violently partisan legacy of these earlier battles. Here Mahon overtly juxtaposes the "white noise of sectarian hate" (Mahon 1999, "Northern Star" line 22) to the "holistic sound" (line 36) of local landscape, making the point that Ulster's "boomtown[s]" (line 19), as his poem "Derry Morning" describes them, drown out both the subterranean patter of civilians and the voices of the phenomenal world. Approaching the North's hostilities as an acoustic ecologist, Mahon's eavesdropping bears out noise pollution in surround sound: "the lanes of Antrim, Down" (Mahon 1999, "Northern Star" line 4) echo with the cries of "killers and victims" (line 34) "drowning out any further words" (line 40). The poem also same-word rhymes the "white noise of sectarian hate" with the "[w]hite noise of gulls at rubbish dumps" (line 33), a chime that faults combatants both for the unwieldy feedback distorting its speaker's clairaudience and for the degradation of the natural world (the "rubbish dumps" are a far cry from the landscapes once hailed by local nature poets). This marks Mahon's unhomely moment: already removed from the North's human community because he falls awkwardly between its political worlds, the poet has tried to "learn to know [his] place" ("Spring in Belfast" line 16) by keeping local ecology within earshot. The conflict, however, redoubles his sense of alienation from place by threatening any possibility of pastoral peace, and the poem's "streams" and "dreams" (lines 27–28) "fade oblivionwards" (line 39), drowned out by the din of anthropogenic decibels. Ultimately in "Northern Star," Mahon offers a sustained critique of Ulster's sonic shrapnel; its lo-fi soundscapes silence local lives, muting even the once-reparative "sound / of blackbirds on a summer night" (lines 36–37).

Mahon's Mushrooms

Mahon's "A Disused Shed in Co. Wexford," his most canonical poem, follows a similar narrative arc to "Northern Star." First published in *The Snow Party* (1975), "Disused Shed" is typically read as a take on the Troubles twice removed: an allegory of the Irish War of Independence offering a deflected view of contemporary conflict. Seamus Heaney (2002, 119) suggests that the poem provides a distanced look at "the frustrations and desolations of lives in Northern Ireland," its untended flat of wild mushrooms standing in for "the familiar shades of [Mahon's] Belfast" both past and present, and Hugh Haughton (2007, 115) says outright, "Mahon's poem is about contemporary violence."[17] This reading is resonant given Mahon's view from his

17. Haughton (2007, 116–17) does caution, however, against an entrenched reading of "Disused Shed," which might rob the poem of its "historical witnessing" and its commitment to "speak[ing] for the masses of the dead from other [wars and] eras." Haughton says that the poem's exclamation, "Lost people of Treblinka and Pompeii!" serves as a broader moment of "mobility on behalf of the immobilized"; beyond his immediate context, Mahon is also interested in "historical memories and analogues" (116–17).

post in London of the violence rending the streets of his youth; the years he spent working on *The Snow Party* (1972–75) were by far the conflict's most lethal. The period included 1281 conflict-related deaths, including 734 civilian casualties, and incendiary events like Bloody Friday (July 21, 1972), when twenty-two Provisional IRA bombs exploded in Belfast city center in a single afternoon. In some ways, these acts of violence broadly generalized Mahon's feeling of home's insecurity and inhospitality: locals' most intimate spaces were brutally defamiliarized as pubs, shops, and well-wandered streetscapes became "holes knocked into holes" (Carson 1989, "Question Time" 61). This widely felt sense of unhomeliness pressed Mahon into writing more persistently about the conflict and into becoming a mouthpiece for those disaffected and dispossessed by its escalating violence. As such, "Disused Shed" opens with a dedication to J. G. Farrell, whose 1970 novel *Troubles* chronicles Anglo-Irish decline and the onset of the Irish War of Independence in 1919. Toward the end of the book, Farrell's Major Archer stores the body of a dead Sinn Féiner in a potting shed, and the scene serves as the seed of Mahon's poem. Mahon explicitly acknowledges the debt by suggesting that his mushrooms, "[p]owdery prisoners of the old regime" (Mahon 1975, "A Disused Shed in Co. Wexford" line 44), have been awaiting rescue "since civil war days" (line 22).

Writing at the height of the Troubles, Mahon uses Farrell's take on the Anglo-Irish War to talk about contemporary conflict—the necessary indirectness of someone suffering from self-diagnosed colonial aphasia: "It's possible for me to write about the dead of Treblinka and Pompeii: included in that are the dead of Dungiven and Magherafelt. But I've never been able to write directly about [the Troubles]" (Mahon 2002, 116). Operating as a "meditation on historical violence and waste, cultural obsolescence and amnesia" at a time when this violence is being re-enacted, "Disused Shed" intimates that partition, the supposed resolution to centuries of conflict following colonial conquest, left Ireland's political divides to "fester and grow, like the [poem's] mushrooms" (Haughton 2007, 112–17).

However, approaching "Disused Shed" (Mahon 1975) stethoscopically yields a second, equally valid reading. The consideration of Mahon's mushrooms strictly as ciphers for victims of violence neglects the undertheorized work of "Disused Shed" on behalf of mute phenomena. A mushroom, for Mahon, is also the thing itself, and the poet bears earwitness to these "weak souls" and ventriloquizes their voices. The collision of these two readings—mushroom as metaphor and mushroom as mushroom—positions the poem as a centerpiece of Mahon's career interests. As an acoustic ecologist, he is concerned with the conflict's cacophony, but his solicitude extends beyond civilian non-combatants to the vulnerable lives of the natural world. Readers familiar with Mahon's work will find the disused shed's "grim / Dominion of stale air and rank moisture" (lines 33–34) redolent of the poet's cloying, claustrophobic representations of Ulster, and there is no doubt that its imprisoned mushrooms stand in for that which Heaney (2002, 119) calls "a whole Lethe of [the North's] doomed generations and tribes, whispering their unfulfilment." Regardless, the poem's first stanza seems as literal as it does figurative, expressing Mahon's desire to rescue his flat of mushrooms—troped here as a "thought" (line 1), a sure sign of life—from the fate of the "echo trapped forever" (line 4): a feedback loop that returns only to itself with no other for auditor. The mushrooms in "Disused Shed" aren't mute, but they have been willfully mut*ed* (Jarniewicz 2002, 95), and Mahon recuperates their protest's tones as his poem's keynote sounds. Landscape, in other words, doesn't simply inspire poetry, as the model of the Wordsworthian idyll suggests, but is rather resonant *with* poetry to the careful close listener. Mahon's mushrooms are agents, affectively charged and actively seeking their emancipation, and the poet grants them authoritative voice: they audibly protest their isolation and "groan / For their deliverance" (lines 38–39), waiting to be reunited with the wider world. A faithful interlocutor, Mahon amplifies all of the mushrooms' otherwise unheeded cries, noting even their fungal jostling for "Elbow room! Elbow room!" (linc 36).

In trying to draw attention to the phenomenal world's crisis of direct address (also a sidelong rebuke to the cacophony of Northern Ireland's "yap[ping] . . . orators" [Mahon 2011, "Afterlives" line 10]), Mahon inspires sympathy for the lives embedded in local landscapes via his poem's own sonic contours. The evocative soundscape that Mahon engineers is precisely the shed's echo-chamber. Imprisoned by the shed's closed door and unable to see beyond its walls, the mushrooms' relationships to the outside world are necessarily mediated by the ear: they "[l]isten . . . to the rooks querulous in the high wood" (line 20) and "hear . . . / trickle[s] of masonry . . . shout[s] from the blue / [and] . . . lorr[ies] changing gear at the end of the lane" (lines 28–30). The poem asks us to testify to the mushrooms' plight by narrating the world from their perspective. Its descriptions abridge vision—the keyhole, after all, is the poem's single source of light—and its perceptual cues come primarily from sonic sense-patterns, such as its penultimate stanza's "cracking lock[s]" and "creak[ing] . . . hinges" (lines 42–43). In fact, light serves these lines more as fodder for fortification and decay—the poem's cycle of horticultural birth and death—than as a medium for making visible. Left so long in a murky twilight, the mushrooms (and Mahon's readers) must re-orient themselves via the heard world.

In the last few stanzas of "A Disused Shed in Co. Wexford," Mahon (1975) develops what might be called a "rhythmic point of view"; he configures his poem's tempi such that his reader-auditors must move *with* his mushrooms. We feel, for instance, their frenetic energy as the poem's meter accelerates with the drivingly hyphenated "flash-bulb firing-squad" (line 47), and we measure with them their long years of abandonment with the multisyllabic drawn-out "interminable departure" of the "expropriated mycologist" (lines 23–24). Mahon's rhythms effect this perceptual alignment by re-timing his audience's bodies, which is a move that conditions affect: our limbic systems associate anxiety with a suddenly hastening pace, and so we begin to feel, however briefly, much like the mushrooms do. The poem therefore legislates compassion for its long-abandoned protagonists, staging the kind of "complementarity" (Bookchin 2005, 266) that Mahon theorizes elsewhere.

Similarly, the poem's onomatopoeic sound effects (its "crack" and "creak" [lines 42–43]) appeal directly to its readers' senses. Mahon asks readers to occupy palpably the mushrooms' poetic posture, to feel their expectancy, and to enact the acoustic alertness of their "feverish forms" (line 48). In so doing, Mahon suggests that mushrooms might teach us about mutuality: many fungi are symbionts, living in intimate awareness of reciprocal exchange between species. In addition, mushrooms break down dead matter (in this case, the "pale flesh" of their brothers "flaking /

Into the earth that nourished it" [lines 31–32]), recycling nutrients for use by the living and sustaining biodiversity. Our continued existence, then, comes largely by their leave, and so Mahon literally moves us to feel in sympathy with his mushrooms' fate. "A Disused Shed in Co. Wexford" invites us into the sensory lives of natural phenomena that we might otherwise think silent and insensate, and it requires its readers to recognize their places in the "socially charged . . . interspecific support systems" (Bookchin 2005, 463) that link human and non-human lives and sustain ecological stability.[18]

As the poem comes to a close, the punctuation of its final stanza reinforces the possibility of its two parallel readings. "Lost people of Treblinka and Pompeii!" (line 54) is a stand-alone line, so the thought is linked associatively (though not with the force of syntax) to the cries of the mushrooms that immediately precede and follow it. The mushrooms are simultaneously figures of "lost people," Northern Ireland's and otherwise, and oft-neglected plants that grow amidst decay. Ultimately, this confluence of political and ecocritical concerns suggests that the poet-speaker faults local conflict both for destroying community and for clogging nature's airwaves with human static.

18. To encourage audience participation in the mushrooms' spatial orientation and sensory awareness, Mahon must have recourse to certain anthropocentric figurations: his mushrooms are made, for instance, to mimic human harkening and stretching. As suggested by the reading of "The Mayo Tao" earlier in this chapter, language often asks the animal and the botanical to approximate the human; "human designations," after all, "express human judgments of nature" (Jung 2001, 276). "Disused Shed" must contend with this troubling puzzle: to resuscitate undervalued voices, it must enter, however tentatively, into these "designations." Even still, Mahon's work is firmly on the side of eco-linguistic criticism, which recognizes the inevitable anthropocentrism of language even while critiquing "the fact that languages not only show the world as humans perceive it, but interpret it so as to show the usefulness of each part of nature for humans [we speak, for instance, of weeds vs. beneficial plants, waste vs. arable land, and so on]" (Fill 2001, 67). "Disused Shed" explicitly reverses this flow of utility, asking instead what human beings might do for a flat of lost mushrooms and displaying a willingness to speak on their behalf even in terms insufficient to the task.

In Pursuit of Silence

Besides critiquing conflict's cacophony, Mahon also takes aim at the sonic ravages of globalization. Many acoustic ecologists, Mahon included, argue that modern mechanization impoverishes the auditory environment. The noise associated with global industry (i.e., manufacturing, travel, mass communication) indiscriminately silences the sounds of natural phenomena, and it also cripples our ability to listen to these sounds where they do still exist. For example, bioacoustician Bernard Krause (1987) conducted a study of the auditory niches of animal and insect species and revealed that animal vocalizations tend to occupy specific frequencies. These frequencies leave open pockets of sound-space into which the sounds of other species can fit. Krause's findings, based on acoustical spectrographic transcriptions of 2500 hours of soundscape recordings, suggest that the noises of urbanization can mask these auditory niches, leaving animal mating calls unheard and unrequited—a muting that could well endanger species.

The idea that we are forcibly earmuffed by the spread of industrialization emerges from a landmark experiment conducted by the late Samuel Rosen and referenced in George Prochnik's 2010 manifesto, *In Pursuit of Silence*. In 1961, Rosen visited a Mabaan tribal village southeast of Khartoum, which was then one of the most noise-free regions in Africa. There he discovered that 53 percent of its inhabitants could readily distinguish sounds that only 2 percent of New Yorkers could hear. Rosen also marveled at the fact that most Mabaans could conduct a conversation in hushed tones, with backs turned, at a football field's distance from each other—a far cry from the abbreviated hearing of his American control group. Prochnik (2010, 60) glosses Rosen's study by saying that "[t]he imbalance between noise and [quiet] . . . dramatically accelerates the aging process of our hearing," and he associates the spread of this "imbalance" with globalizing forces: the flows of capital that hasten industrialization, the population movements accompanying these flows, and the technological advances that occasion such changes. As acoustic ecologist Henrik Karlsson (2000, 11) describes, "sounds are accessories in social interaction connected with territory, power, and economics. . . . [T]he big opponents to a healthy acoustic environment are not individual citizens or even individual nations but neo-liberalism as an ideology and the globalization of the economy." Indeed, aviation, transport, and tourism are among the planet's most egregious noise polluters; the invasively ubiquitous sonic boom, for instance, can today be heard virtually the world over.

As a world-wanderer, Mahon is well placed to observe this sonic "leveling": the enemy of the "quiet [that] enables [auditory] differentiation" and "catalyzes our powers of perception" (Prochnik 2010, 293–94). Mahon has lived intermittently in Northern Ireland, the Republic of Ireland, England, France, Canada, and the United States, and his restlessness allows him to survey the so-called "global village."[19] It is perhaps no surprise, then, that his poetry is interested in preserving the distinctiveness and diversity of the world's acoustic spaces and in protesting the invasion of "shadowy, murmurous sanctuaries" (Mahon 1997b, XI, "At the Chelsea Arts Club" line 11) by "the white noise of late-century consumerism" (line 2), the "raucous trivia" of the globalizing world (line 4).[20] Because Mahon's poetry returns compulsively to Ireland, trying to negotiate a compensatory relationship to a place in which he has never quite felt at home, his work is especially concerned with globalization's feedback as it drowns out the region's sonic phenomena. Mahon (1997b) traces this acoustic arc in "On the Automation of the Irish Lights."[21] A requiem for Ireland's manned lighthouses, the poem frames their gradual automation, thanks to technology's encroachment, as a move to the onset of a "new noisy knowledge" (line 40) from

19. One of Mahon's poems, from his 1995 collection *The Hudson Letter*, even borrows McLuhan's (1964, 6) term "global village" for its title. *The Hudson Letter* has since been retitled "New York Time" (Mahon 2011), but "Global Village" still appears in the sequence.

20. Although some of these lines have disappeared in the revised version of this poem (now entitled "Decadence," Mahon 2011), the poem's sentiments remain the same. "Shadowy, murmurous sanctuaries," for instance, have been replaced by the equally sonic "symphonies in white, / . . . nocturnes consecrating wharf and bridge" (Mahon 2011, "Decadence" lines 11–12), and in both versions of the poem, the tones of the natural world are menaced by the anthrophonic din of "late-century consumerism."

21. This poem does not appear in Mahon's (2011) "Decadence" sequence.

> the dewy, liminal silence . . .
>
> . . . .
>
> [of] an old sea civilization[.] (Mahon 1997b, "On the Automation of the Irish Lights" lines 6–9)

The pressures of global capital, according to Mahon, legislate less and less concern for our lived spaces. The "wave-washed granite and limestone towers" (line 10) that once allowed solitary "rock keepers" (line 29) to "listen . . . to the wind" (line 31) and commune with "grumbling boulder[s]" (line 35) gradually give way to "visitor centres" (line 41), which are centerpieces of a tacky tourist trade where "[w]ind high among stars, solstice and equinox / will come and go unnoticed by the human eye [and ear!]" (lines 37–38).

Mahon (1997b) similarly protests the acoustic onslaught of the "new world order" in "Night Thoughts." Prefaced by an epigraph from Paul Fussell's (1982) *Abroad* ("One striking post-war phenomenon has been the transformation of numerous countries into pseudo-places whose function is simply to entice tourists"), the poem narrates the devastating global currents that lap at Northern Ireland's shores.[22] Mahon composed "Night Thoughts" at the close of the North's lengthy peace process, and the poem remarks on the country's dizzying turn from the 1998 Good Friday Agreement to efforts at economic globalization. Many of these efforts relied uncomfortably on marketing tragedy: Belfast's Titanic Quarter (touted on the city's tourism websites as a "high-profile European waterfront development") sprung up on the former site of the Harland and Wolff shipyard, home of the ill-fated ocean liner (and former workplace of Mahon's father and grandfather), and "mural tours" of sectarian graffiti were popularized by Stormont as local tourist attractions.[23]

22. This epigraph is attached to "Night Thoughts" only in its original form; it is absent from the poem as reproduced in Mahon's (2011) *New Collected Poems*.

23. Many postcolonial theorists have commented on the impact of global tourism on emerging markets and on the industry's inevitable conflict between economic growth and potential cultural exploitation. In particular, elements of core-periphery

In "Night Thoughts" Mahon (1997b) takes aim at the ugly reverberations of this post-conflict corporatization. The poem immediately positions its speaker at its margins. He is sidelined, a stranger to local scenes, and he is literally "lying low" in a Belfast bedroom. Back in the North, Mahon's narthecality is redoubled, and so his speaker hovers at a distance from the streetscapes below (Mahon 1997b, "Night Thoughts" line 17). The speed at which the local "'construction industry' / throws up new office blocks against the sky" defamiliarizes the poet-speaker's childhood city; once soberly industrial, Belfast now seems to be a crassly commercial "Georgian theme park for the tourist" (lines 20–22). This estrangement further legislates Mahon's narrative distance; the speaker in "Night Thoughts" lies abed unseeing and unseen, though not quite out of earshot. The poem therefore filters its world via the ear: although its speaker recalls his town as a place where the wee hours once brought "'impersonal moonlight / audible on steps, railings, sash window and fanlight'" (lines 36–37), he now bears earwitness to the birth of its mechanized din. The poem goes on to reveal congested acoustic spaces that are flooded with industrial detritus and commercial sound bites and are heralded by the symptomatic "thundering[s]" of "transport planes" (line 11)—an earmark that the nostalgic speaker recalls breaking his childhood nights' otherwise peaceful silence. Indeed, the "bird" and "bus" of the poem's third line are less a comfortably alliterative pair than words competing for the same airwaves and laying common claim to a phonemic /b/; the cacophony of tourist throngs, this cue suggests, threatens the sanctity of

---

relationships can continue under the auspices of postcolonial tourism, including cultural representations (infantilization, exoticization) and economic structures (the consumption of margins by center). Although Northern Ireland's situation is unique, given that its economy is bound to that of the United Kingdom, its concerted turn to tourism in the past decade still raises ethical and ideological concerns (e.g., the potential dangers of turning sectarianism into spectacle). In "Selling Conflict Heritage through Tourism in Peacetime Northern Ireland," Sara McDowell (2008) makes precisely this point, arguing that government-funded commodification of conflict heritage often reinforces domestic political divides even though it lends itself to economic development.

local biophony.[24] Readers are asked to perk their ears by the poem's opening: the line-final pair "four" (line 2) and "hour" (line 4), graphemically similar but phonetically dissonant, pit eye against ear and reveal close listening as the most reliable guide to Mahon's sequence.

As "Night Thoughts" (Mahon 1997b) continues, it self-consciously shifts its dominant sense from sight to sound. Mahon's speaker is awake and inspired to song by the night's synesthetically "audible" moonlight; as he "night-write[s] / blind in a bedside notebook" (lines 35–38), his vision is dimmed by the darkness but his ears are carefully attuned. The speaker's poetry is less the characters on the page than the comforting scratching of his "biro break[ing] the silence" (lines 35–38). As Hugh Haughton (2007, 278) explains, this passage "draws our attention to the audible dimension of the writing, the consonantal music of s's and b's, the vowel music of i's and o's in the night-written phrases," and it creates "resistant music" as a consolatory counter to the acoustic hegemony of the "new world order." As daylight breaks, however, the night's—and the poetry's—hushed tones are dispelled by the telling sounds of globalization's ecological and cultural leveling: "air-brake and diesel-chug," all nasal vowels and plosive consonants, "'coaches' throng[ing] the square," and tourists in "baseball caps and nylon leisurewear" "shouting" and "clicking at the front door" (lines 28–33). These descriptions represent the for-profit marketing of Ireland, and the country's capitulation to global capital comes, Mahon suggests, at the expense of both unmolested "night thoughts" and the leisurely rhythms of local eco-phenomena: the soothing sounds of seaside towns that once offset "the plastic / bombs go[ing] off around Belfast" (Mahon 1972b, "Beyond Howth Head" lines 71–72).

These poetic sentiments also carry over into Mahon's prose selections. In his essay "Huts and Sheds," for example, he laments the untimely passing of "[s]ites of reverie: sun porches . . . windows, rivers . . . huts and sheds . . . clearings," places "immune to market forces" that are giving

24. The term "biophony" comes from Bernard Krause's (1987) "niche hypothesis" and refers to the range of sounds that vocal, non-human animals create in a given acoustic environment.

way today to indistinguishable condos, "retail units," and "hideous new developments" (Mahon 2012, chap. 1). Because Mahon believes firmly in the world's interrelatedness, having long been self-professedly invested in "lift[ing Ireland's] droopy eyelid and disturb[ing] it into a sense of relationship and awareness"[25] (Mahon 1997a, 16), he is compelled to take aim at globalization's economic imperatives and their collateral ecological damage. As Mahon (1972b) prophetically suggests in "Beyond Howth Head," the cornerstone of his collection *Lives*, when spaces "where once Molloy, uncycled, heard / thin cries of a surviving bird" (lines 83–84) are absorbed by "[r]oaring . . . ten-lane highways" (line 81), signs of "Washington['s] . . . grisly aim / to render the whole earth the same" (lines 85—86), the ethical writer must raise his voice on behalf of nature's silenced lives. Tellingly, Mahon (2012, chap. 1) resolves "Huts and Sheds" on precisely this kind of acoustic ecological note: "People before profit, please, art before artifice; and much less noise."

25. Mahon's commitment to a dialogical relationship with "elsewhere" is revealed by both his sustained interest in translation and his frequent turns to other languages in generating rhyme. He has a rather prodigious command of language, and his translations include the work of Ovid, Horace, Rimbaud, Baudelaire, Rilke, and Irish-language poet Nuala Ní Dhomhnaill, among others. He also relishes rhymes that bump cheekily against linguistic barriers, chiming, for instance, "crews" with "*Nikolaos*," "*lumière*" with "fare" (Mahon 1999, "October in Hyde Park"), "*Personae*" with "antennae," and "*kalòn*" with "microphone" (Mahon 1984, "A Kensington Notebook").

5

DEREK MAHON

A "Politics of Frequency"

Mahon's Radio Poems

Because Mahon so persistently uses the ear to mediate his relationships with otherwise mute phenomena, it is no surprise that he eventually considers sound as a potential register for reimagining *human* community-building. Mahon (2002, 111) has long admitted to "feeling not at home" in Northern Ireland, claiming that both Protestant and Catholic communities are too narrowly defined by geographical proximity and ideological uniformity and that these myopic attachments leave little room for would-be culture-crossers. In an interview with John Brown, Mahon (2002, 123) explained, "Throughout my teens I had a sense of the immediate community—extended family, the neighbourhood and so on—but I felt that there was something terribly amiss and lacking and skewed about this whole carry-on. It seems a very insufficient community. The question in the back of my mind all the time was, Is this all? Is this it? Is this life? These people, this place?" Mahon readily concedes the intolerance of this position, which neglects the substantial grassroots cross-community work being pursued in the North in service of peacebuilding and reconciliation. Nevertheless, despite these potential prejudices, and despite the "psychological risk[s]" (Mahon 2002, 123) involved in his desire for "deracination," Mahon continues to search for alternate modes of community formation:

Unless otherwise indicated, the versions of the poems referenced in this chapter are drawn from Mahon's (2011) *New Collected Poems.*

modes that are based on affinity and affiliation rather than the tyrannical nearness of neighbors.

Mahon's stance demands a redefinition of "being together." Although we typically think of community as a geographical or visuospatial phenomenon—as a group of people in common place—Mahon finds this rootedness limiting. Conversely, Marshall McLuhan and Edmund Carpenter (1960, 68) assert that soundscape is deterritorialized: "a sphere without fixed boundaries," a space that takes "[t]he universe [as its] potential map." In other words, the soundscape can potentially circumnavigate the globe, reaching ears on both sides of the Atlantic.[1] Mahon taps into these theories in his work; he uses the promise of sound's transnational scope to reimagine community. The possibility exists, Mahon suggests, of hailing like-minded listeners even at a visual distance, and his poems' acoustic contours shape shared auditory geographies. Hugh Haughton (2007, 8), riffing on Mahon's poem "Courtyards in Delft," comments suggestively that Mahon's "idiosyncratic sense of place" comes "in terms of 'the thing made.'" Although Haughton doesn't elaborate further, his insight can be qualified by his later references to Mahon's "poetic space[s]" and "poetics of space" (Haughton 2007, 18): Mahon thinks of his poems as resonant echo-chambers that use rhythm and rhyme to coax reader-auditors into common acoustic spaces and to forge sound-founded communities.

Mahon's "radio poems" first establish this theoretical framework by thematizing aural community. Turning on the radio invites outside voices into the home, and listening to a broadcast involves hearing in time with other ears. This kind of community, although fleeting and tentative, handily transgresses visuospatial bounds and establishes intimacy at a distance. Barry Truax (2001), R. Murray Schafer's one-time colleague and collaborator, defines "acoustic community" as "any soundscape in which acoustic information plays a pervasive role in the lives of the inhabitants (no matter

1. Sound, of course, can also reterritorialize (e.g., national anthems sound the bounds of particular place). However, sound is often unmoored in ways that sight is not, and acoustic space is always *potentially* boundless: its expansive shape and scope are pregnant with the possibility of "being together" beyond the territory.

how the commonality of such people is understood)." Truax explains that "the boundary of the community is [therefore] arbitrary and may be as small as a room of people, a home or building, or as large as an urban community, a broadcast area, or any other system of electroacoustic communication." This definition, he says, "means that acoustic cues and signals constantly keep the community in touch with what is going on from day to day within it. Such a system is 'information rich' in terms of sound, and therefore sound plays a significant role in defining the community spatially, temporally . . . as well as socially and culturally. . . . [T]he *shared experience* of hearing [is crucial to this kind of community-formation]" (65–67). Mahon shares Truax's view: sound, he suggests, redefines space's dimensions, allowing community to stem from the sympathies of common hearing rather than from physical proximity.

As Mahon (2012, chap. 1) suggests in his essay "Huts and Sheds," when one writes in solitude, a television feels "incongruous," but "a radio . . . help[s]" to sketch a shared "psycho-geography." Consequently, Mahon's poetic speakers turn repeatedly to the radio as a meaningful source of solidarity. The untitled opening poem in *The Hudson Letter* (Mahon 1995, line 30), for instance, shifts into plurality when discussing the radio; it slips from the solitary "I" to an inclusive "we" in theorizing "Respighi's temperate nightingale on WQXR" as a shared sonic experience. Although this moment of communion is fleeting, the poem's speaker still relishes the opportunity to select a sympathetic soundscape, and he credits this "radio serendipity" with renewing "the resilience of our lyric appetite" (lines 32–33).

Mahon's "Radio Days" (formerly entitled "Morning Radio"), which is dedicated to John Scotney (who adapts, produces, and dramatizes radio plays for the British Broadcasting Corporation [BBC]), similarly stages the prospect of "acoustic community."[2] As Hugh Haughton (2007, 192) points

2. Mahon has written at least one radio play—his adaptation of *The Bacchae: After Euripides* aired on Raidió Teilifís Éireann (RTÉ)—and the collection of his papers in the Emory archives includes pieces of others. This work suggests his vested interest in Truax's "shared experience of hearing."

out, the poem uses the radio to enable "multiple location": a sound-bound togetherness superseding visual geography.[3] Its opening stanza signals that the poem will be resounding a BBC broadcast: its "art-deco liner" (line 3) is a coded reference to the BBC recording studio, which is housed in a purpose-built broadcast liner in London's Portland Place. Although the BBC is sometimes framed as a colonial tool[4] and although the Unionist government's one-time ban on BBC Northern Ireland's Irish-language programming was indeed politically fraught,[5] Mahon counters lingering tribalism that associates the station with abhorrent Englishness; he prefers to reimagine classical music radio as a potential catalyst to international community.

The opening lines of "Radio Days" also inaugurate the poem's ear-centricity by narrating "[t]he silence of the ether," or radio dead air—a silence that the poem repeats as its ellipsis legislates a breath or brief break (line 1). After this sound effect, Mahon continues by describing in detail an evening's programming. He presents a sequence of musical selections,

3. Louis MacNeice, one of Mahon's major poetic influences, wrote radio plays for precisely this reason. MacNeice (1993, 397) claimed an attraction to the medium because it allowed an author to "take many more liberties with time and place . . . with the help of music and recorded effects"—in other words, because audition can exceed the bounds of visual space. In his essay "MacNeice, 'the War' and the BBC," Mahon (2012, chap. 14) notes the "close relationship between MacNeice's poetry and radio work"; both forms, he says, leave "intimate whispers . . . echoing somewhere in the ether." I argue that the same can be said of Mahon's work.

4. See Dionne Brand's (2002) descriptions of listening to BBC radio broadcasts as a child in colonial Trinidad. "Through the . . . broadcasts," Brand says, "[you are] inhabited by British consciousness. . . . [On the other hand,] the ovular sound of the BBC . . . [tells] you that you are living elsewhere. . . . You have heard it described as an island. . . . You have seen on the borders of maps of islands, natives, nubile and fierce. You are living on an island, banished or uninhabited, or so it seems through the voice of the BBC. You are therefore already mythic" (13, 17).

5. The ban was overturned in 1981 while Mahon was in the midst of composing *The Hunt by Night* (the volume in which "Morning Radio" [now "Radio Days"] was initially collected). Paul Muldoon produced the first Irish-language radio show on BBC Northern Ireland after the injunction was lifted, and he made significant headway with bilingual programming in subsequent years.

a commentator's interlude, and, finally, the seven o'clock news. Just as the orchestra harmonizes, its "stealth of strings" (echoed by Mahon's whispering sibilance) accompanying the woodwinds' soaring melody (line 5), so too do its eager hearers. Once again, Mahon carefully marshals the first-person plural to suggest a set of coordinated ears: "Even as he speaks / *We* can hear furniture / Creak and slide on the decks" (lines 16–18, emphasis mine). This strategic "we" showcases the radio as a source of acoustic community, as does the "we" collectively given pause by the apocalyptic strains of the seven o'clock news (line 14).[6] These cues suggest that tuning in to a radio broadcast is as much about listening to others listening as it is a private aural experience, and Mahon celebrates the potential breadth of his fellow hearers. Chadwick Jenkins (2007), a musicologist who studies classical music radio communities, suggestively explains that

> the radio induce[s] within the listener a sense of engaging in a larger listening community . . . [and therefore] s[eeks] . . . to efface . . . the regional, economic, and political divisions among the constituent listeners. . . . The announcer [Tom Crowe, in Mahon's case] it would seem allows these listeners not to listen to this music (they would be better served by CDs if that was what they wanted) but rather to listen along with another . . . the seemingly private act of listening is transmuted into a communal experience and this sense of community is intrinsic to radio listening. The music becomes complimentary to the communal ethos as such.

In other words, Mahon's "we" is his own imagined community: a community in common close listening. Whereas Jenkins' notion that radio can efface regional and political divides is perhaps too indulgently utopian,

6. The prophesy "[t]hat the world we know / is coming to an end" ("Radio Days" lines 14–15), a sense of finality reinforced by Mahon's strategically end-stopped line, is further amplified by the reverberations of historical tragedy in the poem. The sounds of "furniture / creak[ing] and slid[ing] on the [art-deco liner's] decks" (lines 17–18) recall the sinking of the Titanic, a ship built in Belfast's Harland and Wolff shipyard where Mahon's grandfather contributed to its construction. Mahon (1991, 27) likes to indulge in the rather morbid fantasy that his grandfather's handiwork brought down the liner.

Mahon does suggest acoustic community as a mode of collectivity that compensates, in his estimation, for the North's short-sighted sectarianism.

In Sync: Mahon's "Community of Imagined Readership"

After proposing the power of shared soundscapes, Mahon tries to put theory into poetic practice. Mahon (2012, 119) describes the radio as "an intimate medium" for its listeners, and he attempts to channel this auditory intimacy in his poetry. He seems to envision his verse working like the radio: his poetry, which he describes as "music" (111), or a reminder that "once upon a time this stuff was sung" (117), aspires toward "creat[ing] . . . a circle of reader[-auditors]" (123). As Mahon himself puts it, "Seamus [Heaney] is very sure of his place; I've never been sure of mine. . . . [T]he place that [my] poetry occupies is not a geographical location; it's a community of imagined readership" (quoted in Haughton 2007, 97). He therefore suggests that his poetry might serve as a type of "imaginary homeland" (to borrow a phrase from Salman Rushdie [1992]) and that sound, poetry's proximity to song, lies at the very heart of this homemaking project.[7]

Mahon's neo-formalism, especially his characteristically pronounced rhythm, asks readers to move together to lines' tempi, tapping their toes in time. "[E]ven in the most talky poem," Mahon (2002, 119) argues, one must have a "residual echo of traditional form": a head-bobbing, toe-tapping patter; an "eddy of semantic scruple / In an unstructurable sea" ("Rage for Order" lines 9–10). Although many poets, Carson and Muldoon included, turn occasionally to regular meter, Mahon (2002, 117–18) alone confesses to imagining his poetry's prosody as a source of "control, orchestration, forceful activity." He argues that "being formally arrested" (that is, being

7. On this point, see Elmer Kennedy-Andrews' (2008, 174) *Writing Home*: "Mahon's final resting-place, as he makes clear in [*Harbour Lights*] concluding poem, 'The Seaside Cemetary' . . . is in the deterritorialized, paradoxically shifting, symbolic space of the poem itself." Similarly, Carol Tell (2004, 119–21) argues that for Mahon, "[w]ords form an alternative landscape to geography . . . [they] make solid the unsteady ground upon which [he] travels. . . . What Mahon comes home to, then, is not nation, homeland, or even family, but poetry—*his* poetry."

gripped or absorbed) "promises [a] material arrest" (117–18); in other words, that well-tempered poetry can exert embodied effects. Moreover, Mahon holds poetic sound effects uniquely responsible for re-timing an audience's lived tempi: "[F]ormal arrest . . . has to do with the sound of the thing . . . [with] hearing music loud and clear" (117–18). These comments indicate Mahon's concerted efforts to *move* his readers; his work must "clear its throat and make its presence felt" (117–18) to sound out its community's bounds. Put otherwise, Mahon crafts a common auditory geography for his inner circle, which he imagines as the "creation of a new family" (116–23).

Steve Goodman (2009, xv) frames common vibration as community formation and calls this tactic a "politics of frequency." When noise, Goodman argues, is organized as "a reservoir of rhythmic potential," it also becomes "a locus of affective collectivity" (xv). For example, Afrofuturism—its music forged in the context of depressed urbanism and racial oppression—is a "rhythmic decision-making," enabling collective mobilization (in both kinesthetic and political senses) amid social instability (192). Mahon's poetry likewise aims at affective collectivity: at a group of hearers or company moving together in time. His poetry's rhythms realign bodies around a musical line; they work against militant, forward-marching calendrical time—time marked in the North by incendiary dates like the July 12th Orange Walks, the January 30th commemorations of Bloody Sunday, the August 12th Apprentice Boys parades, and so on. The poet must therefore breach the bounds of his country's competing nationalisms and open up an acoustic space in which alternate belongings might be forged. As Eamon Grennan (1999, 31) says of Mahon, "His poems, without sentimentality, make that offering of the self that is true speech, that entering into genuine relationship . . . with an audience of fellow-creatures who become, in their listening, a community. He brings us in every sense 'to the point of speech,' and we should have no choice but to hear him out."

The hypotheses that robust rhythms can literally move bodies and that this kinesis can serve social cohesion are tried and tested by neurologist Oliver Sacks (2008) in *Musicophilia: Tales of Music and the Brain*. Sacks argues that rhythm autonomically integrates our auditory and motor systems: a cross-wiring called "entrainment" (261). Sound, in other words, has real kinesthetic power: we involuntarily keep time with an external beat. Of course, visual, tactile, and even olfactory rhythms do exist, but Sacks' experiments suggest that it is auditory rhythm alone to which the body inadvertently responds. Moreover, he argues that this rhythm initiates irresistible coordination or "neurogamy"; music is profoundly communal precisely because its beat can bind or "marry" hearers' nervous systems (266). Taken together, these arguments suggest that rhythm turns listeners into participants and then synchronizes their hearts and minds. Therefore, Sacks speculates that rhythm may have had an important cultural and economic function in human evolution, bringing people together and producing a sense of collectivity and solidarity (268).

This sort of community-building certainly resonates with the experience of a poetry reading, but it also works similarly on the page—an important dispensation for Mahon given his discomfort with public performances. Poetic rhythm typically takes its cues from the musical line, which positions the reader as auditor. A poem's patterns cannot be processed until the page's graphemes are sounded and resounded, aloud or in the mind's echo-chamber. Mahon's inflections are often particularly insistent, and it is almost impossible to read his "well-tempered" stanzas (Haughton 2007, 230) without lilting along with their lines. His "community of imagined readership" therefore seems to stem from the idea of an audience—readers past, present, and future—tapping their toes in time with his work: a "family" both aesthetically and physiologically in sync.

"Hearing Music Loud and Clear": Mahon's "Beyond Howth Head"

Mahon's most vigorous rhythms often accompany his wrestling with place and placelessness, suggesting that his sense of unbelonging invests his "politics of frequency" with particular urgency. "Beyond Howth Head" (Mahon 1972b), for example, jarringly juxtaposes metrical drive with existential angst. Written almost entirely in iambic tetrameter with an irresistibly swaying step, the poem's cheery nursery-rhyme cadence seems a strange bedfellow for its macabre meditations on violence and decay. However, Mahon's form is an intentional counterweight to his theme. The unhomely threats posed to Ireland's landscapes and soundscapes demand other possible belongings, in this case the "neurogamous" community of readers moved by Mahon's poetic soundscape. The poem's rhythmic force is evident even from its opening lines: "The wind that blows these words to you / bangs nightly off the black-and-blue / Atlantic" (lines 1–3). So measured they might verge on doggerel in a lesser poet's hands, the couplets' iambic cadences ring clearly in the reader's ear. The experience of hearing these lines chime often evokes involuntary head-nodding and finger-drumming, which Sacks (2008, 260) calls "spontaneous synchronization" or "entrainment." If, as Sacks (2008, 278) claims, one's "face and posture" will frequently "mirror" an overheard melodic "narrative," then here the poem's soundscape literally moves readers' bodies, and its unmistakable meter ensures unison. Mahon's reimagined community, then, becomes a kind of drum circle, keeping time together in response to the poem's irresistible percussive power.

This rhythmic regularity initially seems at odds with the poem's thematic uncertainty. The poem describes the twinned "decline" of Irish culture and ecology, with "rock-built houses . . . collaps[ing]" on "crumbling shores" and "homespun cottage industries," Ireland's now-near-defunct linen mills, gone to ruin (Mahon 1972b, "Beyond Howth Head" lines 4–9). It later faults the country's myopic insularity for its decay; cultural and environmental disrepair come, Mahon suggests, from clinging too tightly to local tribalism while turning a deaf ear to the wider world. Mahon's speaker claims to be "bored to tears by Telefís," or Raidió Teilifís Éireann, Ireland's public service broadcaster—here slyly glossed as "*vox populi vox Dei*" (the Latin is a dig at the self-enclosed self-regard of local Catholicism)—and suggests that he might instead "reach / with twinkling importunity / for good news on the BBC" (lines 19–22). The poem's tone implies, however, that this "reach" for British airwaves in the Republic borders, for some, on blasphemy or even on betrayal. The speaker wonders, "What can the elders say to this?" (line 25). Mahon's compensatory community-building, however, hopes to breach this brand of provincialism as his circle of readers occupy common sound-space but remain geographically and culturally disparate. The verse's sing-song modulations, then, serve as a democratizing tonic to the poem's theme of blinkered insularity. The poem's opening stanza reflects tacitly on these formal aims: the "wind . . . blow[ing] these words to you" (line 1) is framed as an internationalizing force, brushing shores on both sides of the Atlantic and bearing far-flung ocean currents to Dublin's coastline. Moreover, this wind circulates in the poem as a sonic phenomenon: it "bangs" invisibly "off the black-and-blue / Atlantic" and "hammer[s]" insistently on local doors (lines 2–3). The clamorous wind stands in for the poem's own lively soundscape, and the implied metaphor suggests that Mahon's acoustic contours might accommodate a different kind of community: a circle of like-minded listeners against the tyrannies of geographical proximity and cultural uniformity. Mahon's meter therefore seems to self-consciously echo the wind's rolling rhythms and the tide's comforting undulations—the very refrains of the transatlantic relationship that the poem charts.

As "Beyond Howth Head" progresses, this meter must continue to comfort the ear because it accompanies a reproachful enumeration of Ireland's endangered ecologies. Mahon (1972b) describes the detritus of the British Isles as it washes ashore on the Irish coastline ("a boot from Blackpool"; a used condom from Merseyside [lines 62–64]) and carefully chronicles the vulnerable lives of the natural world that are menaced by this circulation of rubbish. Brief disturbances in the poem's regular rhythm and rhyme suggest the scale and scope of these threats to local landscape: in stanza eight, "wild" and "troubled" make for an odd slant-rhyming couple amid clearly chiming pairs, and "troubled" adds a stray syllable to one of Mahon's perfectly tetrametric lines (lines 57–59). Mahon similarly holds the ravages of globalization responsible for local noise pollution; relentlessly "[r]oaring" highways and the earsplitting sonic booms of American B-52 bombers drown out the poem's birdsong (lines 81, 87). The reference to Samuel Beckett's *Molloy* in stanza eleven is resonant: by Beckett's (1955, 123) description, Molloy falls "blindly, in the dark" into a ditch, where he is left awaiting death, but the cries of "birds, skylarks perhaps" offer him perceptual respite. In "Exit Molloy," from *Night-Crossing*, Mahon (1968) makes precisely this point. The poem ventriloquizes Molloy's decline but suggests that it can be deferred by the comforts of passing birdsong: "Strictly speaking I am already dead / But still I can hear the birds sing on over my head" (lines 8–9). "[T]hin cries of a surviving bird" (line 84) enable an intimacy with place, and once they are eclipsed by white noise, their absence amounts to sensory impoverishment and ecological devastation.

Mahon (1972b) also faults local conflict for the country's destructive self-consumption in "Beyond Howth Head." When "[P]lastic / bombs go off around Belfast," detonations sever the final iamb of the ninth stanza's penultimate line and blow its second syllable into the subsequent phrase in service of the poem's rhyme scheme (we *hear* the couplet as "Meanwhile, for a word's sake the plast / ic bombs go off around Belfast" [lines 71–72]). To compound the conflict's cacophony, the strident voices of sectarian politicians compete for local airwaves, and their warring words of "sacrifice" and martyrdom fall "thick" on noncombatant ears (lines 77–78). Mahon once again objects to the unhomely effects of these outcries on both the North's civilian acoustics and the keynote sounds of the natural world. The only peace available amid this clamor, he later suggests, is "the great peace of death" (line 102). Nevertheless, Mahon tries to use poetry's rhythm and rhyme as salves for the sonic static his work describes: even when the sound-schemes in "Beyond Howth Head" are briefly troubled, its jaunty time signature is soon restored. Lines like "And here I close; for look, across / dark waves where bell-buoys dimly toss" (lines 137–38) swing compellingly, their cadences resolving neatly in service of their tempo's social function.

Nevertheless, Mahon's acoustic community can offer at best a fleeting sense of belonging. The moment of moving with a poem passes quickly and is superseded by other sensations. Although the poetic soundscape offers temporary comfort in fellow-feeling, it can neither provide lasting consolation nor compensate for the creeping "shadows of the encroaching night" (line 144) with which "Beyond Howth Head" menacingly concludes. As much as Mahon capitalizes on the possibilities of poetic entrainment, he also recognizes its limits. Poetry, after all, is text, and the rhythms of written sound, however heavy its footfalls, are necessarily open to mis-readings and mis-hearings.

In light of this recognition, Mahon (1972b) builds the impossibility of continuous community into "Beyond Howth Head" by juxtaposing metrical regularity to rhythmic "hiccups." For example, the lines "And placed in Co. Clare, a sign: / 'Stop here and see the sun go down'" (lines 69–70) allow for both measured meter and rhythmic rupture; if we read "Co." as "County," we move naturally with the couplet's iambic lilts, but if we treat the phrase as written, pronouncing Mahon's abbreviation ("Co. Clare"), we break with the poem's prosodic scheme. Likewise, the lines "and spins a single / garage sign behind the shingle" (lines 11–12) from the poem's second stanza allow for a similar disjunction. The stanza explicitly theorizes sound as a source of cross-border community, charting the transatlantic course of "night music" "[f]resh from Long Island or Cape Cod" as it wends its way to "the radio sets that play / from Carraroe to Dublin Bay" (lines 13–18). At first glance, these shared long-distance hearings seem to suggest Mahon's acoustic communities as democratizing alternatives to the tribalisms policed by Belfast's "plastic bombs." However, accent crucially conditions readers' hearings of these lines, enabling the poem's sound to potentially contravene its sense. If we read (and hear) the word "garage" in British English, as Mahon's Irish readers might, we emphasize the first syllable, pronouncing "gah-ridge" (ˈgærɪdʒ) and perpetuating—with some sleight of enjambment—the poem's regular iambic tetrameter ("and *spins* a *sin*gle / *gar*age *sign* be*hind* the *shin*gle"). However, if we pronounce the word "ga-rah-ge" (gəˈrɑ(d)ʒ), stressing the second syllable as is typical of French loanwords in American English, the phrase evades clear scansion and instead invites individuating rhythmic readings. Even when Mahon overtly theorizes common close listening as a source of neurogamous community, his circle cannot always hold. Here Mahon's meter hails only *particular* reader-auditors, a specificity that fragments the poem's audience and even threatens to realign listeners along national or regional lines. "Beyond Howth Head" therefore dramatizes the pull of the individual versus the collective; the social body versus the body proper. This double bind illuminates (or, rather, makes audible) one of the animating anxieties of Mahon's work: the desire for, but unsustainability of, the comforting coherence of self-made community.

Mahon's willingness to theorize this tension even after asserting "the sound of the thing" as the source of his poetic "authority" (Mahon 2002, 117) suggests that he is perhaps reluctant to relinquish his recalcitrant narthecality. As much as he seeks out ways to feel at home, Mahon's "stubborn aloofness" (Said 2002, 561)—his "work[ing] on the circumference"

(Mahon 2011, "The Sea in Winter" line 50)—remains the source of his poetic critique. As Patricia Horton (2000, 356) describes it, Mahon's poetry is "a search for an alternative structure in which the self can find meaning, and which, at the same time, will not threaten the sovereignty of selfhood," and his work is everywhere shaped by these contradictory centripetal and centrifugal forces. "Beyond Howth Head" concedes as much: even while exercising its moving meter in service of a shared soundscape, one of its concluding stanzas stages the speaker's willing withdrawal from the world in the face of its so-called "general mess":

> I too, uncycled, might exchange,
> since 'we are changed by what we change',
> my forkful of the general mess
> for hazelnuts and watercress
> like one of those old hermits who,
> less virtuous than some, withdrew
> from the world circles people make
> to a small island in a lake. (Mahon 1972b, "Beyond Howth Head" lines 105–12)[8]

Postlude: Mahon's Wave Theory

Turning an ear to Mahon's signature sound-patterns eventually reveals the coincidence of his autobiographical and literary rhythms. Mahon's life and work equally evidence "a dialectical rhythm of leaving and returning" (Haughton 2007, 125); seafaring and travel mark both his own restless tempi and his poetry's characteristic cadences. Mahon, in other words, is a kind of poetic mariner, and Edna Longley (2002, 42) therefore describes

8. The line "we are changed by what we change" is purloined from Auden's (2007, II.39) "New Year Letter," a philosophical long poem written on the eve of World War II. Auden's growing disillusionment with modern civilization anticipates Mahon's take on the global village: both poets' hopes for democratizing cosmopolitanism are dashed by the grim realities of industrialization, corporatization, and regressive returns to knee-jerk nationalisms. Mahon would rather withdraw from community altogether, he suggests, than be changed by this changing world.

him as "a sea-poet in the Atlantic tradition." He overhears and resounds the sea's "briny bubble and squeak" (Mahon 2005, "On the Beach" line 3) and "the raw crescendo of the crashing shore" (Mahon 2011, "Somewhere the Wave" line 11), bearing earwitness to ocean ecology. In *Life on Earth* Mahon (2008, "Art Notes: Wave Shadow" line 11) refers self-reflexively to his maritime poetry as "wave theory," and the tide's recursive rhythms do seem to "liberate [poetic] ebb and flow" throughout most of his collections. "Shorelines," for instance, from Mahon's 2005 volume *Harbour Lights*, demonstrates how this sensibility collides with many of Mahon's major themes: his efforts to develop ecological belonging in the face of political alienation; his commitment to sensitive perception; his connection with marine life, its rolling tempi suggesting the rhythms of his own comings and goings; and his attempt to channel these undulating rhythms in his poetry and to move his readers to and fro:

> [A] swirl of incoming tide
> has signed a separate peace
> with sighs and whisperings,
> its ripples silent strings,
> each one a thoughtful stave
> next to the bath-house roar,
> air garden and wind bower
> where each slow-motion wave
> is a blue note designed
> to calm the riotous mind—
> proposing, like a soul breeze
> or random natural noise,
> a new kind of 'found'
> spirit-breathing music:
> not pop, please, but the basic
> tones of an ancient sound[.] (Mahon 2005, "Shorelines" lines 33–48)

"Shorelines" serves as both a personal tonic for unbelonging—a source of imagined community—and a broader ecocritical statement: it exhibits care and concern for the phenomenal world, which is too often crowded out of earshot by the white noise of local conflict and global industry.

Here, the tide's "sighs and whisperings" and waves' "blue note[s]" are part of the "natural noise" that prompts the poet's politics of good feeling—the "music" that lets his "spirit . . . breath[e]." Caught even today between Ulster's two worlds, Mahon's poetry remains on anxious pilgrimage to Ireland, and this consolatory intimacy with place—with "the basic / tones of an ancient sound"—enables at least a temporary respite from his sense of alienation. Moreover, in allowing his poetic soundscape to echo the waves that lap at Ireland's shorelines, Mahon develops acoustic community: a coordinated circle of reader-auditors moving together in time and a place "[w]here each slow-motion wave" demonstrates a perfect unity of form and content, its rolling iambs the very rhythms of the tide. However, this sensory alignment is fleeting, and Mahon's efforts to feel at home remain incomplete; although his marine rhythms are resonant of the island's tides, he will never quite belong in a divided Ireland. As Mahon suggested in an interview with Nicholas Wroe ("A Sense of Place," *The Guardian*, July 22, 2006), this is why he continues to write: "ambiguity," after all, "is poetry. It is the other thing that is the other thing."

6

PAUL MULDOON

Becoming Opera

Muldoon's "Mouth Music"

Paul Muldoon has been called "the most significant English-language poet born since the Second World War" (Stephen Knight, *Times Literary Supplement*, December 25, 1998); he has been accused of writing poetry that is "endlessly evasive, polyvocal and outlandish" (Wheatley 1999, 145–46); and he has been praised for being a "shape-shifting Proteus" who leaves his readers "authentically touched or delighted" (Richard Eder, *New York Times Book Review*, June 10, 2001). Muldoon won the 2003 Pulitzer Prize for Poetry and a coveted post as poetry editor for *The New Yorker*, so his reputation is clearly beyond dispute. However, his poetry's slipperiness (as the above reviews suggest) still ignites heated critical debate. Often contrasted with the rootedness and moral stability of Seamus Heaney's work,[1] Muldoon's protean poetry hinges on its uninhibited wordplay and its intricate inter-referentiality. Word patterns and rhyme schemes echo compulsively between Muldoon's poems and even between his volumes. Further, his poetry shifts undetected between tonal registers and ventriloquized voices, refusing to land didactically on a particular political or philosophical position. Most commentators who critique this

1. In a *Sunday Times* review of Muldoon's work (June 21, 1987), John Carey, one of Muldoon's most outspoken critics, draws the unflattering comparison that "Heaney's poetry seems unforced, deep, natural . . . Muldoon's is tricky, clever, tickled by its own knowingness."

shape-shifting, Rajeev Patke (2008, 282) observes, share the sentiment that "the poet is happy to lose some part of agency to the random potentialities of language as sound." In other words, these critics seem to fear that sound might outstrip a poem's sense. Muldoon has stoked the flames of this critical fire by professing that "devices like repetition and rhyme are not artificial, that they're not imposed, somehow, on the language. They are inherent in the language. Words want to find chimes with each other, things want to connect . . . I believe in the serendipity of all that, of giving oneself over to that" (see Muldoon's interview with John Redmond, *Thumbscrew*, conducted November 2, 1995, published 1996).

In contrast to Muldoon's detractors, I argue that his poetry is far from chiming itself into meaninglessness and contend that it instead approximates opera. Muldoon uses devices like multivocal ensemble and recurring leitmotifs in his poetry, devices that shape and structure (or semanticize) an opera's score. Indeed, Muldoon has long been concerned with clearing a signifying space in which to *sing*. He has often cited Robert Frost as one of his major influences, and Muldoon's preoccupation with poetry's aurality does seem to rely on Frost's notion of "the sound of sense": the idea that "a sentence is not interesting merely in conveying a meaning of words; it must do something more; it must convey a meaning by sound" (*Boston Evening Transcript*, May 8, 1915). That is, if you "think deep enough you think musically."

Muldoon's reference to Joyce's ([1932] 2012) *Finnegans Wake* as a kind of "mouth music" therefore applies equally to his own poetry (Muldoon 2006b, "Finding Music"). As his career has progressed, Muldoon has taken to heart the idea that song and poetry are intimately part of the same world (see Charles McGrath's "Word Freak," *New York Times Magazine*, November 19, 2006). He played for many years with a "three-car garage-rock band" called Rackett (see Belinda McKeon, "Rackett, Rhyme, and Reason," *The Irish Times*, August 22, 2007) and, more recently, he joined the musical collective The Wayside Shrines. He has also written several full-length operas with composer Daron Hagen. In this chapter I focus on these generic cross-overs before turning to Muldoon's opera poems. Although they are almost entirely neglected in the criticism, Muldoon's song lyrics and libretti are indicative of his lifelong literary interests, and they serve as pedagogical primers for his poetry. His music might therefore teach us how to read (and to hear) poetry that is on the threshold of becoming opera. As Elmer Kennedy-Andrews (2005b, 17) describes it, "Muldoon's central poetic concerns [parallel] his excursions into other media. Indeed, operatic theatre's 'mixed marriage' of words and music might well be considered a particularly suitable vehicle for the expression of the Muldoonian vision." But what *is* the so-called "Muldoonian vision"? To what purpose does his poetry so "suitably" harness sound?

A glance at Muldoon's idiosyncratic political perspective offers a point of entry to these questions. Although he conceded in 2006 that "what had been the day-to-day violence of Northern Ireland" still fundamentally shapes his work, Muldoon rarely deals directly with the Troubles; he is inspired instead by sectarian clamor to ideological evasiveness and equivocality. "I've not espoused one [political] position over another," he explains, "because I don't really have much time for [those] positions, all of which tend to simplify the matter. And anybody who knows anything about [the conflict] knows that it's a lot more complex than that" (Muldoon 2006d, 14).[2] But Ulster's strident identity politics were the very stuff of Muldoon's childhood soundtrack: he was born in Collegeland, a small Nationalist enclave in largely Protestant County Armagh (the Orange Order was founded in the neighboring parish of Loughgall). He spent most of the Troubles living in Belfast, the conflict's incendiary epicenter, studying English at Queen's University, and working for BBC

2. During a 2004 interview on BBC Radio 3, Muldoon elaborated on this position: "What you probably won't find in the poems, of course, is anything that smacks of taking a particular position. That's not to say that I'm a person who sits on the fence, but I suppose that put very crudely I can see arguments on both sides as it were there. And frankly I think that's one of the things we have to pursue, all of us. We have to imagine, no matter where we come from, which side we're on as it were, what it's like to be on the other side. . . . [Nevertheless, the violence] is [still an unresolved issue for me] and you know . . . it's still very much part of the, I don't even want to say back of the mind, it's in the front of the mind, constantly." Even at the height of Troubles-era violence, Muldoon disavowed pledges of political allegiance: asked in 1985 by Michael Donaghy, "What are your politics?" Muldoon responded bluntly, "I don't think it matters. I don't think it's of any interest."

Radio between 1973 and 1986. His proximity to the Troubles' violence left Muldoon intimately familiar with Ulster's fractious tribalisms and overexposed to the cacophonous volley of essentialisms—competing claims to kith and kin—that were mobilized on behalf of both Nationalist and Unionist platforms.

As Muldoon developed as a poet, he was increasingly subject to political pressure. Northern Ireland's writers have often been tasked (at least tacitly, and sometimes overtly) with carrying the weight of the country's ideological divides. "Ulster poets today," Edna Longley (1985, 26) argues, are frequently "the victims of improper 'expectations'" and are asked to forfeit "the poet's special passport to *terra incognita*" to take on "a national . . . role." This role is perhaps the legacy of the turn-of-the-century literary revival, during which Yeats and his fellows encouraged work written in the so-called authentic "Irish spirit" as a means of countering "Britishness" or broader European modernism. The scope of this cultural nationalism was narrowed even further by the ardent Irish Ireland movement, which critiqued Revivalists for pandering to the Anglo-Irish Ascendancy—a myopic outlook that would come to propagandistically shape subsequent versions of Republicanism (B. Stewart 2000, 23). Irish Irelander D. P. Moran, founder of *The Leader*, a militantly Catholic weekly broadsheet, drew a strict line in the sand between Gaelic Ireland and Anglo-Ireland (or the so-called "Gaelic mind" versus "the English mind in Ireland"). Moran re-cast Irishness in exclusivist, essentialist terms: "We want to go back to the Gael, the matrix of the Irish nation. If the Gael is to be raised, the proper place for the sympathetic Palesman [i.e., Protestant] is behind the Gael until he becomes absorbed" (quoted in C. O'Brien 1995, 55).

The Leader set discourses of religion, nationalism, and "the soil"—a term that frames place as a hallowed "natal source" for partisan political aims (Deane 1997, 71)—on a collision course, laying the groundwork for the rhetoric of the Troubles. After partition, this divisive "race-consciousness" (Corkery 1931, 212) remained the North's dominant discursive mode. Political speeches from both Nationalists and Unionists throughout the period reveal this enduring essentialism: Bobby Sands referred to his "British oppressors" as "aliens" and "parasites" (creatures beyond the bounds of Republicanism's moral order);[3] and Protestant Ian Paisley starkly cast the conflict as "a matter of Ulster or the Irish Republic . . . a matter of freedom or slavery" and bitterly protested the "appeasement" of Republican "monsters" (Ward 2004, 166). Accordingly, the expectation that poets become propagandists for local politics intensified throughout the Troubles, sending many of the period's up-and-coming Catholic writers to pen paeans to Bobby Sands that sacralized his martyrdom.[4]

Although many emerging poets were pressed into political service—Longley (1985, 26) even calls *An Phoblacht* (*The Republic*, Sinn Féin's official newspaper) "the dustbin . . . of Republican poetry"—the young Muldoon instead favored ideological obliqueness and ambiguity, which to this day remain his signature postures. He assiduously avoids any declarations of political allegiance, instead professing, "I don't have anything to say to mankind. I have nothing to say to a mass audience. I'm suspicious of people who do" (Muldoon 1987a, 36). Muldoon does mine the Irish language as a poetic resource, but this is far from a sign of fervent Republicanism: Gaelic is lodged irreverently alongside the likes of American English in his repertoire. When asked in a BBC interview about the first poem he remembers writing, Muldoon (2004) responded, "[my first poem] was about Charlemont Fort, which was an Elizabethan fort in the vicinity of where we were brought up. And I was drawing some kind of connection between, or actually . . . a lack of connection between that and the modern world and the smell of gasoline. And the word gasoline was a word I was using at the age of whatever, twelve, and what I remember about that was that a teacher said 'gasoline? Do you mean petrol?' So somehow the American lingo was in there already." Even at twelve years

3. See Bobby Sands' diaries, reproduced for PBS' *Frontline* at http://www.pbs.org/wgbh/pages/frontline/shows/ira/readings/diary.html.

4. Muldoon's opinion of Sands can be read, at least obliquely, in "Gathering Mushrooms" (1983), in which he ventriloquizes a Republican dirty protester through the head of a horse: the hallucinatory result of a drug-fueled evening's revelry with Ciaran Carson (or so the story goes). For some nationalist hard-liners, "Gathering Mushrooms" probably verges on blasphemy given Sands' longstanding pride of place as a community martyr.

old, Muldoon was writing about home in a way that countered tradition; he was casting his country not as an insular ideal but as a potentially relational space—Ireland refracted through American.[5] His life's work is borne out of this sentiment: Muldoon treats Ireland (North and South) as a seat of hybridity, which he implies in the title of his 1977 volume *Mules*. His homeplace is porous and open (willingly or otherwise) to the world. As Sean O'Brien (1998, 173) observes, "Muldoon's home ground is always already an elsewhere. The Moy [a river near Collegeland, often mentioned in Muldoon's poetry] is as exotic as it is familiar. . . . If Heaney belongs to a tribe, Muldoon wonders what a tribe is, and comes up with the answer 'Mohawk.'" Indeed, Muldoon seems especially interested in reconfiguring community in ways that contest the North's calcified identity politics and forge connections beyond geographical proximity and cultural uniformity. Repelled by strident sectarianism, his work seeks cross-community and even cross-national (Moy/Mohawk) forms of belonging.

In this chapter I argue that sound is the vehicle best suited to Muldoon's cross-cultural vision (or audition). Although cultural community is typically thought of as a cartographic phenomenon—a unity in visuospatial proximity—Muldoon writes instead with a "migrant consciousness"; his work bristles with multidirectional movement and cross-cultural influence and interactivity (Kennedy-Andrews 2008, 18). Theorizing

5. When asked to edit *The Faber Book of Contemporary Irish Poetry* twenty-three years later, Muldoon made much the same point: the poet, as he writes in his prologue, must be "a sensitive instrument designed to record *anything* which interests his mind or affects his emotions" (emphasis mine), rather than a slave to racial "blood-music" (Muldoon 1986, 18). This sentiment introduces his anthology's non-programmatic, nonpartisan, and worldly selections from poets like Louis MacNeice, Thomas Kinsella, and Derek Mahon. Although Muldoon's edited volume does include Seamus Heaney, he conspicuously omits excerpts from *North* (Heaney 1975), the volume for which Heaney was famously accused by Ciaran Carson (1975, 183–86) of being a national "mythmaker" and a "laureate of violence," and of submitting to the gravitational pull of mythologizing his tribe's violence. The 1986 anthology therefore bears out Edna Longley's (1994, 195) comment that "[b]oth Irish Nationalism and Ulster Unionism must accept the reality of the North as a frontier-region, a cultural corridor, a zone where Ireland and Britain [and the world beyond!] permeate one another."

Muldoon's poetic world therefore requires a clean conceptual break—a means of rethinking community beyond home turf.

Communications theorist Nikos Papastergiadis (2000) offers a viable critical alternative to traditional visions of community in *The Turbulence of Migration*. After examining global population flows (the circulation of people, practices, and products), Papastergiadis (2000, 116–17) argues persuasively for the "deterritorialization" of culture, explaining that community can no longer be "mapped in bounded space" and emphasizing "the need for re-imagining the possibilities of belonging." Although he fails to specify what form this "re-imagining" might take, Papastergiadis does discuss "fusion musics" at length, framing "crossover" genres such as Bhangra as registers in which "diasporic . . . inflections" are voiced and as viable "hybrid representation[s] . . . of cultural identity" (116).[6] This shift from the eye to the ear suggests sound as deterritorialization's political unconscious and allows Papastergiadis to point to an alternate possibility of belonging: community-building in *acoustic* space.[7]

The notion of reconsidering landscape as soundscape is reminiscent of Marshall McLuhan and Edmund Carpenter's (1960) essay "Acoustic Space." McLuhan and Carpenter sketch the contours of Muldoon's poetic project: they take the idea of sound-space seriously and theorize its potential shape and scope. In particular, they argue that acoustic space is theoretically boundless. Whereas visual space, a field that objects move

6. Bhangra, which developed in the United Kingdom in the 1980s thanks to a sudden influx of Punjabi immigrants, exists at the intersection of South Asian, British, and hip-hop cultures. The genre was hybridizing even before export; Sikh folk dance forms merged with many other community traditions after the post-partition scattering of Punjabi refugees.

7. Sound seems to hover spectrally above many different discussions of deterritorialization, suggesting audition as the political unconscious of the entire field. Even Deleuze and Guattari (1994), who originally coined the term "deterritorialization" to connote the unhomeliness of "the thinker"—the philosopher as *conceptually* deterritorialized and in figurative exile—observe the incompatibility of visual space and migrant consciousness. They compare territory and deterritorialization, respectively, to "finite melodic compounds" and "the great infinite plane of composition" (Deleuze and Guattari 1994, 186). See also Obert's (2006) "The Cultural Capital of Sound."

through or are rooted within, is circumscribed by the eye's 180-degree perceptual limits, the soundscape creates its own dimensions and its reaches are dictated by each noise's volume. Sound-space can therefore accommodate modes of community-building far beyond those the eye can see; as McLuhan and Carpenter (1960, 68–69) describe, "[t]he universe" is auditory space's "potential map." This theory is borne out provocatively by Muldoon's poetic practice. To oppose narrow regionalisms, Muldoon proposes community's deterritorialization; he conjures capacious acoustic spaces in which to chime together far-flung people and places.

Muldoon's lyrics and libretti lend *literal* voice to this chiming. Thematically, each of Muldoon and Hagen's operas—*Shining Brow* (1995, first performed in 1993), *Bandanna* (1998), *Vera of Las Vegas* (2003, first recorded in 1996), and *The Antient Concert* (2007, first workshopped in 2005)[8]—juxtaposes dangerous desires for purity with transgressive hybridities: former IRA thugs cross paths with a Vegas transvestite; *Othello* is recast along the Texas-Mexico border. As David Wheatley (2004, 151) remarks in an all-too-rare critical reaction to Muldoon's libretti, "as if in response to the meeting of media that is opera composition, the . . . libretti take as their theme the meetings of worlds." Formally, the operas sound out cross-cultural counterpoints; voices' harmonies and dissonances move alongside Hagen's hybrid musical idioms (neo-Gershwin meets a motif from *der Rosenkavalier* one moment, blues meets mariachi the next). The operas live primarily as recordings (they are infrequently staged) and Hagen and Muldoon's close collaboration suggests that neither the libretti nor the scores serve fully as stand-alone texts (ASCAP 2002). The operas therefore "mak[e] raids" from their acoustic battlements on the monophony of "nationalistically marked" cultural artifacts (Osborn 2000, 355), chiming their way toward these (ever complex, often messy) heteroglossic "meetings of worlds."

Muldoon's poems seem to borrow many of their musical strategies from the libretti, and he fashions them from specific sonic building blocks.

8. *The Antient Concert* is a one-act "dramatic recital for four singers"; for brevity's sake, I will refer to it as an opera.

These building blocks include the poet's wide-ranging ventriloquy, a technique prized for its "allow[ing] the individual to make manifest a multiplicity of points of view, including political points of view, allowing him or her the freedom to shape-shift" (Muldoon 2000, 73), his intricate system of intertextual phonetics, and his obsessively recurring acoustic leitmotifs. Moreover, rhyme works associatively for Muldoon, broadcasting signals between seemingly disparate poetic spaces, and he often marshals these signals in service of surprising cross-culturalities. "[T]he connective force of rhyme," that is to say, allows Muldoon's poetry to travel on "caravans of sound" (Ramazani 2009, 55). For instance, as Sean O'Brien's Moy/Mohawk comment suggests, Muldoon's rhyme schemes frequently intone Ireland with indigenous America, charting a community-in-sympathy based on proximate colonial histories.[9] Muldoon's poetry reimagines belonging beyond the claustrophobic confines of geographical space; soundscape's potential boundlessness allows it to accommodate long-distance connections in ways that visual space cannot. Ultimately, Muldoon's operatic flourishes bring local and global topographies within mutual earshot. Although the poetry can tread on surprisingly specific Irish ground, with frequent references to Belfast and Muldoon's childhood Moy, these details are marshaled not as "roots" but as "routes" (Clifford 1997, 3), chiming their way toward counterpoints with other groups and geographies.

Making a Rackett: Muldoon's Lyrics

Muldoon grew up with one foot in the Moy and one in Motown; his artistic sensibilities straddled the Atlantic. Even while being steeped in Irish bardic traditions at his local grammar school, he was forged poetically in the kiln of burgeoning rock 'n' roll. Unsurprisingly, he cites master lyricists like Leonard Cohen, Bob Dylan, and Warren Zevon as formative aesthetic influences. Poems like "Sleeve Notes" (2001) and "Bob Dylan at Princeton,

9. Never one for oversimplifications, Muldoon does complicate the relationship between the two: on occasion he reminds readers of the collusion of Irish scouts during the conquest of Native America (see, e.g., Muldoon's [1990] eponymous concluding poem in *Madoc: A Mystery*).

November 2000" (2006c) chart Muldoon's life—from his Collegeland youth, to Belfast and the BBC, to New Jersey fatherhood—as a series of albums and shows that evocatively encapsulate time and mood. Muldoon only arrived firsthand on the pop music scene, however, after mailing a fan letter to Warren Zevon. To Muldoon's surprise, Zevon responded and invited the poet to collaborate with him on new material. Together, Muldoon and Zevon wrote "My Ride's Here," which Zevon recorded on his album of the same name and which was later covered by Bruce Springsteen. They also penned "McGillycuddy's Reeks" shortly before Zevon's death in 2003.

After seeing (and hearing) how rich this kind of collaboration could be, and after understanding songwriting as a process that gave full-throated, vibrant life to language's inbuilt musicality, Muldoon decided in 2004 to assemble a "three-car garage-rock band" called Rackett. Muldoon wrote lyrics and played rhythm guitar for Rackett, and in 2010, the band gave way to a new musical collective called the Wayside Shrines (after Muldoon's eponymous 2009 collection). Wayside Shrines enjoys a larger membership (eight musicians compared with Rackett's five) and a more complex instrumental mix, but Muldoon's role as lyricist and amateur musician has not changed, nor have the bass stylings of fellow Princeton professor Nigel Smith.[10]

Based on the published collection of Rackett's lyrics, *General Admission* (Muldoon 2006b), and on the band's recordings on their MySpace page (https://myspace.com/rackett) and their albums *Don't Try This at Home* (2006a), *Standing Room Only* (2006b), and *Resistance* (2007), I argue that the rock song is a stylistic ground bass for Muldoon: a form that his poetry approaches and perhaps even aspires toward. Muldoon's poems, in other words, have an inbuilt sense of their own proximity to music, and his tunes are resoundingly able to realize this fusion of word and sound. As his bandmate Nigel Smith explains, Muldoon's lyrics are "very easy to

10. In this chapter I refer primarily to Rackett because its recordings and published lyrics are more readily available than those of the Wayside Shrines.

write music to, because the music just comes. I think that's because [Muldoon] invests a lot of attention in what you might call chiming. He gets the sounds right as well as the conceptual content and ideas" (quoted in McKeon, *The Irish Times*, August 22, 2007).

In addition to writing lyrics, Muldoon has started writing music to accompany those lyrics, suggesting that melody and instrumentation have become more and more wedded in his mind as a third term to language's sound and sense. Although Muldoon's songwriting has been almost entirely neglected in the criticism (it is typically dismissed as a part-time hobby and divorced from his "serious" literary work), I suggest that the poet's genre-crossings give literal voice to his existing sense of poetry's fundamental aurality. Rackett's tunes can tell us much about how we might eavesdrop on Muldoon's poetic soundscapes.

Songwriting allows Muldoon an especially emphatic means of contesting tribal "blood-music": his songs showcase acoustic space's ability to fashion communities far beyond what the eye can see. As such, Rackett's tunes tend to take cultural mélange, "hodgepodge" ("Saab with Sandi," Rackett 2006b), or "salmagundi" ("It Might Be True," Muldoon 2006b) as a central conceit. They often circulate motifs definitive of native Ireland—as in "Tara of the Kings" (Muldoon 2006b), a reference to the ancient seat of Ireland's high rulers, or "Rapparee Rap" (Muldoon 2006b), a play on the ferocious Irish guerrilla fighters of the 1690s' Williamite War—only to de-sanctify these motifs and to mock their cultural jingoism. For example, "Rapparee Rap" is echoed by "kneecap," a particularly malicious paramilitary practice.

Rackett's tunes often chime Ireland into contact with the voices of "others" to decenter myopic local loyalties and to suggest long-distance connectivity in their stead. As Elmer Kennedy-Andrews (2008) explains in his account of Muldoon's community-building, because "[t]he history of Northern Ireland is bloody testimony to the trouble that arises when discourses of 'home,' 'belonging' and 'nation' are linked to territory and bounded place" (2), Muldoon's work suggests "other ways of imagining community which are not centred in the nation-state or the traditional narratives of cultural nationalism but which cut across many of these boundaries, and provide alternative images of identity and culture" (15). Kennedy-Andrews (2008, 115) also proclaims sound to be the poet's "central organizational principle"—a rhetorical coincidence that can perhaps be read symptomatically. He alludes to the argument I am advancing here: sound can sever community from "territory and bounded place" because acoustic space is a potentially "boundless sphere" (McLuhan and Carpenter 1960, 69). Song therefore seems a suitable vehicle for Muldoon's "global imagined communities" (Hena 2008, 258).

One of Muldoon's most frequently cited political geographies (or political sonographies) is his affiliation of Ireland with indigenous America. This strategic resonance relativizes Irishness, making it "fluid, porous, and globalized" (Hena 2008, 243–44). It also diagnoses "cross-cultural trauma" (243–44) and identifies its treatment via the poultice of "common . . . resistance" (258). Muldoon often charts cross-cultural community based on political sympathies and analogous histories, breaching the bounds of traditionally tribal belonging.[11] In his own words, "[o]ne of the ways in which we are most ourselves is that we have to imagine ourselves to be going somewhere else. It's important . . . to have the notion of something out there to which we belong, that our home is somewhere else . . . there's another dimension, something around us and beyond us" (quoted in Kennedy-Andrews 2008, 103). A Northern Irelander's allegiances to Native America are perhaps grounded in common (post-)colonialism; in

11. In an interview with Dillon Johnston, Muldoon (2008) explains the thought process behind his poetic community-building using the example of his poem, "The Year of the Sloes, for Ishi": "[T]he first [epic poem] I wrote, based largely on Native American material—"The Year of the Sloes" it was called—a combining of the Irish notion of the year of the sloes, a low year, the year of the haw, a braw year, an indicator from what might appear in the hedge row of how the weather might be shaping up. That's before global warming, I suppose. That then tied in with a lot of imagery derived mostly from *Bury My Heart at Wounded Knee*, Dee Brown's great book, but a poem also, the more I think about it, written in 1972, just after the occasion of Bloody Sunday, when in Derry there was a civil rights march where a number of unarmed people were shot down. At some level, this poem was a response to that."

an interview with Lynn Keller, for instance, Muldoon (1994b, 19) identifies his interest in "Indian . . . parallels with the Ireland situation" based on Ireland's historical role as an "imperial testing ground."[12] However, the "meetings of worlds" that Muldoon engineers are often messy, and his community by no means requires uniformity. Muldoon's (1990) poem "Madoc: A Mystery," for example, both outlines the "reverberations created between the colonization of America and that of Ireland" (Kennedy-Andrews 2008, 111) and suggests the history of Irish complicity in New World expansionism. In "Madoc," Muldoon grants Alexander Cinnamond, a vicious Scots-Irish scout, a supporting role in Coleridge and Southey's Pantisocratic fantasy, and he introduces Cinnamond's cruelty to the local Cayuga with a resounding "de dum, de dum" that recalls an Orangeman's ominous lambeg drum.

Muldoon also mines these "reverberations" as one of Rackett's lyrical resources. "Need to Know," from the band's first full-length album *Standing Room Only* (Rackett 2006b), resonantly substantiates Muldoon's cross-cultural community-building. As one of Rackett's few down-tempo ballads, "Need to Know" uses rhyme to chart long-distance connections, but it also harnesses music's associative force. Muldoon's very first lines, "I used to know how Custer / Blew the Little Big Horn," are playful puns thanks to the double meaning of "blew," and they are charged with introducing the checkered conquest of indigenous America.[13] This theme is subsequently underscored by Muldoon's reference to Charles Kingsley's (1899) *Westward Ho!*, a novel whose British protagonist follows Francis Drake to the Caribbean, only to fall in love with/make a fetish object of an "exotic" Indian maiden, and whose title was later adopted to describe Western expansionism along the American frontier. The link between

12. See Neil Corcoran's (1993, 211) "In Ireland or Someplace," Heather Clark's (2006, 107) *The Ulster Renaissance*, and Ruben Moi's (2007, 223) "Transtextual Conceptualizations of Northern Ireland" for thoughtful elaborations of this argument.

13. George Armstrong Custer, a cavalry commander in the "Indian Wars," was infamously held responsible for a disastrous defeat at the hands of a united Lakota-Cheyenne force in the Battle of the Little Bighorn.

these two lines is emphasized acoustically by an associative system of alliterative b's ("*b*lew," "*B*ig," "*B*uster," "*B*uddha").[14] The song then moves from verse to chorus, and from an inter-textual, inter-referential mode into more familiar rock 'n' roll territory: "Now all I know's / On a need to know basis / For I'm lovesick I'm sick at heart" (Rackett 2006b, "Need to Know" lines 7–9).

Musically, although the song begins in F major with Lee Matthew's vocals accompanied by a simple picking pattern on the electric guitar, it modulates at this point into D minor, striking a chord of uncertainty for the lyrics' shift from past to present. Whereas the speaker used to be confidently erudite, with all sorts of esoteric facts at his fingertips, his inconstant lover now "keep[s him] in the dark" (Rackett 2006b, "Need to Know" line 11), and "all [he] knows [is] / On a need to know basis" (lines 7–8). The anxiety suggested here by the music's shifting tonal center is also conveyed by the sound of *language* (the poetry's own aurality): the verse's pattern of perfect end-rhyme and final consonance (ababcdcd) is thrown awry by the slightly off-kilter echo between "heart" and "dark."

"Need to Know" continues with a verse-bridge-verse-chorus progression. Of particular interest is the tune's bridge (from "Who was that thug" to "cut my life support" [lines 25–30]), which breaks markedly from the verses' pace. The tempo accelerates abruptly, the lyrics seem a sudden multisyllabic mouthful, and a percussive cymbal begins to underscore the vocal line. The music's sense of urgency fittingly accompanies the lyrics' emotional climax; here the speaker first suspects his lover's affair, asking apprehensively, "Who was that thug who gave you the hug / On the ambulance forecourt?" The cymbal is an apt complement to the lyrics' medical metaphors, which reflect the speaker's physiological reaction to his lover's betrayal: pulse racing, temples pounding, and almost autonomic stream-of-consciousness ranting, delivered by lead singer Matthew in a rushed

14. This tune suggests the organic connections between Muldoon's music and poetry: he composed it almost concurrently with his sonnet sequence in *Horse Latitudes* (Muldoon 2006c). The collection spans a series of battles that all begin with the letter "B," and it includes battles implicated in both the British occupation of Ireland and the conquest of the American frontier.

monotone: "Is that thug gonna help you pull the plug / And cut my life support?" The bridge's system of compulsive internal rhyme, with "thug"-"hug"-"plug"-"thug"-"plug" returning again and again to a guttural /ʌg/ sound and mimicking the thumping lub-dub, lub-dub of a heightened heartbeat, similarly underscores this point. Continuing at this hastened pace through a final verse and chorus, "Need to Know" ultimately charts lasting panic but little emotional progress. Its speaker remains "in the dark" as the tune concludes; the future of his relationship is still uncertain. When Matthew performs the song, he emphasizes this uncertainty by twice repeating the lyrics' final line, "I need to know my chances of surviving you." Appropriately, the tune's final note is also inconclusive; the song ends abruptly, with no real instrumental denouement after Matthew's last words, and it does not resolve with a convincing final cadence.

Perhaps the most significant moment in the song in terms of its relationship to the Northern Irish conflict, however, is its concluding mention of Edmund Spenser (Rackett 2006b, "Need to Know" line 31). Spenser was an Elizabethan poet who is still celebrated as a foundational figure of modern English verse; he was also implicated in the British conquest of Ireland. Spenser served in the British military during the Second Desmond Rebellion (1579–83), and he received confiscated colonial lands in County Cork as part of the Plantations of Ireland after the rebels' defeat. He later wrote an inflammatory prose pamphlet, *A View of the Present State of Ireland* (Spenser 1633), which actively advocates the eradication of Irish culture and custom and the subjugation by war and "scorched earth" famine of the Irish people as a means of ensuring the territory's submission to the Tudor state. Spenser's fervent belief in British cultural superiority meant that he found "evil" in Ireland's "lawes, customes, and religion," and he thought the "sworde" the instrument best suited to "the reformacon of those evilles."[15]

Although Muldoon doesn't openly take this colonial jingoism to task, he does provocatively distance-chime "Spenser" with "Custer," and

15. The full text of Spenser's pamphlet is available at http://www.ucc.ie/celt/published/E500000-001/index.html.

his rhyme scheme suggests a common imperial, even genocidal, intent. This resonant half-rhyme indicates that the song isn't simply about the speaker's failed relationship, with its bits of school-book trivia serving as lyrical window-dressing; rather, the song's sounds sketch their own second-degree sense. The bridge's racing rhythms suggest the physiology of anxiety and fear and connote the psycho-affective dimensions of political conquest alongside those of personal betrayal. As Nigel Smith explains, "[Paul's] songs often work by fusing two landscapes, which creates an energy in their collision. Something that brings the speaker's world together with something from a world outside is a powerful facet of creativity in literature that both Paul and I recognize" (quoted in Mizell, "Rackett's Rise," *Daily Princetonian*, December 2, 2004). In this case, Muldoon chimes Ireland and indigenous America into collision, and although these two landscapes remain geographically distant, the song's soundscape reveals their (post-)colonial proximity.[16]

Beyond Muldoon's revelatory rhyme, the repeated musical figures in "Need to Know" also chart this common ground. As "reminiscence motifs" (Parker 2001, 219) recall their previous instantiations and register relationships between resoundings, they here exert analogic force. The first verse's "I used to know how Custer" is echoed to the letter by the later

16. The unrecorded song "Hard Cheese and Sour Grapes," which appears in *General Admission* (Muldoon 2006b), is similar in purpose to "Need to Know." Singer Lee Matthew ventriloquizes the character Martin Pawley (played by Jeffrey Hunter), Ethan Edwards' (John Wayne's) half-Cherokee travel companion in John Ford's 1956 film *The Searchers* (Los Angeles, CA: Warner Brothers). The film contends with racism and miscegenation in the early days of the American West and with settlers' violent clashes with displaced Native Americans, and it centrally informs the tune. "Hard Cheese and Sour Grapes," however, refuses to stay on location as it rhymes "Monument Valley," the Utah region where the film was shot, with "Stradbally," a town in Ireland's County Laois. The song's subsequent mention of a "burned-out big house" refers both to the Edwards homestead, torched by local Comanche in the film, and to the so-called "Big Houses" of Ireland (the landed estates of the Anglo-Irish Ascendancy that were targeted by Catholic paramilitaries). Muldoon's acoustics analogize the two contexts; the song's sounds suggest political proximities even if its narrative exposition says nothing of the kind.

"I used to know why Spenser," with each line repeating four counts of D before finally resolving to C. This motif, memorable because it lingers so long on a single note, hovers spectrally in the mind until it is answered by its acoustic pair, allowing the tune to suggestively twin "Irish" with "Indian." Acoustic space therefore becomes the register of Muldoon's newly imagined "translocal" community (Ramazani 2009, 58). As Omaar Hena (2008, 257) describes it, Muldoon's "Indian-Irish connection constructs a counterhegemonic identity formation," resisting both tribal exclusivism and "the seemingly all-totalizing, all-homogenizing operations of globalization."

Rackett's 2007 album *Resistance* is more musically experimental than the band's previous offerings. It introduces a wider instrumental range (including a Hammond organ on "Shocks and Struts" that is reminiscent of The Doors and The Band), dabbles in distortion and synthesized sound, and plays more freely with genre. "Brighton Rock," for example, is an obvious homage to early punk rock, and "11 O'Clock" rings clearly of Santana's signature jazz/rock/salsa blend. This genre-crossing involves cultural border-crossing: genuflections to peoples and places from which Muldoon draws inspiration. The band's nod to Santana, a musician raised in the border city of Tijuana and influenced by both Latin rhythms and instrumentation and African-American blues and jazz traditions, is an important musical counterpart to Muldoon's thematic interest in the U.S.-Mexico border. Like Muldoon and Hagen's (1998) opera *Bandanna*, which documents the dangers of the "zona media," Rackett's (2007) unrecorded song "American Lives" skirts the line dividing Tijuana from San Diego. The song revolves around the folk wisdom dispensed at "Señora Anna's Taco Shack," where would-be migrants, legal and otherwise, hear Anna's take on America as a land of both plenty and peril:

Every sot's F Scott Fitzgerald
Every hero his own herald
Every Stan an Ollie
Every cur a collie

. . . .

Behind every great man

Are at least two great ex-wives
But there are no second bananas
In American lives[.][17]

Students of Muldoon's poetry are well aware that his collections are similarly preoccupied with the border that severs Northern Ireland from the Irish Republic. In "The Boundary Commission," from *Why Brownlee Left*, Muldoon (1980) muses on the paradox of partition: how can a line that arbitrarily cuts a town in two, leaving "the butcher and baker in different states" (line 3), be so heavily militarized, so hotly contested, and so ardently marshaled as a symbol of ethnocultural identity? Muldoon brings Northern Ireland and Mexico into contact in "American Lives" (Rackett 2007) by focusing on the common denominator of lives lived on the "wrong" side of an incendiary border. As critic John Kerrigan (2004, 130) explains, "When [Muldoon] writes about borders in America they share the psychological and linguistic ambiguity of the one bred into him."

Muldoon's music also eloquently features these contact zones: "11 O'Clock" departs from Rackett's typical rock 'n' roll riffs into the territory of Tito Puente's "Oye Como Va"—a song that Santana turned into an international hit by taking the rhythm and tempo of its Latin roots and re-instrumentalizing its riffs for a blues-rock band. Genre-bending in Muldoon's musical collaborations, therefore, is often marshaled strategically: Rackett borrows from Santana the hybrid sounds of Mexican-American borderlands and then strikes these chords alongside tunes thematizing Ireland's margins. "It Might Be True" (from *General Admission*, Muldoon 2006b), for example, discusses the gradual re-negotiation of Irish territory. Its opening reference to things "east of the Shannon" conjures the specter of the seventeenth-century Plantations of Ireland, during which Cromwell reputedly pronounced that displaced Catholic landholders could go "to hell or Connacht"—that is, accept forced migration west across the River Shannon or face death. The song's later chime between "1916" and "Dark Rosaleen" highlights the year of the Easter Rising, which precipitated the

17. The song plays on F. Scott Fitzgerald's famous dictum that "there are no second acts in American lives."

Irish War of Independence and led to present-day partition. Ultimately, the U.S.-Mexico border acts as a "magnet for Irishness" (Kerrigan 2004, 130) in Muldoon's work, and Rackett's tunes make this tactical "meeting of worlds" abundantly audible.

Crossing the Line: Muldoon's Libretti

Many of Rackett's sonic strategies surface again in Muldoon's operas, which are the fruits of an intensive twenty-year collaboration with renowned American composer Daron Aric Hagen.[18] As Hagen has explained, with each new project, the two sit down and co-write a filmic treatment, then Muldoon pens an act, Hagen revises and musicalizes it, plays and sings it for Muldoon, and asks for changes in turn, such that the operas are the products of the partnership's ongoing workshop process ("Daron Hagen's Opera Shining Brow" 2009). These expansive audio-texts are remarkably wide-ranging in both sound and sense, bridging traditional operatic structures with the likes of blues, barbershop, and Broadway and allowing each of their characters to "sing the kind of music that that character demands" (Hagen, quoted in ASCAP 2002). The scope of the operas' scores is well suited to the libretti's common concerns about cultural contact zones: forms of empire-building, the crossfire of competing nationalisms, attachments to purity versus promiscuous hybridity, and politically fraught cross-border transits.

18. The proximity between the poet's lyrics and libretti is far from coincidental. Muldoon has argued that there is little difference between writing a libretto and writing popular song because musicals and opera have exerted such extensive mutual influence in the modern era ("Daron Hagen's Opera Shining Brow" 2009). At one point, the members of Rackett expressed a desire to collectively pen a "rock opera," suggesting the intimately reciprocal relationship between the two genres (Stuart Mitchner's "After a Visit to 'Recording Heaven,' Rackett Is Celebrating a New Album," *Town Topics* [Princeton], August 15, 2007). Muldoon and Warren Zevon actually began co-writing a rock musical about two competing Native American casinos, but it was left unfinished after Zevon's death in 2003. The musical's characters were based loosely on James Fenimore Cooper's *The Last of the Mohicans* (Charles McGrath, "Word Freak," *New York Times Magazine*, November 19, 2006).

In all four of their operas Muldoon and Hagen thematize the dislocation of people from place, and estrangement and alienation are the driving feeling-states in their work. *Shining Brow* (1995), a commissioned piece on the life of architect Frank Lloyd Wright, hinges on the actions of Wright's near-invisible Barbadian servant, whereas *Vera of Las Vegas* (2003) features a pair of former IRA gunmen in Vegas on the run from British authorities. *Bandanna* (1998) charts the fates of a group of migrants at the Texas-Mexico border; in the libretto's preface the group is referred to as "the dispossessed and the disappeared." Finally, *The Antient Concert* (2007) revolves around the reputed showdown in the 1904 *Feis Ceoil* competition between James Joyce and tenor John McCormack.[19] Muldoon and Hagen cast McCormack as a fervent Nationalist who frames British rule as a kind of internal exile, while Joyce pokes fun at McCormack's poker-faced devotion to all things "authentically" Irish.

All of the geographical displacements explored in these operas, exemplified by the staged insecurity of the border zone in *Bandanna*, demand consolatory modes of belonging and community-building. In Muldoon and Hagen's collaborations, these modes are voiced and scored. In other words, when visual orientations are overturned, and the insufficiencies of local tribalisms revealed, Muldoon's casts of migrants and outcasts try to re-negotiate affinities and affiliations in acoustic space. If each character "sings the kind of music that [he or she] demands," and if those demands often take on cultural valences, then we literally hear the pleasures and perils of Muldoon's experimental cross-culturalities. During performances of *Bandanna*, for example, a mariachi band (an earmark of Mexican nationalism) remains onstage and variously chimes with and offsets the opera's pit orchestra. For these reasons, Muldoon's operas are perhaps the ultimate expressions of his career concerns. They are "magnificently mixed genres" (Bernard O'Donoghue, review of *Vera of Las Vegas*, *Times*

19. The *Feis Ceoil*, translated as "Festival of Music," is an annual Irish cultural festival and a longstanding pillar of the country's musical infrastructure. Founded in 1896, the festival now comprises more than 180 competitions and attracts nearly 3,000 musicians of all ages and disciplines to Dublin each Easter.

Literary Supplement, June 29, 2001) that suitably convey what Elmer Kennedy-Andrews (2008, 86) calls "the ambiguous thrill of travel and border-crossing . . . Muldoon's potentially self-destructive engagements with otherness."

Vera of Las Vegas, subtitled by Muldoon and Hagen as "a nightmare cabaret opera in one act," was first recorded in 1996, premiered publicly in New York in 2003, and was revived for an Irish tour in 2004. This subtitle suggests that the opera is a "a stew of postmodern influences" (Hagen, quoted in ASCAP 2002); the piece freely mixes operatic conventions with everything from 1970s power ballads to neo-Baroque antiphony, all the while liberally sampling lyrics from Bob Dylan, African-American spirituals, and Celtic folk songs. Although the libretto has been published in book form (Muldoon and Hagen 2003) and the production staged in two short runs, Hagen explains that its "life [is] mostly in recordings," and he suggests that he and Muldoon consciously patterned the opera after concept albums like Pink Floyd's *The Wall*: immersive record-length acoustic experiences (ASCAP 2002).

The opera's musical blending makes audible its plot's daring border-crossings. *Vera of Las Vegas* revolves around two former IRA volunteers, Taco and Dumdum, who land in Las Vegas while on the run from the MI-5.[20] Doll, an undercover U.S. immigration agent, tracks the two for visa violations, promising them a free Vegas vacation to try to herd them into custody. She directs them to her associate, the eponymous Vera, who is a lap-dancer on the Vegas strip. When the British agents, synecdochally named Trench and Trilby, turn up, it appears they are also seeking Vera (they are trying to stifle her efforts to press charges against an influential former client). Vera, Doll, Taco, and Dumdum flee to the Delphine, a local strip club, where Taco and Vera retire together to a dark corner. Taco discovers that Vera is a transvestite but confesses that his attraction to her is undiminished; men and women, he sings, "are more or less the

20. These characters are themselves inter-textual border-crossers, having first appeared in Muldoon's (1995) play *Six Honest Serving Men*, which follows the violent exploits of an active IRA unit.

same." Vera and Doll, having become fond of Taco and Dumdum, then disclose their affiliation with the Immigration and Naturalization Service, and Vera suggests a pair of "green card weddings" as a solution to their problems. The four head to a drive-through chapel for what promises to be the opera's comic denouement, but tragedy ensues: Taco backs out of the wedding, and the opera's final scene features him in an interrogation center "somewhere near Northern Ireland," being tortured into a murder confession by Trench and Trilby.[21]

As this summary suggests, Muldoon's libretto is centrally concerned with displacement and dislocation; Taco and Dumdum, repentant former paramilitaries, are wanted on one side of the Atlantic and hounded across the other in an elaborate immigration "sting."[22] The production also reflects on internal dispossession, with many of America's "others" consigned to marginal outposts like Vegas' so-called "Glitter Gulch."[23] Vera's sense of unbelonging, for instance, is voiced in an emotional aria in the opera's penultimate scene. An African-American transvestite with the auspicious last name "Loman"—a byword, thanks to Arthur Miller, for America's working classes—Vera's non-normative body has been too often "trodden and trampled" into "powerless[ness]." Muldoon's related interest in empire's latter-day reverberations—in people unhomed by histories of expansionism and enslavement—is suggested by the opera's chorus of

21. *Vera of Las Vegas* overtly acknowledges its indebtedness to the 1992 film *The Crying Game* (directed by Neil Jordan, London: Palace Pictures), in which Stephen Rea plays an IRA operative who becomes intimate with the girlfriend of a former British hostage and stays with her after discovering that she is anatomically male. In fact, when Taco reveals Vera's "secret" to Dumdum, the latter replies, "You mightn't have missed it if you'd seen *The Crying Game*. Didn't I tell you?"

22. One of the opera's latent concerns seems to be the issue of paramilitary prisoner release, which was a controversial component of Northern Ireland's peace process. Given Muldoon's sympathetic portrayal of Taco and Dumdum, it would appear that he feels reform is indeed possible. The characters' even-handed responses to Vera's "secret" are perhaps symptoms of their fresh approach to identities once thought rigidly absolute (Nationalist/Unionist and Catholic/Protestant).

23. "Glitter Gulch" is a nickname for the somewhat seedy area along Freemont Street in downtown Las Vegas.

costumed Pequod Native Americans (at once Caesar's Palace caricatures and specters of New World genocide). In light of these estrangements, the cast of migrants and exiles turns its ears to compensatory community formation. If the opera frames visual space as "deceptive . . . malleable, and liable to change" (Jonathan Allison, "Covert Operations," *Irish Literary Supplement*, September 22, 2002)—a suspicion of fixed geographies that Allison calls Muldoon's "antipastoral" mode—then rethinking place in acoustic space suddenly seems an affective imperative. Furthermore, given the opera's motley crew, the *kinds* of community that strain toward audibility in the opera are decidedly "translocal" (Ramazani 2009, 58); Muldoon invokes a capacious hybridity that demands sound-space's boundless sphere.

First and foremost, Muldoon and Hagen use musical genre-crossing to sound out the cultural miscellany in *Vera of Las Vegas*, and Hagen artfully synthesizes wide-ranging sonic styles. When the opera's characters are pushed to the margins of nation-space, they find community, however conditionally, in pursuit of sonic syncretism. The score tends toward bluesy brashness, with lots of smoky saxophone and bass clarinet—a sonority well suited to a so-called "cabaret opera." The blues evolved in America from slaves' work songs and "field hollers": participatory performances that contested the power of plantation owners and overseers by initiating group communication and communion. By bringing this history to opera, a genre often associated with decadence and privilege, Muldoon and Hagen signal a desire to democratize the stage and suggest subterranean community-building as one of the major themes of *Vera of Las Vegas*.

Although the blues genre is the score's backbone, the opera's soundscape is sweepingly inclusive, and the styles it incorporates often self-consciously carry cultural weight. The pit band occasionally breaks into U2's (1987) "I Still Haven't Found What I'm Looking For," which modulates melodically in the "Forum Shops" scene with the oboe's repetition of the opera's casino motif—the jazzy juggling of a D harmonic minor scale's sixth and raised seventh (B♭ and C#). Throughout the "Wedding Chapel Chorus," the lyrics to the African-American spiritual "Joshua (Fit the Battle of Jericho)" are superimposed on a musical background of liturgical antiphony reminiscent of Roman Catholic vespers. The opera therefore painstakingly defines a hard-won auditory multiculturalism as the characters' relationships develop; we hear Taco and Dumdum's Irishness gradually harmonize with Vera's African-American traditions and playful Sondheimian sensibility. Remarkably, the score throws all of these genres into rich euphony. As Jonathan Allison (*Irish Literary Supplement*, September 22, 2002) describes in his review of *Vera of Las Vegas*, "[t]he inclusiveness and eclecticism of the music . . . does not make the opera disintegrate into fragments—it is not a mess of allusions—since the thing is sustained by a firm musical narrative, under whose control there is scope for radical variations."

This musical diversity, a kind of operatic creolization, peaks in the opera's reveal scene ("Duet"), during which Taco and Dumdum learn of Vera's transvestitism and choose nonetheless to keep her close—a decision to sustain togetherness-in-difference that precipitates the characters' wedding preparations. "Duet" opens with long-held chords in the strings, prompting the vocal lines to provide their own rhythmic accompaniment. Initially, Dumdum's name is used by Taco as a percussive backdrop to the scene's lines; his staccato "dum-dum-dums" approximate the sharp, hollow rings of a djembe and offer a robust counterpoint to Dumdum's mellifluous Irish brogue. Taco soon takes over the vocal lead, however, to disclose the news that Vera "isn't everything she seems. . . . I gave her a peck on the cheek. Her chin's like sandpaper. . . . She has an Adam's-apple." Dumdum chimes in with a chorus of "hey nonny nonnys," a common refrain from old Celtic folk tunes and an antiquated euphemism for "vulva" that here alludes to Vera's anatomy. This passage initially seems to herald the return of Taco and Dumdum's one-time tribalism. The characters' turn to Celticism, combined with their caustic comments about Vera's gender ("Dumdum, when I had a feel of little Lady Day she had this huge fucking horn"; "It's like something out of a dirty book"), suggest the imminent collapse of the opera's experimental cross-culturalities. However, the score then takes a sudden turn for the lyrical and the earnestly heartfelt; the scene's music is gesturing, as Hagen explains, to the characters' sincerity of feeling even though its dialogue seems crass (ASCAP 2002). The opera's sounds, therefore, sometimes modify its scenes' meanings: we can hardly take Dumdum's flippant references to Vera's "middle leg" at face value when they are accompanied by a delicately melodic violin duet and a warm modulation from a minor to its relative major key. Indeed, as the score approaches pop balladry, it prompts Taco's climactic admission of both his affection for Vera and his newfound suspicion of things ostensibly "pure":

> A strange thing happened. It just came to me.
> That these are just different forms
> of one thing. That there's no right way.
> There's no right. No left. There's no centre.

Taco's vocal line soars above a shimmering string accompaniment as he becomes Muldoon's momentary mouthpiece, voicing a suspicion of rigid ideologies and fixed identities. After Taco sounds these sentiments, Doll and Vera promptly enter stage right and reclaim the airwaves monopolized by Taco and Dumdum throughout "Duet." Muldoon and Hagen's acoustic border-crossing is once again at play, and Vera's marriage proposal will soon be in the offing.

Another of the major catalysts to community in *Vera of Las Vegas* is its series of recurring leitmotifs or melodic fragments. An important part of modern opera's technical oeuvre, leitmotifs were first popularized in the nineteenth century by Richard Wagner, who used repeated musical phrases to lend tonal coherence and provide so-called "guides-to-feeling" (*Gefühlswegweisern*) for his expansive *Ring Cycle*.[24] As Roger Parker (2001) explains in his comprehensive *The Oxford Illustrated History of Opera*, Wagner drew on an earlier tradition of "reminiscence motifs," "recollections" of a chord or timbre or melodic fragment used "for associative purposes" (219), and he made of these passing "melody memories" an intricate system of musical "presentiments and reminiscences . . . enabl[ing] key ideas to resonate through the score like 'emotional signposts'" (224). These memories are passed from mouth to mouth as they drive the score forward

24. See Wagner's ([1893] 1995) *Opera and Drama*. Full text available at: http://users.belgacom.net/wagnerlibrary/prose/wlpro063.htm.

and gradually accrue connective force; once in sympathy, characters often end up carrying the same tune.

Leitmotifs are traditionally exchanged in opera duets, with musical and lyrical phrases passed between partners such that the score reveals their intimacy (Jarniewicz 2005, 237). In *Vera of Las Vegas*, however, this repetition is granted broader scope, and the opera's primary *dramatis personae* are eventually brought together in an elaborate echo-chamber (see Allison, *Irish Literary Supplement*, September 22, 2002). The opera therefore makes one of Muldoon's signature moves: it forces hermetic exclusivisms, such as Taco and Dumdum's militantly Republican allegiances, to gradually give way to the cultural alchemy of the contact zone. Although *Six Honest Serving Men* (Muldoon 1995) found Taco and Dumdum myopically preoccupied with their own oppression, *Vera of Las Vegas* (Muldoon 2003) hears them harmonize with *other* "others": with the opera's Pequod chorus and, most compellingly, with the race- and gender-bending Vera. Dumdum Devlin is himself symptomatically resounded by these new affiliations; his surname, an earmark of Catholicism shared with famous Republican activist Bernadette Devlin, is repeatedly pronounced "Devine"—a "drag-Irish" handle of a kind.

The leitmotifs in *Vera of Las Vegas* hit fever pitch as the opera's plot reaches climactic communion: the eve of its would-be side-by-side weddings. As Scene XV opens, Trench and Trilby are hounding and hunting Taco and Dumdum, driving them out of their temporary refuge at the Delphine. This insecurity is indicated by the percussive, off-kilter D-A-B♭-A progression that Muldoon and Hagen typically associate with Trench and Trilby's ominous machinations, which is played throughout the opera by the trombone, French horn, synthesizer, and electric bass, and in this scene is taken up by the vocal line. However, as the weddings are poised to foil the agents' plans, the score takes an optimistic turn for the operatic, with pairs of characters singing melodiously *a due* and then opening to quartet. Although Muldoon's outcasts and misfits remain restless, nervously temporary, and hovering at the nation's margins, they here sing their way toward consolatory common ground. As the passage progresses, its echoes become increasingly insistent, with characters passing lyrical and musical fragments back and forth like acoustic batons:

> TACO: It has to do with being able to transform
> lead into gold, Dumdum.
> DOLL: You must transfigure and transform
> yourself, Dumdum. You must find a way
> not to stand in your own way.
> You must become an alchemist.
> DUMDUM: Mist is the word, Taco.

The words "cloud," "mist," and "centre/centaur" flit infectiously from mouth to mouth, and the passage eventually verges on a musical round.[25] "Cloud" alone is repeated nine times over the course of two pages (less than three minutes of performance time); its sound ricochets between the four characters to define shared airwaves as the weddings approach.

Recurring musical motifs similarly serve as collective refrains in *Vera of Las Vegas*. In the above lines, for instance, Dumdum's name is sung in parallel perfect fifths, with the interval first ventured by Taco and then mimicked by Doll. In classical music, consecutive fifths are typically discouraged on the basis of "voice leading" because convention dictates that voices operate independently rather than by call-and-response. Muldoon and Hagen, however, temper these rigid demands with jazz's participatory sensibility, and they allow even fifths and octaves to travel freely between vocal lines. *Vera of Las Vegas*, in other words, turns Muldoon's characteristic poetic echoes into live echolocation: literally, a twinned sounding and listening or a pattern of shared speech-sounds. Critical geographer Paul Carter's (2001) theory of "echoic mimicry" therefore resonates with the

25. This observation is thematically revealing; as John Kerrigan (2004, 131) explains it, Muldoon and Hagen "put a border condition in the middle of things" in *Vera of Las Vegas*. "Clouds" and "mist" replace clarity as the opera's status quo, and "centaur" is a suggestive homonym of "centre" given Muldoon's preoccupation with daring border-dwellings. Vera, who is herself a type of centaur (identifying as female but remaining anatomically male), sings convincingly in her aria that "I who seem to be on the periphery / of things am, truth to tell, / at the very centre." Her hybridity, these lines suggest, is more honest than fantasies of purity and manufactured truths, and the opera positions identity politics—like Taco and Dumdum's one-time Republicanism—as the products of "a little illusion, a little sleight-of-hand."

opera's soundscape. Carter theorizes reciprocal sounding—an effort to try and arrive at a mutual understanding—as a means of ethical cross-cultural encounter in the migrant moment. Echoic mimicry amounts, Carter (2001) says, to the "production of a common place" in the absence of anything else to market there, and "the sound in-between" becomes a register in which to belong. This is precisely the opera's agenda; the concluding scene suggests that acoustic space can provide "placedness" if not "place" in its traditional (i.e., visual) sense, theorizing the comforts of a common auditory topography. As directed by the libretto, the four characters are "transported" by "the flood of emotion" precipitated by their shared sounds, and they are soon moved to exchange passionate embraces. Dumdum even cathartically confesses the trauma of the Troubles to try and expunge his old allegiances before committing to his new community: "I saw a bomb go off in the centre of Belfast. At the Europa Hotel. [Dumdum *seems spent.* Doll *holds him reassuringly*]." This near-orgasmic moment comes directly out of the characters' acoustic exchange; the opera's leitmotifs become more and more urgent as the characters prepare for their redemptive marrying of fortunes.

At the height of this climactic scene, Dumdum repeats a line from *Shining Brow*, conjuring Muldoon and Hagen's (1995) first collaborative effort as a spectral intertext. Leitmotifs circulate both within and between their operas, leaving later libretti laden with previous performances' historical weight. This long-distance echo is especially suggestive: the repeated line, "a cloud no bigger than a [man's] hand," operates in *Shining Brow*—as it does in its original context, the Biblical Book of Kings—as a harbinger of a deluge to come. In *Vera of Las Vegas*, it suggests the same, allowing Muldoon and Hagen to qualify their characters' ecstatic communion and to anticipate the limits of the opera's cross-cultural consolations. Commissioned by the Madison Opera Guild of the Madison Civic Music Association, *Shining Brow* stages the life of architect Frank Lloyd Wright, and it is structured around one of his most dramatic biographical subplots: his extended affair with his one-time client, Mamah Cheney. The opera includes Mamah's eventual death, which occurred when the Wright's Barbadian chef, Julian Carleton, intentionally set fire to their Wisconsin summer home, Taliesin (Middle Welsh for the opera's titular "shining brow").

In *Shining Brow* Muldoon and Hagen (1995) cast Wright's approach to architecture as its own brand of empire-building; he sings of bringing order from chaos and "making his mark" on both the "clean slate of America" and the "well-worn slate of Europe." As Tim Kendall (1996, 189) describes, *Shining Brow* treats "[t]he impulse to build [a]s an impulse towards expansionism, which in turn displaces or destroys precursors," and Wright's will-to-territory is seemingly indefatigable. Indeed, even after Mamah's death, he sings repeatedly of resurrecting Taliesin as a memorial monument. Wright's colonial impulses are emphasized by the fact that his home is conspicuously manned by black hired help—a cast of shadows sung *to* but denied voice. Carleton, in particular, is near-mute throughout the piece: in Act II, Scene 2's "Canapé Variations," he silently takes and obeys orders, serving more as a cocktail party prop than a fully realized character. When he finally is acknowledged, it is to be scolded by Mamah for using her first name; as it turns out, she has (unapologetically) misheard his interrogative "Ma'am?" This misunderstanding precipitates a brief exchange between master and servant, an exchange remarkable for the fact that Carleton remains beyond the bounds of music throughout. The onstage piano trio, playing snippets of the "seduction theme" from Strauss' (1911) *Der Rosenkavalier*, falls tacit, and while Mamah sings *a cappella*, Carleton can only speak in response: "Might everything be in order, ma'am? . . . Whatever you say, ma'am." His voice, in other words, becomes the score's unincorporable residue; his speech-sounds fall flat alongside Frank and Mamah's soaring vocals, starkly marking his alterity. When he makes a second entrance later in the scene, his presence cues a disruption, prompting melodic instrumentals to give way to the percussive beat of a snare drum—more unassimilable noise than unobtrusive acoustic texture.

Suddenly, as the scene concludes, Carleton takes center stage, seizing the opera's sound waves and virtually *becoming* its score. His rhythmic chanting assumes the force of bardic incantation, and each of his verse's lines begins with "I," as though he is willing himself for the first time into being:

> I am the birch stripped of its bark.
> I am a raven swooping over the squadron.

I am a hangnail on a finger.
I am the eye that looks askance.
I am a flint that holds no spark.
I am the rain falling at a slant.
I am a half-moon-shaped gold torc.
I am a sponge steeped in vinegar.
I am the hart. I am the hind.
I am the green and burning tree.
I am the cloud no bigger than a hand.
I will go down in history.

Although the passage approximates Whitman's ([1855] 2001) "Song of Myself" (Carleton's I "contain[s] multitudes" [Whitman 2001, line 53]), it also ventriloquizes the ancient Irish poet Amergin, who was a druid and bard of the Milesians (proto-Gaelic Celts) in the Irish Mythological Cycle. Some of the early medieval Welsh poems attributed to the bard Taliesin, the namesake of Wright's home, are reputedly Amergin's—a connection that explains this scene's unity of setting and style. In particular, Carleton's recitation echoes Amergin's "Incantation to Ireland," a rann composed in honor of the island when the Milesians arrived on its shores to overthrow the resident Tuatha Dé Danann. The incantation suggests the transformative power of the bardic word: Amergin's recitations foretokened victory, and the Names of Power he granted the land—including Ériu, from which the Irish Éire derives—shaped space for years to come. Despite his poetry's authority, however, Amergin himself remained a liminal figure. Muldoon (2000, 5) explains that Amergin often associated himself with thresholds, even delivering his incantation poised in an "unhewn dolmen arch." This sense of being between worlds, Muldoon suggests, has for centuries been Irish literature's driving feeling-state; it is a "terminal narthecality" that the poet later yokes to Ireland's postcolonial predicament: "[S]uccessive invasions of the country le[ft] a sense for many so-called native Irish people of their own invisibility" (Muldoon 2000, 9).

Carleton, like Vera, is peculiarly attuned to Irishness. Out of place throughout the opera, he is uniquely open to possession by Amergin, and he becomes a vessel of poetry's promiscuous power. In particular,

Carleton's polyphony points to the proximity of African and native Irish histories throughout the British Caribbean. Colonial Barbados, for instance, imported both Gold Coast slaves and Irish Catholics displaced by Cromwell as manpower for local planters. Carleton even delivers his lines in a thick Irish brogue, prompting Mamah to wonder aloud whether "all the natives of Barbados speak with an Irish [accent]" and suggesting the possibility of "Barbadoed" interbreeding and cross-voicing between Irish and African slaves.[26] This suggestion is far from speculative; Irish intonations still inflect English throughout the Caribbean and are particularly prevalent in Montserrat, where Cromwell shipped tens of thousands of Irish prisoners of war. The passage therefore sounds its way toward sympathy in common subjection, and Carleton seems at the brink of a bardic will-to-power on behalf of empire's "others" as he commandeers the opera's airwaves.

Just as the audience thinks, however, that Carleton is near redemption, having located agency in acoustic space and common cause in cross-cultural audition, things come undone. Carleton, it turns out, can neither envision nor even hear a way out of a paradigm of enslavement and social death beyond physical death—his own and Mamah's. After his incantation, the opera's stage directions indicate a lengthy blackout, during which jarring music—staccato chromatic triplets from the strings, shrill piccolo trills, and, suggestively, the sounds of a slap-stick and whip—ensues, eventually giving way to the police sirens heralding Mamah's death. There are some things, the opera suggests, for which one cannot

26. John Kerrigan (2004) points out that Carleton's name also alludes to William Carleton, a nineteenth-century Tyrone writer linked to Amergin in *To Ireland, I* (Muldoon 2000) for his own vexed liminality and transgressive border-crossing: Catholic by birth but Protestant by choice, Carleton wrote as a daring "double agent." Kerrigan (2004, 129–30) further allows "Muldoon's preoccupation with cultural and racial hybridity of the Carleton sort" to reflect back on "the mixed state" of Northern Ireland itself, "an entity . . . articulated by a contingent and permeable border that can only constitute an edge, or double-edge, by running through the middle of things and creating a zone of transit." Muldoon's work aims to illuminate—or, more aptly, to make audible—these culture-crossings at every turn.

be compensated, and this scene consciously marks the limits of its own consolatory community-building.

When Taco from *Vera of Las Vegas* repeats Carleton's line, "I've seen a cloud no bigger than a man's hand," we can similarly expect the opera's newly forged "auditory topographies" to give way, and indeed this is the case. Shortly thereafter, Taco backs out of his wedding to Vera and is returned to Northern Ireland, where he is re-subjected to tribal retributions and their rigidly binaric terms: Protestant and Catholic, purity and contamination, perpetrator and victim.[27] The curtain finally falls on the sights and sounds of torture: the ominous "ticking" of an MI-5 parcel, Vera's far-away "wail[s]," and "the judder of blood in [Taco's] ears" brought on by Trench and Trilby's repeated "slaps." Muldoon's migrant consciousness is therefore palliative but far from utopian. Although the operas sound shared structures of feeling by way of reimagining community, their moves away from the "cultural wholeness . . . claimed by nationalist ideology" (Kennedy-Andrews 2008, 113) and toward the idea of "homecoming . . . as a combination of here and there, self and other" necessarily remain as "balancing act[s] on the border between rootedness and disintegration" (116).

27. In many ways, this conclusion reflects contemporary events in the North: Muldoon and Hagen were working on *Vera of Las Vegas* during the lead-up to the first paramilitary ceasefire (1994), and this early (and tenuous) period of the peace process inspired a violent backlash. There were 68 civilian deaths in the country in 1993—the highest recorded number since 1976. Consequently, many in Northern Ireland remained skeptical that a peace accord could be reached, particularly because the conflict had been so protracted and seemingly intractable, and the issues of disarmament and paramilitary prisoner reintegration upon which Vera touches proved particularly difficult obstacles for cross-community negotiations. Even today, almost twenty years after the Good Friday Agreement (1998) and well after large-scale decommissioning, splinter groups such as the RIRA (Real IRA) and CIRA (Continuity IRA) continue to commit sporadic paramilitary violence directed primarily at army and policing targets.

7

PAUL MULDOON

Poetic Sonography

Hot and *Bóthar*-ed: Muldoon's Forked Tongue

Muldoon's poetry has always been abundantly aware of its own musicality; his collections operate as intricately structured song cycles with fragments of rhythm and rhyme that resound between poems and even between volumes. As Muldoon (2006a, 384) has written, "aurality [is] at the heart of . . . poetry," and verses' acoustic spaces consistently lend themselves to his capacious cross-culturalities and his efforts to "bring diversity into a harmonizing net of sound" (Kennedy-Andrews 2005a, 125). In his review of Muldoon's (2006c) *Horse Latitudes*, critic Brian Lynch compares Muldoon's "nifty rhym[ing]" and his poetic "rattle and hum" to the show-tune stylings of Irving Berlin (Lynch, "Paul Muldoon: Rattle and Hum of a Great Poet," *The Independent*, January 6, 2007). Lynch suggests that in Muldoon's hands, the lyric always verges on lyrics.

This bardic sense of poems' proximity to music was probably nurtured by a few of Muldoon's most influential teachers. Seán O'Boyle, who taught Muldoon Irish language and literature as a boy, sang unaccompanied *sean-nós*, and he "presumably often sang a few bars [in class] to demonstrate a point about poetic rhythm and metre or to illustrate, as he does in his book *The Irish Song Tradition* (1976), how a slowed down reel corresponds to '*an rannaíocht mhór*' or how another bardic metre, *séadna*, can be speeded up to a jig" (O'Connor 2011, 139). Muldoon has suggested that

Unless otherwise indicated, the versions of the poems referenced in this chapter are drawn from Muldoon's (2001) *Poems, 1968–1998*.

his own work is shaped by "the ancient Gaelic tradition that made little or no distinction between poetry and song," and he has claimed "the song as a genre that might be considered as part of the general poetry world" (quoted in Charles McGrath, "Word Freak," *New York Times Magazine*, November 19, 2006). He particularly prizes skilled songwriters' facility for marrying language with musicality and harnessing sound's semantic power. As his idol Bob Dylan once said, "[t]he . . . meaning is all in the sound of the words. The lyrics are your dance partner" (quoted in Johnston 2007). This is precisely why it is useful to read and to hear Muldoon's poems through the lens of his libretti: the poetry approximates opera, and these cross-genre reverberations reveal the internal logic of the collections' acoustic contours. Muldoon suggests that his collaborations with Hagen have left him newly attuned to his literary soundscapes,[1] but the libretti also reflect on their poetic predecessors, amplifying their elaborate echoes and multiculturalizing multivocalities. Muldoon's operas provide the opportunity to re-read the poet's oeuvre with ears perked and to listen closely to his remarkably resonant lines.

Muldoon's volumes have always used sonic phenomena to add degrees of latent content to their manifest themes. Their carefully plotted rhyme schemes, for instance, aim at capturing Frost's "sound of sense" (*Boston Evening Transcript*, May 8, 1915). An opera's chimes can reveal subterranean sympathies between characters, and although these chimes ring aloud in performance or recording, they also resonate on the poem's page. Likewise, leitmotifs (same-word rhymes or long-distance lyrical echoes) circulate freely in Muldoon's work. Eavesdropping on his collections often means overhearing the uncanny whispers of poems past. Muldoon therefore borrows from opera's acoustic playbook by asking repeated sounds to operate as poetic "presentiments and reminiscences" (R. Parker 2001, 219). This strategy charges present contexts with the affective force of things gone by, and it often complicates seemingly simple sentiments. A leitmotif

1. In conversation with Lynn Keller, Muldoon (1994b, 9) explains, "The poems I've been writing since [*Shining Brow*] have been influenced in a strange way; I still haven't quite broken free of the mold of it. . . . [I've been using] repetition in [new] way[s]."

that once rang ominously retains its emotional valence even when repeated at apparently innocuous moments. Muldoon's poetic polyphony—his subtle shifts from mouth to mouth—allows far-flung voices to sing *ensemble*, undermining the authority of the lyric "I" and enabling characters to forge choral connections as if part of an opera's score.

As such tactics suggest, Muldoon's operatic investments in "cultural corridors" (Longley 1994, 195) and in-between spaces carry over into his poetry, accounting for critical takes on his collections as shape-shifting or slippery. This slipperiness, however, is far from postmodern nonsense; rather than perversely "resisting intelligibility" (Helen Vendler, "Fanciness and Fatality," *New Republic*, November 9, 2006), Muldoon's work is pregnant with political possibility. As Muldoon has said, "I hope the mischief I make is of a rewarding kind, not that of a practical joker, and will outline the complexities of being here" (quoted in Kennedy-Andrews 2008, 96).

The poem "Cows," originally published in Muldoon's (1994a) collection *The Annals of Chile*, offers an introduction to such "meaningful mischief": its playful frontiersmanship relies centrally on its soundscape's scope. Muldoon prefaces "Cows" with a dedication to Dermot Seymour, a Belfast artist whose paintings routinely juxtapose livestock with religious and military iconography. Seymour explores "the anxiety, bewilderment and absurdity of the situation in Northern Ireland . . . with definite imagery but in an oblique and obscure way"—an approach to representation near and dear to Muldoon's own (*Culture Northern Ireland* 2006). On the heels of this preface, the poem begins, "Even as we speak," which throws us into its action *in medias res*. Our heroes (whoever they are) are immediately issued an aural alert: a "smoker's cough," heard but not seen, ominously stops them "dead in their tracks" (Muldoon 1994a, "Cows" lines 1–2). Although trouble's clearly afoot, we are told only that "a cattle-truck / all but sent [them] shuffling off this mortal coil" before the poem's plot is suspended in favor of an extended etymological riff (lines 4–5). Nevertheless, the *Hamlet* reference suggests that something's rotten in the state of the North, and if we have read Ciaran Carson, we might also find cattle-trucks suspect (commandeered as they often are in his poetry for paramilitary attacks). The half-rhyme that cheekily chimes "Gael" (line 7) with "coil" (line 5) similarly suggests something of this sectarian divide: are IRA men behind the wheel?

No sooner are we reminded of this divide, with Troubles-era violence spilling out into an otherwise pastoral scene, than Northern Ireland is opened up as a cultural frontier via the questioning of the conflict's rigid terms. For example, "Had Hawthorne been a Gael" (Muldoon 1994a, "Cows" line 7) is a clever piece of transnational role-play, especially when Hawthorne's final consonance is echoed by the subsequent stanza's Gaelic "boreen" (line 12). "Hawthorne" is not simply harnessed as a convenient rhyme-word; as Shane Alcobia-Murphy (1996, 84) argues, "Muldoon's intertextual references are neither arbitrary nor meaningless: they are, rather, carefully chosen to provide unforeseen analogies and comparisons." In this case, the intended connotation is likely Brook Farm, the failed Transcendentalist utopian community of which Hawthorne was a founding member. Utopian experiments have proved one of Muldoon's enduring fascinations, largely because their efforts at regulated uniformity tend in practice to breed contempt. "Madoc: A Mystery" (Muldoon 1990), for example, revolves around what might have happened had Samuel Taylor Coleridge and Robert Southey's envisioned Pantisocratic utopia been realized.[2] For Muldoon, Brook Farm, based largely on a shared theological-philosophical outlook and a romanticization of the rural idyll,[3] "recalls a Republican 'race-consciousness' rooted in place" (Corkery 1931, 212): the kind of belonging Muldoon's poetry consistently contests.

At this point in "Cows," Muldoon (1994a) begins to blur the line between Irish and English by letting loanwords ring, a move that reflects on Catholic/Protestant divides in light of the longstanding yoking of

2. In the late 1970s Coleridge and Southey devised the notion of Pantisocracy: a utopian community in which all would govern equally and all would labor for the collective good. However, the scheme fell apart a few years later when the two poets could not agree on an appropriate location for the colony and when financing the community proved all but impossible.

3. Brook Farm's members retired to the New England countryside—with "New England" itself proving ideologically freighted in this context—and tried unsuccessfully to live off the land.

language to identity politics in the North. The Irish language has been linked to nationalist resistance ever since the Elizabethan conquest's efforts to de-Gaelicize the Isles made English their official tongue. The ideological weight of this link intensified throughout the early twentieth century as Irish Revivalists responded to the dual pressures of Gaelic's gradual decline and the lingering persuasions of language-based models of European nationhood. The Revivalists began tirelessly promoting Irish Gaelic as a vehicle of cultural transmission; their efforts influenced the Free State's adoption of the Irish language as a potent symbol of national independence (O'Reilly 2001, 78–83).

In post-partition Northern Ireland, the relationship of language to identity politics became an increasingly polarizing issue, with "competing versions of the significance of Irish . . . [serving] as part of an ideological struggle to define Irish identity and to have this identity officially recognized" (O'Reilly 2001, 86; see also Tymoczko and Ireland 2003). Tensions intensified as the Troubles approached; the North's Unionist government tried to mute Irish-language instruction in the country's schools and banned Gaelic programming from BBC Radio Northern Ireland,[4] while Republican activists, particularly Sinn Féin, began to mobilize the language as a central pillar of their political platform. Even the peace accords of the 1990s couched questions of Irish Gaelic's place in the North in the language of "two traditions," casting Irish as the exclusive province of the Catholic community and largely excluding the possibility of Protestant interest in a shared heritage.

Muldoon was one of the few students in the pre-Troubles North who had access to Gaelic as an elective subject in school, and he even honed his conversational Irish by spending immersive summers throughout his teens in the Republic's Donegal *Gaeltacht* (a native Irish-speaking community). Muldoon's Irish-language teacher, Seán O'Boyle, situated Gaelic

4. Paul Muldoon (or Pól Ó Maoldúin) was the producer of the first Irish-language radio program broadcast on BBC Northern Ireland when the statute was overturned in 1981 (O'Connor 2011). Much of his work for the BBC was thereafter bilingual; his English translations of Gaelic poems allowed the station's readings to reveal unexpected cross-fertilizations between the two languages and traditions (O'Connor 2011, 135–36).

in the context of comparative linguistics and used song and poetry recitation to reveal Irish/English reciprocities. Because of O'Boyle's sensitivity, Muldoon was largely immunized against the linguistic segregationism of the period. Instead, the young poet came to understand Irish and English as diachronic, and he developed an interest in the languages' points of historical contact and their contemporary synchronicities (O'Connor 2011, 140, 152). Although written thirty years beyond O'Boyle's classroom, Muldoon's "Cows" features precisely this linguistic flexibility. "Boreen," a translingual borrowing used in the poem, is evidently "a diminutive form of the Gaelic *bóthar*, 'a road,' / from *bó*, 'a cow,' and *thar* / meaning, in this case, something like 'athwart'" (lines 13–15). This explanation suggests mutual influence and interplay between languages and cultures that are often kept distinct, and the poem speaks in this forked tongue via the translingual chime of "*thar*" and "athwart." Here we see one of Muldoon's signature strategies in action: given the poet's propensity for harnessing rhyme's associative force, this cross-cultural sounding realigns and redefines community, revealing reciprocal contamination between otherwise segregated groups.[5] As Tim Kendall (1996, 205) describes it, "[i]n Muldoon's poetry, similar-sounding words are an aid to analogic progression, as they are shown to possess some deeper, inscrutable relationship."

If language-based theories of nationhood demand monophony as a means of drawing borders—a demand that explains both Unionist antipathies and Nationalist attachments to Irish Gaelic[6]—then "Cows" pokes holes in this model and mocks the myths of purity on which it depends.

5. Physical segregation remains a major concern in Northern Ireland's cities; although cross-community interactions in the workplace have improved, the places where people live, go to school, shop, and socialize remain almost exclusively divided along communal lines (see Hughes et al. 2007).

6. Sometimes these attachments are more symbolic than functional; there are very few fluent Irish-language speakers in Northern Ireland today (in part because of the country's history of prohibition against Irish-language education, television, and radio programming). According to the 2011 census, only 10.65 percent of Northern Ireland's population has "some ability in Irish," and a mere 3.74 percent reports that they can "speak, read, write and understand Irish" (NISRA 2012, 18).

Although nation-states do begin and end at defined (if sometimes redefined) visual borders, and although the North's segregated British and Irish communities do similarly stratify the country's urban spaces along strictly defined geographical lines, sound often slips across borders that bodies cannot or will not cross. Muldoon's etymological excavations in "Cows" expose the ways in which words travel and suggest acoustic space as a breeding ground for unexpected, perhaps even unwelcome, cross-cultural affinities and affiliations. As if to make this point outright, Muldoon (1994a) writes in "Cows" that "'boreen' has entered English 'through the air'"—that is, by way of spoken word—"despite the protestations of the O.E.D. [Oxford English Dictionary]," an etymological guide limited by its deference to print culture's "authoritative" archive (lines 16–17).[7]

Muldoon's exploration of his poem's aural possibilities only intensifies as "Cows" continues. The poem's plot likewise thickens: the cattle-truck pulls over to broadcast some threateningly cryptic tail-light Morse, and our speaker and his companion hear, too close at hand for comfort, "[t]hat smoker's cough again: it triggers off from drumlin / to drumlin an emphysemantiphon / of cows" (Muldoon 1994a, "Cows" lines 22–24). Here is yet another loanword, this time left unremarked: "drumlins," from the Gaelic *druim* (back, ridge), are long, low hills that are the topographical remains of ancient glacial tilt. The fact that Muldoon circulates purloined terms without commenting on their etymological drift suggests the extent of the cross-community influence indicated by his borrowed "boreen"; furthermore, it implies that things thought to be pure, including the Queen's English, are often hybrid through and through.

As the stanza continues, the smoker's cough menacingly "triggers" a so-called "emphysemantiphon / of cows," a convoluted coinage that suspends the poem's temporal flow and demands an elaborate sounding out. Readers must assemble "emphysemantiphon," almost necessarily aloud,

7. Indeed, the Oxford English Dictionary (http://www.oed.com) can only trace "boreen" as far back as S. C. Hall's (1841) *Ireland: Its Scenery, Character, Etc.*, although the loanword had probably long been in colloquial circulation.

from its constituent phonemes: a strategy that draws attention to the poem's status as echo-chamber. This particular word seems to be the product of compulsive compounding. Its lexical building blocks include "emphysema," "semantic," and "antiphony," the latter being a call-and-response style of singing; in this case, the lowing cows are startled into echoing the rasps of the none-too-clandestine field agent. Whereas "emphysema" is a syntactical stand-in for said "smoker's cough," "semantiphon" is defined literally as "the meaning is in the singing": a maxim that could be applied to the poem itself.

The rhyme schemes in "Cows" are especially extravagant: in stanzas 8–10 alone, a system of nasal consonance links "drumlin" with "emphysemantiphon," "trampoline," "divine," "incline," "Devon," and "Japan." The poem semantically divides Irish cows from their Devon(shire) counterparts and from Japanese "metaphysicattle" (line 29):

> This is no Devon
> cow-coterie, by the way . . .
> . . . .
> these are earth-flesh, earth-blood, salt of the earth[.] (Muldoon 1994a, "Cows" lines 27–32)

These lines' antiphony betrays a fundamental connectivity: both "Devon" and "Japan" chime with the Irish-derived "drumlin." Furthermore, the way in which sound lends second-degree sense to this passage suggests a satirizing of Irish stereotype; "earth-flesh, earth-blood, salt of the earth" rings far too resoundingly of D. P. Moran's (2006, x) "primal Irishness," which is fundamentally rooted in rural civilization, to be taken at face value.[8] The poem's cows therefore reflect back on the conflict's climate.

8. This "meaning in singing" is perhaps Muldoon's (1998a, 125) answer to his own "question of that inevitable cattle-truck and its inevitable freight. . . . How does [the Irish writer] find an adequate reprise to the latest reprisal, a strophe equal to the latest catastrophe?" "Getting Round," the title of the essay from which this question is excerpted, reverses the declaration in "Cows" that "there's no getting round this cattle-truck," suggesting that Muldoon's modes of representation have found a way through political roadblocks, however partial and provisional that way might be.

They are at once themselves, fixtures of Muldoon's own childhood scenes, and vehicles whose tenor seems to be the dangers of political myth-making. Apropos of this point, "Cows" goes on to take the concept of "kith and kine" (in Old English, literally "friends and cattle"), the premise of local tribalism, to task (line 35). Although the poem's cows, apparently operating with the power of "blood-music" in mind, claim their roots in the Bethlehem herd "that presided over the birth / of Christ," the speaker instead suggests that they have long been "tramping" the rather more homely ground of local "cwms and corries"—Welsh and Scottish Gaelic synonyms, respectively, for the Irish "drumlin" (lines 36–40).

"Cows" also references Cuchulainn, a mythological figure often invoked as an icon of both Irish Nationalist and Ulster Unionist identity. Cuchulainn is framed either as the canonical Celtic hero (as in Yeats' plays or Oliver Sheppard's statue commemorating the 1916 Easter Rising) or as an Ulsterman ardently defending his province from southern enemies (as in several prominent Belfast murals). In "Cows" Muldoon (1994a) chimes his name with "Céline" and "Celan" (line 49), conjuring the specters of both fascism and suicide. The poem's soundscape therefore occasions bathetic call-and-answer encounters to subvert the conflict's most militantly held and stridently professed beliefs.

As "Cows" concludes, we are treated to a final ludic coinage: "oscaraboscarabinary." This word is near impossible to parse, even with the legend we are offered: "*Oscaraboscarabinary*: a twin, entwined, a tree, a Tuareg; / a double dung-beetle; [etc.]" (Muldoon 1994a, "Cows" lines 46–47). "Scarab" is synonymous with "dung beetle," and "Arab" is perhaps a suitable enough substitute for "Tuareg," whereas "oscaraboscara" suggests the name of Muldoon's family dog, Oscar MacOscair, who was already immortalized in "Oscar" (Muldoon 1994a). But what does all of this accomplish for the poem? Turning binaries into "twins, entwined" seems to be Muldoon's aim in "Cows," given his apparent desire to deconstruct the dualisms underpinning Northern Ireland's identity politics, but "oscaraboscarabinary" otherwise proves a red herring. The poem here marks the limits of its own agency: "However I might allegorize / some oscaraboscarabinary bevy / of cattle there's no getting round this cattle-truck" (lines 42–45). This line echoes the proclamation in "7, Middagh

Street" (Muldoon 1987b) that "history's a twisted root / with art its small, translucent fruit / and never the other way round" (lines 78–79).

In an interview with John Redmond (*Thumbscrew*, Spring 1996), Muldoon indicated that "One thing 'Cows' is saying is forget that world, forget about the meaning of 'oscaraboscarabinary.' It is saying that *is* completely by the way, that *is* irrelevant compared to the reality of standing on a road on a dark night and not knowing what is going to happen next." Muldoon's point proves particularly salient in light of the "plain / and simple hi-firing party" (Muldoon 1994a, "Cows" lines 48–49) likely crouched in the back of the cattle-truck. This cautionary note prompts the poem's frank, unadorned conclusion: "Now let us talk of slaughter and the slain / the helicopter gun-ship, the mighty Kalashnikov: / let's rest for a while in a place where a cow has lain" (lines 56–58). Such a check to Muldoon's acoustic enthusiasm resonates with the concluding flourish of *Vera of Las Vegas*, which suggests sound-space's possibilities and allows song to source cross-cultural community, but ultimately veers away from the utopian promise that sound might somehow contain conflict and reframes harmony as a temporary salve. Similarly, although "Cows" charts common ground between English and Irish, allowing their histories of intimacy to strain toward audibility, Muldoon must yet face the conflict's material conditions and he remains suspicious of grand claims to art's political agency: "[Poetry] has to have efficacy at some level. Now we're not talking about necessarily changing the world . . . [only something] as simple as the fact that *ideally* one should never be able to look at [the subject of the poem] again in exactly the same light" (Muldoon 1998b, 67).

Ultimately, Muldoon's "Cows" is of two minds. Although there is perhaps "no getting round this cattle-truck," and although the conflict's terms are still splashed across the canvases of the North's cities, the poet's consolatory "semantiphony"—his effort to "sound together" visually partitioned people and places and to blur ostensibly clear political and philosophical boundaries—makes for palliation if not reconciliation.

Meeting the British: Muldoon's Translocal Poetics

Beyond shedding new light, however modestly, on Catholic/Protestant divides, or perhaps simply muting their political static, Muldoon is more broadly concerned with ways to expand home's horizons. Nationalism and Unionism, Muldoon suggests, depend on such strident demands for sameness and such deeply felt ties to home turf that their terms are almost unbearably claustrophobic. Moreover, even the least politically partisan Ulster regionalists, like Seamus Heaney and John Hewitt before him, consider culture and identity to be (to some degree) immanent in place. Muldoon, ever suspicious of such essentialism, often makes the point that what seems most intimate can in fact be most jarringly foreign: what does a civilian make of a paramilitary Kalashnikov; how does the living really "talk of the slaughter and the slain"? His work therefore moves against this myopia, operating as an amplifier to increase belonging's potential bandwidth.

As previously suggested, Muldoon's poetic connections are characteristically translocal: his volumes try to reimagine solidarity via soundspace's potentially boundless scale and scope. In other words, poetry's "rhythmic and sonic coordinations of distances" (Ramazani 2009, 14) can enable extraterritorial travel and cross-cultural identification. One of Muldoon's most commonly cited political sonographies, a feature that his poetry shares with Rackett's tunes, is his affinity for associating Ireland with indigenous America. This long-distance community-building is juxtaposed against the twinned tyrannies of visuospatial proximity and cultural uniformity, and it is rooted instead, as Ramazani (2009, 141) suggests, in "the transnational affiliations that form the basis, sometimes paradoxically, for anticolonial poetic solidarities."

"The More a Man Has the More a Man Wants" (Muldoon 1983) centrally features this strategic trans-Atlanticism even while conceding its thorny political complexities. Here Muldoon's poetic process suggests his interest in shared structures of feeling; "The More a Man Has the More a Man Wants" superimposes Native America on Northern Ireland, loosely transposing Paul Radin's (1956) version of the Winnebago Trickster cycle to Muldoon's native Ulster.[9] Muldoon also redoubles his efforts at coalition

9. Radin, an anthropologist, spent many years doing fieldwork with the Winnebago in the early twentieth century, and he was one of the first Westerners to transcribe the tribe's version of the Trickster story. The Trickster is a mythical figure shared by many

building in this poem by covertly casting his two main characters as doppelgangers (perhaps flip sides of the slippery Trickster). The paramilitary Gallogly and the visiting Apache Mangas Jones are at thematic cross-purposes, with Jones trying to "trac[e] the family tree / of an Ulsterman who had some hand / in the massacre at Wounded Knee" (lines 227–28) while Gallogly perpetrates violence of his own. However, Muldoon gradually muddies the *formal* waters between the two, leaving their voices virtually interchangeable by the poem's end. "The More a Man Has the More a Man Wants" is therefore one of Muldoon's signature "opera poems": it crosses oceans, enabling community that far exceeds what the eye can see, and instead demands sound's deterritorializing energies. The poem's acoustics—its multilingual chimes, its repeated refrains ricocheting from stanza to stanza, and its almost choral ventriloquisms—are opposed to the stultifying, short-sighted approach to home characterized by the "For God and Ulster" shibboleths scrawled across the city's walls.[10]

At the outset of "The More a Man Has the More a Man Wants," Muldoon (1983) introduces Gallogly and Jones in turn, keeping their tales at arm's length. The poem's opening stanzas set two distinct scenes: Gallogly is in Belfast, as both the nearby River Farset and the characteristic black taxis suggest, and the vernacular "skedaddled" is thrown in for local lexical flavor. Mangas Jones, on the other hand, has freshly arrived at Aldergrove (now more commonly called Belfast International Airport), which is approximately eleven miles outside of the city. Although his visit's motivations are still under wraps, his name does conjure the specter of his own past conflict: Mangas Coloradas was an infamous Apache chief who defended his tribe against Mexican bounty hunters around the Rio Grande and would-be American occupiers of the tribe's northern territories (now

First Nations peoples; she or he can typically shape-shift, taking on different animal forms at will, and is generally associated with humor, impulsiveness, energy, and appetite.

10. "For God and Ulster" is the rallying cry of the Ulster Volunteer Force (UVF), one of Northern Ireland's most notorious Loyalist paramilitaries (decommissioned in 2009). In the context of the poem, though, it might also be attributable to a passing Ulster Defense Regiment (UDR) patrol, suggesting the widely reported collusion of the British Army with Loyalist paramilitaries during the Troubles.

southwestern New Mexico). Coloradas' nickname, "Red Sleeves," supplies the first tacit clue that the poem will chart cross-cultural proximities; it suggestively evokes the "Red Hand of Ulster," a symbol mobilized by combatants on both sides of Northern Ireland's divide.

Jones' introduction, however, sets up resonances to come; Muldoon begins plotting subterranean acoustic connections that will soon murmur toward audibility. Although both Jones and Gallogly pledge tribal allegiances and consider their political grievances to be singular states of exception—as Muldoon says of Gallogly with satirical bite, "[s]uch is the integrity / of [his] quarrel" (Muldoon 1983, "The More a Man Has the More a Man Wants" lines 177–78)—the poem's broader sound-sense or semantiphony chimes its own common ground. Muldoon's passing mention of "Hertz" (line 28) cues this interpretive approach; although the word refers diegetically to the car rental company, its metadiegetic function as a unit of audio frequency (Hz) signals the worth of bearing careful earwitness to the poem. Jones' stanza, for instance, mines multilingualism for rhyme and brings distant tongues together: "Apache" rings with "attaché," and "Mescalero" with "arroyo" (lines 15–28). "Arroyo" means "brook" in Spanish, indicating the confluence of cultures at Coloradas' colonial frontier, but as an English loanword it designates a wash or dry ditch. Already a hovering synonym, "ditch" is anchored by its echo in the following page's "sniffer . . . bitch," the Constabulary's "Labrador" (line 77) that is hot on Gallogly's heels and is itself a phonetic answer to the call of the airport's "corridor" (line 27). The so called "swoop" (line 80) on the suspect's safe house in turn shares a distinctive /u:/ with a nearby line that misidentifies Jones as an "Oglala Sioux" (lines 235–36). "Oglala" also operates as a near-homophone of the poem's sighs of "O Gallogly" (line 617). Bringing the passage full circle, "Sioux" is finally paired with "sheugh," Irish for "ditch": the trench where we find a fleeing Gallogly concealed (line 267). Although this hideout seems a far cry from Aldergrove's halls, an intricate acoustic chain tethers one ditch to the next; Jones and Gallogly, whether they know it or not, are intimately in tune. As Sean O'Brien (1998, 176) explains, "rhyme is the spinal column of Muldoon's work, linking the noises in the poems' heads to their rhythmic fleetness and swerving passage." In this case, the poem's carefully orchestrated chimes force plotlines to cross and accentuate potentially common postures. Muldoon's subterranean community-in-sympathy therefore counters his characters' tribal exclusivisms, destabilizing the sense of singularity used by "victims" to legitimize retaliatory violence.

In the next passage of "The More a Man Has the More a Man Wants," Muldoon (1983) immediately begins to deconstruct the word "sheugh," undermining its function as a Nationalist shibboleth: "*Sheugh*, [Gallogly] says. *Sheugh.* / He is finding that first 'sh' / increasingly difficult to manage" (lines 272–74). Besides charting the betrayals of a native tongue, with Gallogly losing his grasp of a password required for admission to the ranks of kith and kin, these lines also offer Muldoon's parodic response to Seamus Heaney's (1972) poem "Broagh." Heaney suggests that vocal inflections that are shared by islanders but are unwieldy to "strangers," represented in "Broagh" by the titular word's "black *O*" and "last / *gh*," indicate cross-community commonalities and therefore potential steps beyond the conflict.[11] For Muldoon, however, Heaney's terms remain excessively hermetic; they excuse what Muldoon ("The Key" 197) derisively calls "defending that same old patch of turf." Muldoon instead deftly moves from Belfast slang ("glipes," "craythur"), to Dante's ([1317] 2002) *Inferno* ("*lo perfido assassin*"), to the brusque language of the conflict's violent bric-a-brac ("Armalites," "gelignite"), to colonial loanwords ("Algonquin," "Chesapeake," "Winnebago"), and finally to passages of untranslated Irish ("*Beannacht Dé ar an obair*"). These multilingual reverberations consciously resonate against myopic reverence for "the territory."

The poem continues by narrating Gallogly's devastatingly destructive countryside caper: he steals a car, tars and feathers a young woman,[12]

11. I am indebted to Neil Corcoran (1993, 206) for suggesting this connection in his chapter, "In Ireland or Someplace," from *English Poetry Since 1940*. Corcoran argues that "'The More a Man Has' writes back to Heaney's 'Broagh,' where spoken language is an index of potential Catholic/Protestant community—here the final 'gh' of 'sheugh' seems easy, while the initial 'sh' comes across as stage-Irish, the sign not of community but of stereotype."

12. Tarring and feathering was a signature act of the Provos (Provisional IRA) in the early years of the Troubles. It was considered retaliatory justice for young Catholic women who were in relationships with members of the largely Protestant Royal Ulster

booby-traps a local councilor's car with a mercury-tilt bomb that leaves its victim in "smithereens" (Muldoon 1983, "The More a Man Has the More a Man Wants" line 387), and shoots a UDR corporal, all ostensibly in the name of a united Ireland. He then takes a drug (perhaps mescaline, in keeping with Mangas Jones the "Mescalero") that induces an elaborate hallucination, imagining himself in America as a mercenary messenger in search of illegal arms. During the course of his "trip," he consorts with a woman named Alice, whom he kills after a tip-off that she's a "telltale" (line 448). Down Gallogly's drug-induced rabbit-hole, Alice, who is in death seemingly interchangeable with Beatrice (the woman who was tarred and feathered, her "lovely head . . . chopped / and changed" [line 112]), rises as an apparition and begins to sing:

> *Was she Aurora, or the goddess Flora,*
> *Artemidora, or Venus bright,*
> *or Helen fair beyond compare*
> *that Priam stole from the Grecian sight?*
> *Quite modestly she answered me*
> *and she gave her head one fetch up*
> *and she said I am gathering musheroons*
> *to make my mammy ketchup.* (lines 491–98)

At first glance, this song reads like an aisling: the specter of Mother Ireland appears to the sleeping speaker in the guise of a young woman, at once beatific and rooted in local landscape, who arrives to predict the revival of Irish fortunes. The aisling was a medieval genre tailored to political purpose by eighteenth-century Irish Jacobites. These poet-patriots mobilized the genre's energies to foretell the "rightful" restoration of the House of Stuart to its rule over the Gaelic world. An aisling often involves the speaker awaking to a beautiful woman and believing her, as we see here, to be a Greek goddess or a storybook heroine before she is revealed

Constabulary or British security forces. See also Seamus Heaney's (1975) "Punishment," which is controversial for its speaker's concession that he is both "outrage[d]" (line 42) by and somehow accepting of this "tribal, intimate revenge" (line 44).

as the embodiment of Erin.[13] Muldoon's first four lines are in fact lifted wholesale from an anonymous 1790s aisling called "The Colleen Rue" (a transliteration of *cailin ruadh*, a red-haired girl), which was set to music in the nineteenth century and is now a popular tune of traditional musicians. The interpretation of Muldoon's stanza as a prophetic dream-vision is additionally encouraged by the invocation of Beatrice, Dante's spiritual guide, who, like Erin, matches erotic appeal with maternal comfort.

However, this reading of "The More a Man Has the More a Man Wants," which risks legitimizing Gallogly's Republican cause by romanticizing the motherland, is called into question by the broader aural resonances in *Quoof* (Muldoon 1983), the collection in which this poem appears. Muldoon's volumes are assembled operatically, with structuring leitmotifs—in this case, literally snippets of song—recurring and reciprocally re-inflecting one another. Leitmotifs shape and semanticize scores, and they serve *Quoof* in a similar way: Muldoon's tunes carry his poetry's freight by recalling their previous soundings and gradually accumulating symbolic weight. In this case, Alice/Beatrice/Erin, whom we might call Muldoon's chorus, sings back to "Aisling," the poem immediately preceding "The More a Man Has" in the collection. "Aisling" explicitly satirizes "the sexist myth of the nationalist siren" (Hufstader 1999, 161). The poem purloins from "The Colleen Rue" the lines "Was she Aurora, or the goddess Flora, / Artemidora, or Venus bright?" and adds "or Anorexia, who left / a lemon stain on my flannel sheet?" as their brusque postscript (Muldoon 1983, "Aisling" lines 8–9). By casting Erin as "Anorexia," an ignoble hunger-striker and a sexual conquest circulating not cause for self-sacrifice but sexually transmitted diseases, Muldoon completely deflates, even defames, the myth of Mother Ireland. "The More a Man Has," in echoing the same traditional air, also takes on this bathetic valence, suggesting that there is more to the poem than meets the eye.

Similarly, the latter four lines of Alice/Beatrice/Erin's song recall "Gathering Mushrooms," the opening gambit of *Quoof* (Muldoon 1983).

13. Erin is a Hiberno-English derivative of Éirinn, the dative case of Éire, which is the name given to Ireland in local folklore by the poet Amergin after the matron-goddess Ériu.

"Gathering Mushrooms" lifts the lines "*And she stooped so low gave me to know / it was mushrooms she was gathering O*" from a song of the same name, which was first recorded by County Armagh traditional singer Robert Cinnamond in the 1950s and was more recently popularized by the Celtic folk group Clannad. The song's lyrics approximate an aisling's sentiments: the speaker spies a "fair maid" gathering mushrooms—a beautiful young woman in a typically rural pose. She is both chaste, answering his queries "modestly," and powerfully erotic, "pressing" her "parting breast" on the speaker's own as the song comes to a close. In Muldoon's (1983, "Gathering Mushrooms") work, however, the maid's mushrooms are pharmacological rather than pastoral; as the poem's speaker confesses, "We were thinking only of psilocybin" (line 25). Rather than stirring the speaker's "blood-music," Erin more crudely "blow[s his] mind" (line 46). Once again, Muldoon's operatic recursiveness in "The More a Man Has" enables a kind of interpretive counterpoint. In the wake of "Gathering Mushrooms," the poem's genuflections to the motherland seem more the stuff of spoof than sympathy. Muldoon's airs are his volume's anchoring arias: they resonate where they are first sounded and are later associatively recollected. In the case of "The More a Man Has," the repeated leitmotifs allow Muldoon to satirize the Republican voice—a voice that might otherwise worryingly cast Gallogly's violence as warranted sacrifice.[14]

Eventually roused from his hallucinatory dream-vision by the "dunt and dunder / of a culvert-bomb" (Muldoon 1983, "The More a Man Has the More a Man Wants" lines 499–500), Gallogly awakes surrounded by "a snatch-squad of Paratroopers" (line 512). Finally cornered and cowed,

14. This was precisely the criticism leveled at W. B. Yeats' ([1937] 1991) play *Cathleen Ní Houlihan*: in suggesting that Mother Ireland's youth and beauty could only be renewed by a young man's blood sacrifice, Yeats appeared to justify, even to encourage, martyrdom for the Republican cause. Although deconstructing Yeats' sentiments seems a crucial part of Muldoon's program here, Muldoon's (1987b) "7, Middagh Street" tempers this stance by prescribing skepticism in the face of art's supposed political power. Muldoon asks in "7, Middagh Street," "If Yeats had saved his pencil-lead / would certain men have stayed in bed?" (lines 76–77). He then responds with a convincing, full-chiming "Certainly not" (line 75).

> Gallogly, or Gollogly,
> otherwise known as Golightly,
> otherwise known as Ingoldsby,
> otherwise known as English,
> gives forth one low cry of anguish
> and agrees to come quietly. (lines 513–18)

Gallogly's list of aliases enables a kind of improvisatory riff, with each of his name's permutations shifting by a single syllable or speech-sound until the poem arrives at the provocative "English." His four short degrees of separation from his sworn enemies undermine his "obsession with tribal purity . . . confirming the cultural mongrelism even of those most fanatically assertive of their antediluvian origins" (Kendall 1996, 111). As Adam Newey ("Connections at the Keyboard," *The Guardian*, May 15, 2009) has argued, repetition in Muldoon's poetry operates as does "a jazz pianist's modulation of key, in which a central motif is heard from different tonal angles," and in this case, his sliding key signatures reveal surprising proximities.

If "Gallogly" is one of the poem's keynote sounds, as indeed it seems to be (it is repeated fifteen times in twenty-one pages), it is *further* modulated in the poem's penultimate stanza with the word "gallowglass" (line 760). Gallowglass, an anglicization of the Gaelic *gallóglaigh*, meaning "foreign soldier," was a medieval Irish term used to refer to a mercenary warrior caste of Gaelic-Norse Scots, many of whom migrated to Ireland to support the internecine warfare of local chieftains and later helped to combat British occupation. Gallogly's very name, then, suggests that home is the stuff of imports and hybrids, undercutting his fidelity to "race-consciousness" and his claim of being "Celtic at the core." Moreover, under what critic Andrew Osborn (2000) calls Muldoon's system of "fuzzy rhyme," a pattern of line-final chiming based on proximately articulated consonantal pairs, "gallowglass" distance-rhymes with "English"; the phonemes /s/ and /ʃ/ are one of Muldoon's signature couplings. Osborn (2000) argues that "fuzzy rhyme" serves as an acoustic invitation to "unprecedented associations" (341); its "sound and shape . . . attest to a permeability of physical and national borders: physical insofar as fuzzy rhyme discounts syllabic boundaries, walls of sound created by friction between air and the mouth; national insofar as their simulation of etymology recalls the fact that cognates pass freely through customs and other concepts smuggle themselves across into familiar territory through folk etymology" (355).[15]

When listening to "The More a Man Has," hearing "English" and "gallowglass" as a rhyming pair makes audible a second set of associations. Although the Gaelic-Norse *gallóglaigh* once fought the British on the side of the Irish Catholics, they were later classed with the Scottish Presbyterians settled under the Plantation of Ulster as Ulster-Scots. Ulster-Scots as an ethnocultural category has been fervently mobilized in the North in support of political Unionism. Therefore, the *gallóglaigh* in the poem skirt the border between Republicanism and Loyalism: a particularly stark example of passing through territory both foreign and familiar. Not only, then, is home fundamentally hybrid, but its carefully constructed ethnopolitical divides are perhaps more slippery than their most zealous defenders might like to think.

As "The More a Man Has the More a Man Wants" concludes, it moves beyond post-partisanship to sound out broader translocal connections. Here Muldoon most explicitly charts the potential (if complex) sympathies between Northern Ireland and indigenous America: a move foreshadowed by the poem's offhand reference to Gallogly as a "hot-foot from a woodcut / by Derricke" (Muldoon 1983, "The More a Man Has the More

15. Although the first of Osborn's two points is relatively straightforward, the second is usefully elaborated by another passage in his essay. Taking the example of Muldoon's "The Right Arm," in which Muldoon states that he would give that eponymous limb "to have known" (line 9) how his childhood hometown of "Eglish was itself wedged between / ecclesia and église" (lines 10–11), Osborn (2000, 337–38) argues that the poem's "punful rhymes not only substitute for etymology; they simulate it." The principle of "fuzzy rhyme," "which identifies the proximate consonantal sequences in Eglish, ecclesia, and église as equivalent, each word featuring a velar stop (/g/ or /k/), the liquid /ı/, and an alveolar or palatal fricative (/s/, /z/, or /s/)[,] bears an uncanny resemblance to the unconscious principles behind etymological and folk etymological shifts. . . . Muldoon treats as equivalent many of the consonants which linguistic sound rules show to have been systematically substituted over time and across national boundaries" (337–38).

a Man Wants" lines 761–62). "Hot-foot" suggests the stereotype of Native Americans as "overwhelmingly physical creatures" (Churchill et al. 1979, 23): rough, rude, and morally wanting. Cartoonist A. P. Adams' popular "Hurry Up Hot-Foot" panels in the *Cincinnati Enquirer* channeled this sentiment as late as the turn of the twentieth century; his serialized strips depicted a caricature of a "Plains Indian" winning assorted athletic events by variously assaulting or cheating his competitors. Muldoon conjoins this image with John Derricke's *The Image of Irelande*, a poem and accompanying illustrative woodcuts that were first published in 1581 and recirculated by Sir Walter Scott in 1809. Under the patronage of Philip Sidney, the son of Elizabeth I's Lord Deputy of Ireland, Derricke mounted an elaborate defense of imperial intervention by casting the Irish as "wantone" and "wilde" and claiming that their warrior woodkern were "barbarous" and underhanded in combat.[16] This juxtaposition suggests Gallogly and Jones' proximate histories and highlights both their common subjection and their resistance to the incursions of "civilizing" missions.

Muldoon's final stanza strategically ventriloquizes this proximity when it projects Jones' voice from Gallogly's body. The poem's plot introduces this convergence by having Gallogly escape from prison only to find himself at the scene of another crime as a witness to the robbery of a nearby gas station. The young thugs leave a black plastic bucket as a suspicious "memento" (Muldoon 1983, "The More a Man Has the More a Man Wants" line 766) before pulling away, at which the incoming Gallogly aims an absentminded kick. Unaware that the bucket is a makeshift explosive, "packed with fertilizer / and a heady brew / of sugar and Paraquat," this is the last move Gallogly will ever make, and the poem draws to a grisly close with the station's pump attendant picking up his scattered pieces (lines 768–70). As the attendant whispers an act of contrition into Gallogly's "frazzled ear," he "overhear[s] / those already-famous last

16. Images of Derricke's plates are archived online by the Edinburgh University Library and can be viewed at http://www.lib.ed.ac.uk/about/bgallery/Gallery/researchcoll/ireland.html. The term "woodkern" was used to describe native Irish soldiers who fought in the forests of Ireland; the word "kern" is an anglicization of the Irish word *ceithern*, meaning a group of fighting men.

words / *Moose . . . Indian*" (lines 776–80). With his final breath, Gallogly mouths Mangas Jones' last words, which were already famous for having been Thoreau's notoriously cryptic final gambit (see Harding 1970, 464–65). Thoreau revered "natural man"—his respect for the aboriginal verged on noble savagism—and whether Muldoon's recapitulation is homage or satire, it most certainly falls under Jones' rather than Gallogly's narrow purview.

Although critics have called this scene the poem's final "metamorphosis" (Brown 1995, 153) and a moment of climactic "shapeshifting" (Wills 1998, 107), it seems less a sequential shift than a simultaneity or a two becoming one. Jones speaks through Gallogly, making audible the set of (post-)colonial intimacies to which the poem has tacitly alluded throughout. Although its characters' avid allegiances to the tribe never waver, the poem's carefully orchestrated aural encounters chime their way toward newly imagined communities—communities not in blood-sanctioned identity but in common cause. Muldoon's sound effects again lend his story second-degree sense; their acoustic contours accommodate long-distance border-crossings and coalition-buildings against Gallogly's short-sighted "squat[ting] in his own pelt" (Muldoon 1983, "The More a Man Has the More a Man Wants" line 8).

The final convergence of "The More a Man Has" is characteristic of Muldoon; his poem "Yarrow" (Muldoon 1994a) cleverly christened this effort to connect Ireland and indigenous America "Gaelakota" (line 380). Muldoon (1983) "drops" both the ardent Republican and the avenging Indian from "the mast[s their] colours are nailed to" ("The More a Man Has the More a Man Wants" line 142), suggesting a model for political resistance beyond retaliatory violence: strategic sympathies based, as the title of Muldoon's 1987 collection suggests, on a mutual *Meeting the British*.

Muldoon's Leitmotifs

Paul Muldoon's poetry lurks at the limits of music, and in recent years it has breached these limits. His poems have become song lyrics and opera libretti that lend his experimental soundings fully embodied voice, and his musical ventures have in turn re-inflected his poetic soundscapes. This give and take between poetry and opera suggests that sound is a register particularly appropriate to Muldoon's signature themes: he resists the short-sighted identity politics that underpin Northern Ireland's "Troubling" sectarianism and instead tries to reimagine community in auditory space's boundless sphere. As Adrienne Janus (2007, 181–82) argues in her essay, "In One Ear and Out the Others," Muldoon follows Beckett in adopting and adapting "the iconic acoustic image of a poetics that extends the possibilities of language beyond the limits of national identity." Muldoon's poetic sound-play is therefore far from a "Joycean game of baffle-the-reader" (Helen Vendler, "Anglo-Celtic Attitudes," *New York Review of Books*, November 6, 1997); it is rather a considered effort to increase belonging's bandwidth.

Muldoon's poem "The Key" cues this analytical approach. Set in a Foley artist's dubbing suite (a place where sound effects for films are concocted) the poem explicitly highlights the value of acoustic design. "The Key" opens with Foley at work on a new film project: he is editing a sound-sequence of a victim confronting a suspect line-up, and the poem's speaker is looking on and listening in. The scene's victim-perpetrator face-off triggers the speaker's memory of a so-called "'identity parade' in which [he] once took part," a phrase that minds the gap between American and British English ("identity parade" is the British equivalent of the colloquial American "police line-up") and conjures the sectarian spectacle of Northern Ireland's parade season. Muldoon is clearly keen to exorcize the specter of this tribalism, and although the poem's speaker is initially inclined to share his memory, he is soon distracted by Foley "emerg[ing] from his sound booth like a diver from a bathysphere" to offer "a tidbit that taste[s] . . . of mesquite." This sensory reorientation pushes the speaker's recollections aside; newly focused on flavor, he instead finds himself "savoring the play between 'booth' and 'bathy-,' 'quits' and 'mesquite,'" allowing alliterative sounds and pararhymes to trip lightly off his tongue (197). The poem therefore suggests that there is a palpable pleasure in language's musicality; in other words, rhythm and rhyme feel good in one's mouth. This sentiment resolves itself in a playful limerick:

When he sookied a calf down a boreen
it was through Indo-European.

When he clicked at a donkey carting dung
your grandfather had an African tongue. (197)

While suggesting that sound satisfies, this bouncing quatrain plays with loan-words and even loan-sounds to make the point that spoken word travels. "Sookie" is a Scottish cow-call, and "boreen," recalling the poem "Cows," is an Irish term for a narrow rural road that "entered English 'through the air' / despite the protestations of the O.E.D." (Muldoon 1994a, "Cows," lines 16–17). Muldoon deploys multiple versions of English at the same time here, undermining claims to the language's purity, and he also illuminates surprising proximities between English and Irish.

Muldoon's efforts to muddy these waters are doubly revealing. First, because sound can slip across borders that bodies cannot, it navigates mutual exchange, even intimacy, between the North's Catholic and Protestant communities. Second, sound enables *reciprocal* influence in colonial contact zones, and colonized tongues disrupt the supposedly one-way flow of power's authority (see Bhabha 1994 and Stoler 2002). Both of these points expose cross-contaminations between otherwise segregated groups: contaminations that complicate the North's strictly policed identity politics. The stanza's latter couplet further expands these horizons: "[w]hen he clicked at a donkey carting dung," Muldoon ("The Key" 197) trippingly intones, "your grandfather had an African tongue." These lines provide, as Michael Allen (2004, 63) observes, an "international slant" to the poem; they open Ireland to the world beyond and suggest the soundscape's potentially global scope. If the various flows of transatlantic populations, like that which carried the poem's speaker from the Moy to Los Angeles, are irrevocably "deterritorializing" culture and leaving us in need of new forms of belonging (Papastergiadis 2000, 117), then Muldoon proposes sound-space as a register of reimagined community. Shared geography gives way to what might be termed "sonography" as a source of connection in Muldoon's work; his poems, lyrics, and libretti all chime their way toward wide-ranging "meetings of worlds."

8

CODA

"The New North"

Sound-space as Shared Space

As I have suggested in the preceding chapters, Northern Ireland—and Belfast in particular—is a place acutely attuned to its own soundscape. In fact, Belfast has become a nucleus of the emerging field of sound studies, and the pioneering work at the Sonic Arts Research Centre (SARC; opened in 2004) at Queen's University Belfast (QUB) has prompted the city toward an increased acoustic awareness. For example, SARC's Belfast Sound Map, a website to which the public can upload local sound recordings to flesh out a sense of the city's characteristic soundscape, encourages "communal reflection upon sound experiences in the city."[1] The Sound Map, which is constantly evolving and expanding, now hosts hundreds of discrete recordings, including audio clips from cross-community spaces like the city center and the areas surrounding the university as well as single-community spaces like Sandy Row and west Belfast's Bog Meadows. Similarly, "Sounds of the City," a sound installation commissioned by the Metropolitan Arts Centre (MAC) and first exhibited in 2012, is based on a series of workshops conducted by artists from SARC with single-identity community groups in north and east Belfast. During the workshops, both groups were asked to reflect on "the relationship between sound and memory, sound and place" as it bears out in their everyday lives

1. For details of the Belfast Sound Map project, see http://www.belfastsoundmap.org and http://143.117.78.104/soundsofthecity/?page_id=1144.

and to document the details of their "personal auditory experience" of the city.[2] The installation hosts these reflections side by side, asking listeners to consider both the specifics of the city's various acoustic niches and the elements that are shared across these niches. SARC also developed the Belfast Soundwalk smartphone app, piloted in August 2013, in collaboration with the Belfast City Council and piloted it in August 2013. The app's goal is to "sonically enhance the experience of a number of areas of the city, including destinations that may not traditionally be accessed by visitors and/or [are] disregarded or undervalued by local residents."[3] It uses an inbuilt GPS system to track the listener's location in the city and plays corresponding sound materials as he or she reaches various waypoints. The app prompts users to move physically through these "disregarded or undervalued" spaces to access its prerecorded sounds, and it occasionally urges walkers to transgress community bounds in service of immersing themselves in their city's soundscape.[4]

Although SARC's ambient sound recordings do indicate that some sound-signals are unique to rival communities on opposite sides of Belfast's "Peace Walls," they also reveal that many sonic phenomena cross the city's visual barriers to provide common perceptual experiences. In other words, sound-space in the city is often shared space: a crucial concept for reconciliation efforts in Northern Ireland.[5] Projects that bear earwitness

2. See the Sounds of the City project description at http://www.socasites.qub.ac.uk/soundsofthecity/.

3. The Belfast Soundwalk smartphone app can be downloaded, and its various walks previewed, at http://143.117.78.44/~belfastsoundwalks/.

4. SARC's scope of work continues to grow; a new project called Recomposing the City, piloted by the QUB Institute for Collaborative Research in the Humanities, asks how "sound artists and architects working in collaboration [can] generate new ways of analysing, understanding, and transforming urban spaces" (see http://www.recomposingthecity.org/about). The importance of sound-space in apprehending and understanding place is being more and more widely promoted throughout Belfast.

5. The Belfast and Derry/Londonderry City Councils, the Northern Ireland Community Relations Council, and the European Union Programme for Peace and Reconciliation in Northern Ireland, among other bodies, centrally promote shared space initiatives to foster positive contact and dialogue between deeply divided communities.

to sound as a source of common ground can potentially promote cross-community ties to place and can foster a broadly shared Belfast identity as a means of moving beyond the city's pathologically divisive political and religious allegiances. For example, the "A Place Like This" soundwalk,[6] developed by Fionnula Fagan and Paul Stapleton for SARC's smartphone app, explores both sides of the Cupar Way wall, and it requires pedestrians to pass through the security gate on Northumberland Street that divides the Shankill from the Falls. (This is only the most provocative of the walks' many transgressive moves; other recordings shift between largely segregated spaces near Ormeau Park and the Lagan Towpath.) While highlighting characteristic acoustic cues on opposite sides of the wall, the soundwalk also encourages attention to sounds shared *across* the wall—sounds unrestricted by even the most imposing of visual obstacles. The app's success in promoting cross-community movement and exchange is difficult to gauge as of yet, but the rich acoustic experiences it offers give the Belfast auditor reason to be hopeful.

Although these ventures do not explicitly aspire to peacebuilding, the ways in which they invite collective reflection on acoustic space and democratize access to this space clearly promote a shared sense of place. Belfast Sound Map users, for instance, can move virtually through "foreign" territory, and several of the mobile soundwalks prompt users to physically cross community divides in pursuit of auditory experience. I suggest that many contemporary young Belfast poets tap into the same sentiment; their work bears careful earwitness to the city, and it more often figures sound as a register of possible reconciliation than as a harbinger of destruction to come.

In his 2008 poetry anthology, Chris Agee defines this generation of writers in "the new North" as a group whose publishing careers "straddle . . . the last years of the Troubles and the first [following the 1998 Belfast Agreement]" (xxxii). According to Agee, these writers inherit much from the previous two publishing generations—groups that include, in his

6. This walk is available at http://143.117.78.104/belfastsoundwalks/?portfolio=fionnuala-fagan-paul-stapleton.

estimation, Carson, Mahon, and Muldoon, along with Heaney, Longley, and McGuckian—but they also reflect "a North of old and new immigration, diaspora, bilingualism, and cultural interchange between the islands, all under the aegis of a new political dispensation that is rapidly weakening the old certainties enforced by the Troubles, towards a destination as yet undetermined" (xxxiii). Having come of age as writers under this "new dispensation," it is perhaps unsurprising that many contemporary Belfast poets participate in the reimagining of sound-space as shared space; they are forging a potential path toward this invisible (but already faintly audible) "destination."

In this chapter I focus on the work of Gearóid Mac Lochlainn, Leontia Flynn, and Alan Gillis, all of whom were born in Belfast and have been substantially involved with QUB at one time or another. Although it is difficult to gauge the extent of their investment in SARC's projects, their poetry is steeped in the surrounding soundscape and therefore echoes the center's efforts. However, their collections are far from prescriptive about poetry's role in local peacebuilding: as Gillis described in an interview with *The Edinburgh Review*,[7] such self-consciousness about "belonging" and "identity" is "curdling." Instead, Gillis claims to investigate the "ecosystem of the city" and to "earn your ear and create an examination of something like home." Lending their own ears to Belfast's keynote sounds, Mac Lochlainn, Flynn, and Gillis imagine their way toward more comfortable—and perhaps more conciliatory—paths to belonging in a notoriously uncomfortable place.

Stream of Tongues

Gearóid Mac Lochlainn was born and raised in west Belfast, first near the Falls Road and later in Twinbrook estate, home of Bobby Sands, who was twelve years Mac Lochlainn's senior. He grew up in the heartland of the Troubles—a space that was constantly under siege—and he has always considered himself a staunch Republican (Mac Lochlainn 2003). Nevertheless, rather than becoming involved in the violence that surrounded

7. See http://edinburgh-review.com/extracts/alan-gillis/.

him as a young man, Mac Lochlainn became fascinated by the political possibilities of poetry and song and their long histories of anti-colonial resistance. Immersed in the cultural traditions of the Belfast *Gaeilgeoir* (Irish for "Irish speakers" or "Irish language enthusiasts"), especially *sean-nós* singing, Mac Lochlainn chose to begin learning Irish at age eleven, hoping to connect himself to the "aural spell" (Mac Lochlainn 2003) that the Irish language "wove . . . on [his] . . . ear" (Mac Lochlainn 2002, 190). Because he is both captivated by this "spell" and frustrated by the expectation that Northern Catholics "bite the bit, hold our tongue, play the game" (Mac Lochlainn 2003), it is unsurprising that the spoken word remains the adult Mac Lochlainn's weapon of choice. Today he is a musician, performing with the Irish-language reggae band *Bréag*, and a poet with four volumes to his name.

The first two of these volumes (*Babylon Gaeilgeoir* [1997] and *Na Scéalaithe* [1999]) were published only in the Irish language. Mac Lochlainn claims that these collections rely on a sense of poetry as "mouth music" and as a form of *oideas béil*, or "oral education." His writing, with its "rhythmic pulse" and its feeling of "incantation," demands vocalization and is rooted in "the voice, body, eyes, movement, flow, the sensuality and presence of sound and soundings" (Mac Lochlainn 2003). Of course, given the discontinuities that the Irish language has suffered in the North, Mac Lochlainn's Irish is necessarily "creolized," a product of the code-switching required of a "disaffected underclass" (O'Connor 2009, 79). His writing is full of "the colloquial speech of Belfast *Gaeilgeoirí*" (Ní Dhomhnaill 2002, 16) and is therefore already redolent of local soundscape.

It is in Mac Lochlainn's (2002) third volume, *Sruth Teangacha/Stream of Tongues*, which includes a set of poems in the original Irish and *recto* translations by Mac Lochlainn and by other notable Irish poets, that he captures an acoustic absolutely unique to his community. The acoustic of this collection is a "macaronic . . . jam session" between two languages that reveals the shared spaces (as well as the reciprocal influences) between Belfast's Irish-English and English-Irish (Mac Lochlainn 2002, 190–91). This volume includes a compact disc of "field recordings" (192): a set of poems selected from the book and self-recorded in performance by Mac Lochlainn. These recordings were not made in sound studios, but rather in spaces around Belfast city, including some community-specific (the Hercules Bar, the Water Works, and the Protestant Shankill Road) and some non-sectarian (Belfast city center) locations. Mac Lochlainn's language is refracted through Belfast's urban dynamics; it is edgy with shrapnel and looping with pub talk, and the recordings' intentional inclusion of the city's ambient sounds further emphasizes his efforts to bear earwitness to his surrounding soundscape. Moreover, the poet's openness to cross-community recording sites, in combination with his treatment of translation as "a healing process"—one that requires "the English versions of the poems to have some organic connection to the Irish but also . . . [allows Mac Lochlainn's] English speaking self to draw breath" (188)—highlights the fact that the city's sound-space is often common ground. Despite Mac Lochlainn's firmly Republican politics, his poetry resonates with a sense of shared Belfast identity.

As Mac Lochlainn (2002) proposes in his "Author's Notes" to *Sruth Teangacha/Stream of Tongues*:

> Let's say we are reading a poem about a landscape (or cityscape) in Irish. The poet has selected his words because each word in any language has a certain soundscape or sound-contour of its own. The soundscapes in the words (or groupings of words) the poet uses may be used for what they echo of the landscape (for already the poet is translating sensory or psychic impressions of the thing-in-itself to the audio-visual format of the poem and words) and become an aural map for the reader. These original soundscapes of words and word groupings are lost in language translation. Music is lost. The translations are an attempt to win back music. (189)

Mac Lochlainn's description of his writing process immediately suggests a conjunction between Belfast's rattle and hum and the sound-contours of his own poetry. The work, he argues, tries to capture "sensory . . . impressions" of the world and to "echo" the "cityscape," and it can therefore serve as an "aural map" to place. *Sruth Teangacha/Stream of Tongues*, for example, sketches the Twinbrook soundscape of Mac Lochlainn's childhood. "Stream" ("Sruth") is about the young boy escaping to "a secret place / on the edge of the new estate" (lines 1–2): a small glen that "hum[s] with music" (line 8) and is filled with "grasshoppers crooning" (line 12), "[i]nsects buzzing" (line 17), and "the corncrake's tragic dirge" (line 26). Although many of Mac Lochlainn's (2002) poems are situated firmly in specific spaces (e.g., "the pet-shops in Gresham Street" from "The Irish-Speaking Mynah"/"An Máine Gaelach" line 4; "Springfield barracks / in . . . Cavendish St.," from "Patrol"/"Patról" lines 1–2), others limn the edges of things, taking their music from spaces *between* communities, or interface space. Mac Lochlainn's "glen" is likely Colin Glen Forest Park, which is a natural defensive barrier that is surrounded by "Peace Lines" and separates Unionist Suffolk from its surrounding Catholic communities. The earmarks that the young Mac Lochlainn finds there are sounds shared across community lines, which are allowed to flourish in a pastoral "no man's land" and can slip across even the most daunting of the area's steel fences.

Other poems in Mac Lochlainn's 2002 collection, such as "Friday Night and Grounded"/"Oíche Aoine sa Bhaile" (the poem that he records on the Shankill Road), detail the confines of conflict. The poet-speaker is virtually incarcerated in his living room even while he "want[s] to be out / roaming the concrete fields of the city" (lines 30–31). In "Saturday Night on The Town"/"Oíche Shathairn sa Chathair," he is seen out at pub "sessions" (line 16), with "pipes wail[ing]" (line 21) in "wild reel[s]" (line 19): an acoustic escape from "the vertigo radio reports" (line 29) of friends' deaths.[8]

I am most interested in Mac Lochlainn's (2002) liminal poems in *Sruth Teangacha/Stream of Tongues* because of their implications for

8. I should note here that, unfortunately, I do not read Irish, and so my observations are largely limited to Mac Lochlainn's translations; I am not the bilingual "ideal reader" of the volume that Mac Lochlainn (2002, 191) envisions. I am, however, indebted to Laura O'Connor for her comments on the Irish-language version of "Rambling"/"Seachránaí," which have aided my reading of the poem here, as well as for her marvelous essay, "Translation through the Macaronic: Gearóid Mac Lochlainn's *Sruth Teangacha/Stream of Tongues*" (O'Connor 2009), which initially introduced me to Mac Lochlainn's writing. In any case, I hope that this analysis inspires future work on the acoustic give and take between Irish and English in Mac Lochlainn's poems.

reconsidering interface space as shared space in the most severely sectarian territory in Belfast. "Rambling"/"Seachránaí," for instance, a poem translated by Ciaran Carson, opens by describing its speaker's jangled nerves, which are set on edge by "the buzz-word gabble" (line 2) of local news reports and the onomatopoeic "thrum and buzz" (line 30) of hovering helicopters. Feeling unbearably claustrophobic, the poet-speaker leaves the house, and the poem traces the path he describes along the Falls, through Clowney Road, past Lanark Way with its "new security gates" (line 41), and along the Springfield/Shankill "Peace Line" to Springfield Park. Along the way, if we compare *verso* and *recto*, we note many untranslatable terms that have entered the Irish from English. These terms are a shared set of shibboleths having to do with violence and surveillance: "foot patrols" (line 39), "Checkpoint Charlies" (line 39), "body searches" (line 40), and, eventually, "no-man's-land" (line 58). It is in this "no-man's-land" that the poet-speaker finds his refuge: the curious respite of Springfield Park. As in Colin Glen, and in the likes of north Belfast's Alexandra Park, green space is used here as a buffer zone, dividing working-class Catholics from their Protestant counterparts so as to avoid potentially violent cross-community contact. However, this use of parkland and waste ground as security barriers also provides a surprising amount of "clairaudience," or clear hearing, for nearby communities. This often makes for a strange contrast between soothing pastoral tones and visual noise: towering fences, barbed wire, and paramilitary graffiti.

In Springfield Park, for example, which is "[d]eaf to the distant traffic" (line 62) of the city, Mac Lochlainn's (2002, "Rambling"/"Seachránaí") speaker hears the calls of "wildfowl, / swans and seagulls" (lines 61–62) and the hypnotic "cluck . . . and slap" (line 67) of the pond water. These sounds are unrestricted by their surrounding visual barriers; they can easily pass through mesh fences and top breeze-block walls. The gulls' open-throated caws, in particular, undoubtedly carry into nearby backyards on both sides of the divide given their high pitch and brassy timbre. Mac Lochlainn's "close listening" is therefore political as much as it is personal: these lines suggest that some embodied experiences—in this case, the park's biophonic keynote sounds—are shared across interface communities' seemingly insurmountable barriers. This in turn introduces the possibility of cross-community ties in Belfast's interface neighborhoods, even if those ties are unacknowledged or undesired. Shared sound-space makes for a shared sense of homeplace: a sentiment that rubs against the grain of interface areas' mutually exclusionary visual cues.

In addition, the park's music is so calming that Mac Lochlainn's (2002, "Rambling"/"Seachránaí") speaker falls asleep for a time; he says the park is the one place where he can "get a grip" (line 58), curled up on a sheltered bench. Although he eventually awakes with a paranoiac start, imagining himself murdered by militants in the park, he nevertheless manages to steal a few quiet moments away from the conflict's cacophony in this in-between space. By dramatizing this brief peace, "Rambling" offers the possibility of sound as a tonic for visual unhomeliness. Moreover, by listening in on a liminal space where rival communities abut, Mac Lochlainn suggests local soundscape as a basis for shared Belfast identity.

"Bat-squeaks in a Cave"

Leontia Flynn's background is rather different from that of Mac Lochlainn. She grew up on a farm in Ballyloughlin, County Down, and relocated to Belfast in 1994 to study at QUB. She completed both her bachelor's and doctorate degrees at QUB, taking a brief hiatus for a master's degree in Edinburgh, and she now works at the Seamus Heaney Centre for Poetry at QUB. Her three published volumes (*These Days* [2004], *Drives* [2008], and *Profit and Loss* [2011]) are relatively reticent about her religious and political affiliations, and she rarely speaks or writes directly about Northern Irish politics. Nevertheless, place is often at the heart of her poetry, with the "ordinariness of life" in Belfast serving as a backdrop for much of her work (see "Leontia Flynn's Profit and Loss," *Culture Northern Ireland*, September 2, 2011).

As with Mac Lochlainn's writing, soundscape often "echo[es] . . . landscape" (Mac Lochlainn 2002, 189) in Flynn's poetry; it is through her collections' sonic contours that the city can best be sensed. In an interview with J. P. O'Malley, Flynn (*Culture Northern Ireland*, September 2, 2011) explains, "I think in poetry you go a funny way around the houses to get your meaning across. I do tend to make noises and sound effects sometimes, rather than use words. Poetry is always aware of this non-linguistic other part of itself." It is unsurprising that Flynn uses this architectural metaphor to account for her poetic sound effects because noise and space are so frequently yoked in her work. Her pedestrian poet-speaker visits Golden Mile coffee shops ("The Myth of Tea Boy," 2004), wanders across the Albert and Ormeau Bridges ("It's a Wonderful Life," 2004), and imagines a bird's eye view over north Belfast's Waterworks ("Sky Boats," 2008), all the while tracing their acoustic textures. Elsewhere, Flynn (2011, "Letter to Friends" II.24) mentions the echolocative function of "bat-squeaks in a cave," suggesting that sound can work "to steer us in the dark." This is perhaps her view of her own poetry: a volume can be a sound-map of a sort—a perceptual guide to place.

Flynn is a member of the Literary Belfast project, which has paired with SARC's Belfast Soundwalks initiative to better "engage the public through novel ways of disseminating creative writing and sonic arts associated with the city" (see http://www.qub.ac.uk/sites/sarc/News for more information). The Literary Belfast iPhone app now includes a locative media function called "Belfast through Writers' Eyes," which enlists local writers as listeners' guides to walking the city. Flynn serves in this context as an acoustic escort through the Cathedral Quarter; she describes the area's maritime history, mentions its current reincarnation as a hub of Belfast night life, and then reads her poem "The Amazing, Disappearing."[9] Although it is difficult to gauge if her participation in sound projects has influenced her writing in any immediate way, her contribution to the Literary Belfast app underscores her poetic conviction that the ear can be a conduit to deep dwelling in the city—a way of "steering in the dark."

An auditory approach to Belfast city like that of the Literary Belfast app seems particularly necessary given that Belfast remains a bit of a visual puzzle. Between its labyrinthine cul-de-sacs (designed to better segregate divided neighborhoods) and its defensive fortifications (walls and

9. Her contribution to the project can also be viewed as a YouTube video at http://www.youtube.com/watch?v=DxMgs57issY&list=PL3D44F9AC8B85FE01&index=6.

fences that have proliferated rather than faded from view since the Peace Agreement[10]), its streets can be a challenge to navigate. In several poems, Flynn mentions the Catholic Newington area near the New Lodge/Tiger's Bay interface that abuts Alexandra Park: a neighborhood that virtually defines architectural confusion given its patches of waste ground, burnt-out houses, security fences, and "execrable litter-blown" dead-ends (Flynn 2008, "Leaving Belfast" line 6). The fact that "Leaving Belfast" also highlights one of the area's most widely shared earmarks—the warbles and whistles of starlings (line 8)—is telling; Flynn's poetry prescribes a perceptual reorientation in the face of this visual bewilderment.

Even more prominent in Flynn's collections than these markers of conflict, however, are concerns about city redevelopment, which have reared their heads in recent years as overt violence in the city has waned. Many of Flynn's poems are anxious about preserving Belfast's distinctive spaces even as architects "paper over the cracks / with car parks and luxury flats" (Flynn 2008, "Leaving Belfast" lines 12–13) in an attempt to will away lingering divides and to lend the city an air of generic European urbanity. Belfast's City Council has aggressively pursued this "urban renaissance" strategy since the late 1990s, and major building projects have included the Victoria Square shopping complex, the Titanic Quarter's waterfront regeneration scheme, which encompasses the hulking Odyssey Arena, rows of "yuppie flats" (Patterson 2006, 64) aimed at young, wealthy professionals, the landmark Titanic Museum, and the City Quays residential/retail project alongside the Lagan. Many urban planners have commented on the city's studied attempts at normalization and neutralization, arguing that the current building boom rewards anodyne, sanitized, non-indigenous architecture and exhibits a kind of "cultural cringe" (Neill 2004, 307). As Belfast rebuilds with an eye to becoming a "neutral, modernizing place" (Murtagh 2008, 3), something of the city's character is being lost. According to Anne Devlin, "[T]he planners are our bombers now" (quoted in Craig 1999, 399).

10. See BIP 2011. The report identifies ninety-nine defensive barriers in total in the city as of 2012, with a full one third of these having been built since the 1994 ceasefires.

In response to this cultural leveling, Flynn's work highlights the importance of holding on to that which makes Belfast unique. This sentiment is not just a symptom of preservationist nostalgia; rather, given that intergroup reconciliation in the city is still painfully underdeveloped, promoting a shared Belfast identity by way of local particularity remains a pressing political concern. However, the few architectural landmarks that survived the conflict seem today to be increasingly blocked from view or dwarfed by insipid new corporate builds (e.g., the famous Harland and Wolff cranes now "slouch in the background" of the Odyssey Arena, "cowering under the presence of this sign of the new" [Neill 2004, 165]). As a result, Flynn suggests that longstanding earmarks can instead provide a common place-consciousness.

"Letter to Friends" (Flynn 2011) performs this perceptual bait-and-switch: where it describes Belfast city center's new skyline, it clearly reveals its disillusionment. However, the poem's energetic acoustics point to sound as a kind of antidote for its speaker's disappointment; its rollicking lines are giddily pleasing to the ear. Flynn writes, "Belfast, long the blight / and blot on lives has now brought to an end / or several ends, its grim traumatic fight; / the pay-off packet and the dividend / amid the double-dealings, halts and heists: / a building boom and shopping malls thrown up / like flotsam by our new security. / Here are our palaces of snow and ice, / 'and so folks with *esprit de corps* we'll shop / ourselves to civilised maturity'" (lines II.68–76). As the poem narrates its visual surroundings, its outlook seems bleak; Flynn frames contemporary Belfast as both the post-conflict remains of Carson's "demolition city," with its urban "blight / and blot," and as the bland canvas of the city's recent builders, their "shopping malls thrown up / like flotsam." Although the poem's acoustics are not heavy, the passage is rife with internal and line-end rhyme ("blight"/"fight"/ "heists"/"ice," "end"/"dividend," "security"/"maturity," "blot"/"brought") and with bursts of alliteration, and it is ornamented by lightly tripping /b/ and /d/ sounds and breathily aspirated h's—a far cry from the discordant tones one might expect from such a scathing stanza. In a sense, then, the poem's soundscape provides relief from its own thematic landscape, and this sentiment also guides Flynn's take on place.

Many of Flynn's other poems follow the lead of "Letter to Friends" and explicitly highlight Belfast's keynote sounds as pleasantly rooting for the lone pedestrian and as a potential source of common ground in the city. As I have noted, Flynn's work occasionally features starling-song, but it also asks us to call the "delighted shriek[s]" of gulls to mind (Flynn 2011, "Five Obvious Catullus Versions" line V.14), "the air flocking and beating around the[ir] still wings" (Flynn 2004, "It's a Wonderful Life" line 9). Gulls' caws are in many ways definitive of the city; they serve as a biophonic reminder that Belfast is a seaside town. This proximity to the water is otherwise easily forgotten throughout the city, given that visual views of Belfast Lough are often obscured at street level by row housing and hulking downtown high-rises. However, no matter where one lives in Belfast, one is reminded aurally if not visually of the Atlantic's brackish immediacy, and Flynn's poetry repeatedly registers this maritime clamor.

Similarly, the wind that blows off Belfast Lough reverberates incessantly throughout the city. Its howls respect no borders as they probe nearly every nook and cranny of both Protestant and Catholic neighborhoods. This earmark echoes in each of Flynn's volumes; "The Girl Upstairs (2011)," for instance, listens intently while "[o]utside the rising wind / rumbles the bins and makes the drinkers shout" (lines 4–5). The wind's briny whines, which here rumble trashcan lids and elsewhere rattle traffic signs (Flynn 2008, "Drive" line 3), gradually accrue geophonic weight throughout her work, emerging as an important acoustic anchor and a sound widely redolent of place. In exploring local soundscape, Flynn's (2004) "Two Crossings" also observes that the city speaks "with one leviathan and clattering *accent*" (line 3); some few community particularities notwithstanding (*aitch* versus *haitch*), the quick, clipped urban Belfast dialect is distinctive and is broadly shared throughout the city. Even if Belfast is still wrenchingly divided, Flynn reminds us that it very nearly speaks with one voice.

Flynn's (2011) "I Once Lived in a Railway Carriage Flat" reflects on the pleasure to be found as an urban eavesdropper. At one time its poet-speaker lived over a busy Belfast street "where yells and scraps of talk rose up like smoke." As bars shut up shop in the early hours, she could hear the patrons' "hoot and crash," and, feeling at one with the voices below, would find herself "humm[ing] . . . like a fridge, delighted, in the dark" (lines 3–5). Despite the "*harsh attempts at buyable beauty*" that define Belfast's new architectural scheme—the "mock-colonnades" and "tapas bars" that pander shamelessly to tourists and erase the city's particularity (Flynn 2008, "Belfast" lines 9–11)—many of its sounds are still satisfyingly grounding. Furthermore, given that most of the local notes Flynn sounds are shared across community lines, a common (and a more conciliatory) Belfast identity might be well founded on their ground bass. Therefore, both Mac Lochlainn and Flynn encourage SARC and Belfast City Council's recent sound projects. As the city's built environment is either increasingly factionalized (as in interface neighborhoods) or increasingly sanitized (as in the city center and along the Lagan), acoustic space has the potential to source a shared sense of place.

"This Gabble-clinkered Music"

Alan Gillis was born in Belfast in 1973, and he grew up in an overwhelmingly Protestant and Loyalist housing estate in the nearby town of Newtownards. After earning an undergraduate degree in Dublin, where he felt constantly "under scrutiny" as a "Northern prod," he returned to Belfast city and spent the peace process years writing and "incubating" himself in local literary life.[11] Although he now teaches in Edinburgh, each of his three published volumes (*Somebody Somewhere* [2004], *Hawks and Doves* [2007], and *Here Comes the Night* [2010]) returns home to his experiences in Belfast and reckons with the city as it is today: noisy, rowdy, and a work vociferously in progress.

As a writer of firmly urban poetry, Gillis notes his constantly frustrated urge to make sense of the city as "a place where you can locate yourself with some stability . . . with some degree of communal belonging." Gillis also explains to *The Edinburgh Review* that his collections are primarily concerned with "sonic ambiance," their acoustics working to animate "language itself . . . with anxiety and yearning for transfiguration,

11. See Gillis' interview with *The Edinburgh Review*, http://edinburgh-review.com/extracts/alan-gillis/.

imprinting deep through the inner ear an intuition of some potential plenitude." Taken together, these sentiments suggest his volumes' drive—despite their own skepticism—toward "potential plenitude" and "communal belonging," and they identify the "inner ear" as a possible conduit to this "transfiguration." Miriam Gamble's (2009) analysis of Gillis' first two collections underscores this point: Gamble notes the poet's desire to negotiate a "post-ceasefire identity" while refusing "easy conclusions"; he "test[s] imaginative potential against the recalcitrant facts of a culture which . . . remains in limbo" (362). Despite this recalcitrance, however, Gillis' Belfast is "mnemonic" (Gamble 2009, 367), and it is precisely in close listening that the poetry finds its imaginative potential and perhaps its conciliatory power. "The Ulster Way," the opening poem in Gillis' (2004) first collection, clearly signals this auditory possibility: its final line enjoins the reader, "Everything is about you. Now listen" (line 21). And listen we must.

However, it is not exactly the *language* of place to which Gillis would have us lend our ears. Even the simplest of terms are often freighted with political baggage in Northern Ireland, so if we are to move past partisanship, past "washed-out slogans" and angry acronyms and admini-speak (Gillis 2007, "Laganside" line 135), we cannot rely on our existing "word-hoard" (as Heaney's [1975] *North*, following *Beowulf*, would have it). Indeed, Gillis' (2007) "Carnival," which describes a group of Orangemen on parade, associates brusque brand names and bathetic pop-cultural references with sectarian performance: men in "[b]lack buffed leather-tongued brogues with oat- / meal socks and khaki Y-fronts, pleated slacks, / pert navy and gold striped double-windsored tie[s] / on . . . twill non-iron white hassle-free shirt[s]" (lines 1–3) march in formation against their "unwashed brethren," then return home, "content with [their] labours, / to watch *Countdown* and [their] favourite, *Neighbours*" (lines 16–18). The language of the poem is as much a standard-issue uniform as are the marchers' brogues and pleated slacks; these words are spent, exhausted, and insufficient to describe the transfiguration that Gillis seeks.

Gamble (2009, 363) argues that Gillis "links mastery (or otherwise) of [local] terrain with the possibilities inherent in language, suggests regional identity as something which, whilst needing renovation, is only in the process of finding a new shape, and registers the sense, in poetry as in society, of being on the cusp of something 'new.'" I further suggest that Gillis' effort to find a new approach to local terrain involves eschewing well-worn words and approaching pure sound: the "unfathomable score," the "reverb or hum," and the "numinous crack" that is the language of place (Gillis 2004, "Porter" lines 6–8). Gillis does his best to echo the city rather than simply describing it, and this infuses his poetry with an incredible musicality. His verse is rife with onomatopoeic groans and grunts, sound-based coinages, and resonant portmanteaux—so much so that his writing verges on scatting.

Like Flynn, Gillis (2007, "Laganside" lines 107–8) is "a bit bamboozled / by this crash and build of trees and concrete," the marks of a newly "neutralized" cityscape. Accordingly, he takes his poetic energies from Belfast's acoustic spaces: from the "coo-coos" and "tra-la twitterings" of the Lagan Towpath's nesting birds ("Laganside" lines 28–30), and from the river's "slurp and bebble and girny-gab glissando," its "billow-warped refrain" (Gillis 2004, "Big Blue Sky and Silent River" lines 196–99). Gillis (2007, "After Arcadia" lines 4–6) exhorts his reader to "[g]ive [her] ears to this gabble-clinkered music / that chitters my wits all through the claggy morning / and skitters my senses until whiskey snigs the night"; that is, to imagine the "inner ear" as a path to "potential plenitude" in the post-conflict city (see Gillis' interview with *The Edinburgh Review*).

Gillis (2007) makes the important point in "Laganside" that Belfast's heard world is not yet entirely harmonious by identifying all-too-familiar aural triggers of trauma: "a timer's tick-tock, confused with the cistern's drip-drop, / keeping you up to panic at a midnight knock-knock, / which is just a drunk neighbor who thought / his missus must ive change da fuckin front-dure lock" (lines 57–60). In addition to this noise is parade season's partisan cacophony, which Gillis (2007) describes in "Carnival" as strident lambegs and fifes that serve as sonic claims to territory (line 8).

In the acoustic contours of poems like "Wasps," Gillis (2007) incorporates found sound to describe the shape of something new. At first glance, "Wasps" appears to be a parochial Protestant east Belfast poem: it depicts a boat's arrival in Belfast harbor, a dockyard disembarkation, and a drive past George Best Airport out to Newtownards. Its opening stanzas are laden with visual markers of the community's shipbuilding history: a "gymnasium / of cranes" and a "mangle / of rusted hulks" (lines 9–11). However, Gillis dispenses with the well-worn idioms of east Belfast—the grim shipyard scenes of Heaney's (1966) "Docker," where "[m]osaic imperatives bang home like rivets" (line 9) and workers are allergic to the "Roman collars" (line 7) of their Catholic compatriots across the Lagan—and reframes the area as the seat of the city's shared maritime soundscape. The port is the source of Belfast's marine earmarks, and is therefore, Gillis suggests, the heart of the town's heard world. Its rhythms resonate throughout "Wasps," which tries centrally to capture the harbor's "sonic ambiance" (see Gillis' interview with *The Edinburgh Review*). As Gillis' boat arrives, for example, he observes how "the water treacled and brined / around the fudged ferry chugging / carbon flukes to berth in the slime" (lines 14–16). These sounds are themselves tidal: "treacle," "brine," and "fudge" are oral descriptors, but so too are they aural, mimicking the turbulent notes of the boat's sludgy wake. The lines' internal rhyme ("fudged" chiming with the ferry's onomatopoeic "chug") also emphasizes the sound of the frothing lough as the boat churns the murk beneath. These waters are thick with the seabed sleech (the sand, gravel, and muck) on which Belfast city was built—Gillis later describes the inlet as a gash of "tide-locked tar-water" (line 75)—and so they are literally redolent with home's most fundamental tones. Gillis repeats these tones in a number of poems, suggesting their ubiquity the city over. In "In Whose Blent Air All Our Compulsions Meet," for example, Gillis (2010) observes "how the sound / of each wave's crash and suck-back into the hoo-ha / of the sea can soothe and creep under your skin" (lines 6–8): in other words, how familiar sounds can shape and shelter local bodies.

After docking, the narrator in "Laganside" drives out on the A20 highway toward Newtownards, "chugging" along (the car's climb echoing the ferry's engine-whine) past George Best Airport and driving beneath the sound of airplane flight paths, which Gillis (2007, "Saturday Morning" line 63) elsewhere describes as "the bow-wow whooshing of a sonic jet-stream." He proceeds "under herring-gull cries" ("Laganside" line 108) toward the "green-rocked lump-and-frumped hills" (line 22) that ring the city, their "bluebell-blared slopes" peopled by "amber-fizzed bees" (lines 28–29). As his "Picasso or Civic" (line 17) cleaves this sectarian heartland, it is not the row of paramilitary murals that catches his eye, but the landscape beyond that holds his ear in thrall. Gillis' efforts to echo all he hears demand some surprising poetic coinages: "lump-and-frumped," for instance, uses acoustic descriptors to capture visual space. The emphatically repeated "umps," parted by an unaccented "and," sketch the shape of hills and valley but also imitate the sound of the narrator's battered hatchback's shocks as the car crests the hills' "rocked rump and hump" (line 8). As the narrator moves toward the city's outskirts and away from the airport's "babbling hoodoo" (Gillis 2007, "Saturday Morning" line 77), he can more clearly connect with local biophony: gulls' cries, which again evoke Belfast's seaside soundscape, and the onomatopoeic bee-buzz of the flowering valley that is captured by Gillis' "fizz." Together, Gillis' poetic acoustics work to rehabilitate Protestant east Belfast and the marina beyond. This is not the tourist-targeted normalization of the area being pursued by Belfast City Council, but rather a radical recasting of a resolutely segregated neighborhood as a source of "regional identity" (Gamble 2009, 363). Gillis' Newtownards Road is undoubtedly a sectarian streetscape, but it can also be reimagined as the wellspring of the city's shared soundscape.

Gillis (2007) also situates "Lagan Weir" in an in-between space; the weir is a liminal zone between Protestant east Belfast and the more integrated city center; it is also the point at which the waters of the Farset and the Lagan converge. Located between the M3 Bridge and the Queen Elizabeth II Bridge, Lagan Weir is a gateway to the incredibly sectarian Newtownards Road, where today there are more Loyalist murals, Union flags, and reams of bunting to be found than virtually anywhere else in the city. Although the weir is hardly of architectural interest—it is essentially a series of concrete blockades topped by a footpath—it is nevertheless the source of a very vibrant soundscape. Moreover, despite the weir's own liminality, indicated by Gillis' narrator "stand[ing] in two minds" (line 5) in the middle of its bridge, its acoustic features exert significant bidirectional influence over neighborhoods beyond. Because the weir controls tidal levels to cover the riverbed mud flats, it plays a major role in regulating the river's sounds, and it also serves as a convenient stopover for local wildlife (which is itself the source of many of the city's familiar earmarks).

For example, the poem's narrator follows a flock of starlings as it "skirls back on itself, then swerves forward, / swabbing and scrawling the shell-pink / buffed sky" (lines 4–6). Immersed in his sonic surroundings, he variously hears the flock's "hue and cry" (line 28), its "braying" (line 24), its "swish" (line 20), and its "flickered, fluttered hurry-scurry" (line 19) as he stands beneath its flight path. Gillis resounds these surroundings in his verse, such that his stanzas echo the starlings' voices ("hue and cry," "bray"), their wing-beats ("flicker," "flutter," "hurry-scurry"), the wind displaced by their currents ("swish," "skirl"), and their scrabbling talons as they perch on the bridge ("swab," "scrawl"). Similarly, the river beneath the footpath "slooshes its dark way / to open harbours and the glistering sea"—an onomatopoeic rendering of the water's pool and flow as it moves over the weir wall (lines 8–9).[12] Again, these sounds reach ears on each side of the Lagan: they are the tenor of riverside walking paths fronting both the young, hip, integrated Cathedral Quarter and the sectarian patchwork of the Republican Short Strand, the Protestant Mountpottinger Road, and the staunchly Loyalist Cluan Place.

From his perch above the river, the narrator in "Lagan Weir" also hears "the hurly-burlyed, / humdrummed traffic belch to a stop, / fugging, clacking, charring the clotted air" (lines 14–16). These lines suggest that landscape's muted tones must compete with anthrophonic cacophony even astride the Lagan. As in many cities, the din of passing traffic has increasingly dominated Belfast's soundscape in recent decades, particularly since urban planners have frequently routed major roads through disputed territory to create "buffer zones" between rival communities. Although Gillis' lines can be read as a noise complaint—a lament for the birdsong and river ripples overcome by rush hour's discord—they can also be interpreted as yet another gesture toward the city's shared soundscape. Vehicular sound is undeniably an annoyance, but it is nevertheless the

12. Gillis (2004) styles the sounds of the river in "Big Blue Sky and Silent River" as its "popple and papple" (line 86), its "[p]urling bubble" (line 65), its "puggling . . . torrent" (line 199), and its "pizz-popping jingle-jangle" (line 197), so bearing earwitness to local waters clearly drives him to acoustic innovation.

sensory fiber of Belfast's urban texture, and pedestrians of all persuasions live daily with its boisterous tones. The struggle between the city's maritime strains and its "spree of zooms and fumes" (Gillis 2010, "Rush Hour" lines 18–19) is Belfast's definitive ground bass. In other words, even Gillis' more grating sounds—the "belch," "clack," and "fug" of traffic and its whining "*nnyaao, nnyaao, nnyaao*" (line 17)—are a source of common ground. Like "Laganside," "Lagan Weir" rehabilitates a historically divisive space, in this case the entryway to Protestant east Belfast, for more conciliatory aims. This rehabilitation is not the studied neutralization that the Laganside Corporation envisioned as it raised the weir in 1994, but rather the radical reclamation of a contested space as a conduit to "communal belonging"—a belonging "imprint[ed] deep through the inner ear" (see Gillis' interview with *The Edinburgh Review*).

If sound-space is often shared space in the post-conflict city, then perhaps it is also a potential path toward a "shared future," to borrow the terms of Northern Ireland's "Good Relations" policy framework.[13] Of course, Belfast is still a gravely divided city, and any efforts to suture that divide will be partial and provisional at best. Nevertheless, despite all of Belfast's angrily fortified "Peace Lines" and graffiticized gable ends—visual cues that suggest sectarianism almost beyond repair—even the most divided of the city's communities daily share some commonly embodied experiences. In particular, if we turn an ear to the sound signals that link locals to their lived spaces in the city, we will often find more in harmony than out of sync. Poets like Carson, Mahon, and Muldoon anticipated this avenue to peacebuilding by attending carefully to the heard world throughout the Troubles and considering sound's sheltering consolations even amidst conflict. Writers of "the new North" like Mac Lochlainn, Flynn, and Gillis—poets whose publishing careers have largely followed the Peace Agreement—take up this mantle, going so far as to suggest acoustic space as a possible register of reconciliation. Although their work avoids political prescriptions, it often resonates with the conciliatory tones of

13. See the website for the Office of the First Minister and Deputy First Minister of Northern Ireland, http://www.ofmdfmni.gov.uk.

local earmarks—sounds that cross even the most hostile of community bounds. Recent Belfast sound projects similarly flaunt borders, suggesting that even in the face of Belfast's sectarian spectacle, we are collectively immersed in auditory space. A new generation of Belfast poets and sound artists is therefore working to democratize sense experience, hoping that our ears might orient us toward "potential plenitude" in the wake of conflict (see Gillis' interview with *The Edinburgh Review*). Let us take their counsel to heart, and let us hope for thoughtful listening in the North in years to come.

WORKS CITED

INDEX

WORKS CITED

Agee, Chris. 2008. "Introduction." In *The New North: Contemporary Poetry from Northern Ireland*, xxi–xli. Winston-Salem, NC: Wake Forest Univ. Press.

Ahmed, Sara. 2004. *The Cultural Politics of Emotion*. New York: Routledge.

Alcobia-Murphy, Shane. 1996. "Obliquity in the Poetry of Paul Muldoon and Medbh McGuckian." *Éire-Ireland* 31 (3–4): 76–101.

Alexander, Neal. 2010. *Ciaran Carson: Space, Place, Writing*. Liverpool: Liverpool Univ. Press.

Alighieri, Dante. [1317] 2002. *The Inferno*. Translated by Ciaran Carson. London: Granta.

Allen, Michael. 2004. "Pax Hibernia/Pax Americana: Rhyme and Reconciliation in Muldoon." In *Paul Muldoon: Critical Essays*, edited by Tim Kendall and Peter McDonald, 62–95. Liverpool: Liverpool Univ. Press.

Allison, Jonathan J. 1995. "'Everything Provisional': Fictive Possibility and the Poetry of Paul Muldoon and Ciaran Carson." *Études Irlandaises* 20 (2): 87–93.

Andrews, J. H. 2002. *A Paper Landscape: The Ordnance Survey in Nineteenth-Century Ireland*. 2nd ed. Dublin: Four Courts.

ASCAP (The American Society of Composers, Authors, and Publishers). 2002. "Daron Hagen and Paul Muldoon." ASCAP Audio Portrait. Last modified December 16. http://www.ascap.com/audioportraits/h/daron_hagen_paul_muldoon.aspx.

Auden, W. H. 2007. *Collected Poems*. New York: Random House.

Batten, Guinn. 1995. "Ciaran Carson's Parturient Partition: The 'Crack' in MacNeice's 'More Than Glass.'" *Southern Review* 31 (3): 536–56.

Beckett, Samuel. 1955. *Molloy*. New York: Grove.

Bettermann, Henrik, Dietrich von Bonin, Matthias Frühwirth, Dirk Cysarz, and Maximilian Moser. 2002. "Effects of Speech Therapy with Poetry on Heart Rate Rhythmicity and Cardiorespiratory Coordination." *International Journal of Cardiology* 84 (1): 77–88.

Bhabha, Homi. 1994. *The Location of Culture*. New York: Routledge.

Bilbro, Jeffrey. 2011. "Sounding the Darkness and Discovering the Marvellous: Hearing 'A Lough Neagh Sequence' with Seamus Heaney's Auditory Imagination." *Irish Studies Review* 19 (3): 321–40.

BIP (Belfast Interface Project). 2011. "Belfast Interfaces: Security Barriers and Defensive Use of Space." Last modified November. http://www.belfastinterfaceproject.org/sites/default/files/publications/Belfast%20interfaces.pdf.

Blesser, Barry, and Linda-Ruth Salter. 2006. *Spaces Speak, Are You Listening? Experiencing Aural Architecture*. Cambridge, MA: MIT Press.

Boal, F. W. 2002. "Belfast: Walls Within." *Political Geography* 21 (5): 687–94.

Bonacci, Giulio G. 2001. "A City of the Mind: Ciaran Carson's Belfast." *Prospero* 8: 5–34.

Bookchin, Murray. 2005. *The Ecology of Freedom: The Emergence and Dissolution of Hierarchy*. Oakland: AK Press.

———. (1980) 2009. "Theses on Libertarian Municipalism." Reprint, *Boletín CF+S* 40 (June). http://habitat.aq.upm.es/b/n40/amboo.en.html.

Brand, Dionne. 2002. *A Map to the Door of No Return: Notes to Belonging*. Toronto: Vintage.

Brearton, Fran. 2001. "Mapping the Trenches: Gyres, Switchbacks, and Zig-Zag Circles in W. B. Yeats and Ciaran Carson." *Irish Studies Review* 9 (3): 373–86.

Brown, Terence. 1995. "Telling Tales: Kennelly's *Cromwell*, Muldoon's 'The More a Man Has the More a Man Wants.'" In *Poetry in Contemporary Irish Literature*, edited by Michael Kenneally, 144–57. Gerrards Cross, UK: Colin Smythe.

Brydon, Diana. 2007. "Dionne Brand's Global Intimacies: Practising Affective Citizenship." *University of Toronto Quarterly* 76 (3): 990–1006.

Bull, Michael, and Les Back, eds. 2003. *The Auditory Culture Reader*. Oxford: Berg.

Carson, Ciaran. 1998. *The Alexandrine Plan*. Loughcrew, Ireland: Gallery Press.

———. 1999a. *The Ballad of HMS Belfast: A Compendium of Belfast Poems*. London: Picador.

———. 1989. *Belfast Confetti*. Winston-Salem, NC: Wake Forest Univ. Press.

———. 2003. *Breaking News*. Winston-Salem, NC: Wake Forest Univ. Press.

———. 1975. "Escaped from the Massacre?" *The Honest Ulsterman* 50: 183–86.

———. 1993. *First Language: Poems*. Loughcrew, Ireland: Gallery Press.

———. 2009a. "For All I Know: Ciaran Carson in Conversation with Elmer Kennedy-Andrews." In *Ciaran Carson: Critical Essays*, edited by Elmer Kennedy-Andrews, 13–27. Dublin: Four Courts.

———. 2008. *For All We Know*. Winston-Salem, NC: Wake Forest Univ. Press.

———. 1990. Interview by Rand Brandes. *Irish Review* 8: 77–90.

———. 2002. "Interview with John Brown." In *In the Chair: Interviews with Poets from the North of Ireland*, edited by John Brown, 141–52. Cliffs of Moher, Ireland: Salmon Poetry.

———. 2012. *In the Light Of.* Loughcrew: Gallery Press.

———. 1987. *The Irish for No.* Loughcrew, Ireland: Gallery Press.

———. 1986a. *Last Night's Fun: In and Out of Time with Irish Music.* New York: North Point.

———. 1976. *The New Estate.* Belfast: Blackstaff.

———. 2009b. *On the Night Watch.* Winston-Salem, NC: Wake Forest Univ. Press.

———. 1996. *Opera Et Cetera.* Newcastle upon Tyne, UK: Bloodaxe.

———. 1986b. *Pocket Guide to Irish Traditional Music.* Belfast: Appletree.

———. 2001. *Selected Poems.* Winston-Salem, NC: Wake Forest Univ. Press.

———. 1997. *The Star Factory.* London: Granta.

———. 1999b. *The Twelfth of Never.* New York: Picador.

———. 2010. *Until Before After.* Winston-Salem, NC: Wake Forest Univ. Press.

Carter, Paul. 2001. "Ambiguous Traces: Mishearing and Auditory Space." Australian Sound Design Project. Last modified July 16. http://www.sounddesign.unimelb.edu.au/site/papers/mishearing.html.

Churchill, Ward, Norbert Hill, and Mary Jo Barlow. 1979. "An Historical Overview of Twentieth-Century Native American Athletics." *Indian Historian* 12 (4): 22–33.

Clark, Heather L. 2006. *The Ulster Renaissance: Poetry in Belfast, 1962–1972.* Oxford: Oxford Univ. Press.

Clifford, James. 1997. *Routes: Travel and Translation in the Late Twentieth Century.* Cambridge, MA: Harvard Univ. Press.

Close, Charles. (1926) 1969. *The Early Years of the Ordnance Survey.* Reprint, Newton Abbot: David & Charles.

Clough, Patricia Ticineto, ed. 2007. *The Affective Turn: Theorizing the Social.* Durham, NC: Duke Univ. Press.

Collins, Lucy. 2006. "Marking Time: The Influence of Irish Traditional Music on the Poetry of Ciaran Carson." In *Back to the Present: Forward to the Past; Irish Writing and History Since 1798*, edited by Patricia A. Lynch, Joachim Fischer, and Brian Coates, 241–54. New York: Rodopi.

Corcoran, Brendan. 2008. "'Persisting for the Unborn': Derek Mahon's Elegaic Poetics." *New Hibernia Review* 12 (2): 87–105.

Corcoran, Neil. 1993. *English Poetry Since 1940*. Harlow, UK: Longman.

———. 1992. "One Step Forward, Two Steps Back." In *The Chosen Ground: Essays on Contemporary Poetry of Northern Ireland*, 211–33. Bridgend, UK: Seren Books.

Corkery, Daniel. 1931. *Synge and Anglo-Irish Literature*. Cork, Ireland: Cork Univ. Press.

Craig, Patricia, ed. 1999. *The Belfast Anthology*. Belfast: Blackstaff.

Crosson, Seán. 2008. *The Given Note: Traditional Music and Modern Irish Poetry*. Newcastle upon Tyne, UK: Cambridge Scholars.

———. 2004. "Performance and Music in the Poetry of Ciaran Carson." *Nordic Irish Studies* 3 (1): 101–11.

Culture Northern Ireland. 2006. "A Profile of Dermot Seymour." Last modified January 5. http://www.culturenorthernireland.org/article/486/a-profile-of-dermot-seymour.

Damasio, Antonio. (1994) 2005. *Descartes' Error: Emotion, Reason, and the Human Brain*. Reprint, New York: Vintage.

———. 1999. *The Feeling of What Happens: Body and Emotion in the Making of Consciousness*. New York: Houghton Mifflin Harcourt.

"Daron Hagen's Opera Shining Brow." 2009. Naxos, podcast audio, April 14. http://blog.naxos.com/2009/04/14/podcast-daron-hagen-opera-shining-brow/.

Dawe, Gerald. 2003. "The Revenges of the Heart: Belfast and the Poetics of Space." In *The Cities of Belfast*, edited by Nicholas Allen and Aaron Kelly, 199–210. Dublin: Four Courts.

Deane, Seamus. 1997. *Strange Country: Modernity and Nationhood in Irish Writing Since 1790*. Oxford: Oxford Univ. Press.

Debord, Guy. (1967) 1983. *The Society of the Spectacle*. Translated by Ken Knabb. Reprint, London: Rebel.

Deleuze, Gilles, and Felix Guattari. (1987) 2004. *A Thousand Plateaus: Capitalism and Schizophrenia*. Reprint, London: Continuum.

———. 1994. *What Is Philosophy?* New York: Columbia Univ. Press.

Derricke, John. 1581. *The Image of Irelande*. London: Ihon Daie. http://www.lib.ed.ac.uk/about/bgallery/Gallery/researchcoll/ireland.html.

Derrida, Jacques. 1984. *Signéponge/Signsponge*. Translated by Richard Rand. New York: Columbia Univ. Press.

Devine, Brian. 2006. *Yeats, the Master of Sound: An Investigation of the Technical and Aural Achievements of William Butler Yeats*. Gerrards Cross, UK: Colin Smythe.

Ercegovac, Peter. 1999. "Competing National Ideologies, Cyclical Responses: The Mobilisation of the Irish, Basque and Croat National Movements to Rebellion Against the State." PhD diss., Univ. of Sydney. http://www.nationalismproject.org/articles/Pero/title.html.

Falci, Eric. 2012. *Continuity and Change in Irish Poetry, 1966–2010*. Cambridge: Cambridge Univ. Press.

Farrell, J. G. (1970) 2002. *Troubles*. Reprint, New York: NYRB Classics.

Fey, Marie Therese, Mike Morrissey, Marie Smyth, and Tracy Wong. 1999. *The Cost of the Troubles Study: Report on the Northern Ireland Survey; The Experience and Impact of the Troubles*. Derry/Londonderry: INCORE.

Fill, Alwin. 2001. "Language and Ecology: Ecolinguistic Perspectives for 2000 and Beyond." *AILA Review* 14: 60–75.

"Finding Music in '*Finnegans Wake*.'" 2007. *All Things Considered*, National Public Radio, November 11. http://www.npr.org/templates/story/story.php?storyId=16203872.

Flynn, Leontia. 2008. *Drives*. London: Jonathan Cape.

———. 2011. "Leontia Flynn's *Profit and Loss*." Interview by J. P. O'Malley. *Culture Northern Ireland*, September 2. http://www.culturenorthernireland.org/article/4343/leontia-flynn-s-profit-and-loss.

———. 2011. *Profit and Loss*. London: Jonathan Cape.

———. 2004. *These Days*. London: Jonathan Cape.

Forster, E. M. 2000. *Howards End*. London: Penguin.

Frawley, Oona. 2005. *Irish Pastoral: Nostalgia and Twentieth-Century Irish Literature*. Dublin: Irish Academic.

Freud, Sigmund. (1914) 1966. "Remembering, Repeating, and Working-through." In *Standard Edition of the Complete Psychological Works of Sigmund Freud*, Vol. 14, translated and edited by James Strachey, 147–56. London: Hogarth and Institute of Psycho-Analysis.

Friel, Brian. 1981. *Translations*. London: Faber & Faber.

Friel, Brian, John Andrews, and Kevin Barry. 1983. "Translations and a Paper Landscape: Between Fiction and History." *The Crane Bag* 7 (2): 118–24.

Fussell, Paul. 1982. *Abroad: British Literary Traveling between the Wars*. New York: Oxford Univ. Press.

Gamble, Miriam. 2009. "'The Gentle Art of Re-perceiving': Post-ceasefire Identity in the Poetry of Alan Gillis." *Irish Studies Review* 17 (3): 361–76.

Gillis, Alan. 2003. "Ciaran Carson and History." In *The Cities of Belfast*, edited by Nicholas Allen and Aaron Kelly, 183–98. Dublin: Four Courts.

———. 2007. *Hawks and Doves*. Loughcrew, Ireland: Gallery Press.
———. 2010. *Here Comes the Night*. Loughcrew, Ireland: Gallery Press.
———. 2014. "Interview: Alan Gillis." *The Edinburgh Review*. Accessed January 25. http://edinburgh-review.com/extracts/alan-gillis/.
———. 2004. *Somebody, Somewhere*. Loughcrew, Ireland: Gallery Press.
Goodby, John. 2009. "'Walking in the City': Space, Place, and Surveillance in *The Irish for No* and *Belfast Confetti*." In *Ciaran Carson: Critical Essays*, edited by Elmer Kennedy-Andrews, 66–85. Dublin: Four Courts.
Goodman, Steve. 2009. *Sonic Warfare: Sound, Affect, and the Ecology of Fear*. Cambridge, MA: MIT Press.
Graham, Colin. 2003. "Belfast in Photographs." In *The Cities of Belfast*, edited by Nicholas Allen and Aaron Kelly, 152–67. Dublin: Four Courts.
Grennan, Eamon. 1999. *Facing the Music: Irish Poetry in the Twentieth Century*. Omaha, NE: Creighton Univ. Press.
Hall, S. C., and A. M. Hall. 1841. *Ireland: Its Scenery, Character, Etc.* London: Jeremiah How.
Harding, Walter. 1970. *The Days of Henry Thoreau: A Biography*. New York: Knopf.
Haughton, Hugh. 2002. "'The Bright Garbage on the Incoming Wave': Rubbish in the Poetry of Derek Mahon." *Textual Practice* 16 (2): 323–43.
———. 1992. "Place and Displacement in Derek Mahon." In *The Chosen Ground: Essays on Contemporary Poetry of Northern Ireland*, edited by Neil Corcoran, 87–122. Bridgend, UK: Seren Books.
———. 2007. *The Poetry of Derek Mahon*. Oxford: Oxford Univ. Press.
Heaney, Seamus. 1966. *Death of a Naturalist*. London: Faber & Faber.
———. 1975. *North*. London: Faber & Faber.
———. 1998. *Opened Ground: Selected Poems 1966–1996*. New York: Farrar, Straus and Giroux.
———. 2002. "Place and Displacement." In *Finders Keepers: Selected Prose 1972–2001*, 112–33. New York: Farrar, Straus and Giroux.
———. 1984. *Preoccupations: Selected Prose, 1968–1978*. London: Faber & Faber.
———. 1972. *Wintering Out*. London: Faber & Faber.
Hena, Omaar. 2008. "Playing Indian/Disintegrating Irishness: Globalization and Cross-Cultural Identity in Paul Muldoon's 'Madoc: A Mystery.'" *Contemporary Literature* 49 (2): 232–62.
Horton, Patricia. 2000. "Degree Zero: Language, Subjectivity and Apocalypse in the Poetry of Derek Mahon." *Irish Studies Review* 8 (3): 353–65.

Howe, Stephen. 2001. *Ireland and Empire: Colonial Legacies in Irish History and Culture*. Oxford: Oxford Univ. Press.

Hufstader, Jonathan. 1999. *Tongue of Water, Teeth of Stones: Northern Irish Poetry and Social Violence*. Lexington: Univ. Press of Kentucky.

Hughes, Eamonn. 2009. "'The Mouth of the Poem': Carson and Place." In *Ciaran Carson: Critical Essays*, edited by Elmer Kennedy-Andrews, 86–105. Dublin: Four Courts.

———. 2002. "'Weird/Haecceity': Place in Derek Mahon's Poetry." In *The Poetry of Derek Mahon*, edited by Elmer Kennedy-Andrews, 97–111. Gerrards Cross, UK: Colin Smythe.

Hughes, Joanne, Andrea Campbell, Miles Hewstone, and Ed Cairns. 2007. "Segregation in Northern Ireland: Implications for Community Relations Policy." *Policy Studies* 28 (1): 35–36.

Ihde, Don. 2007. *Listening and Voice: Phenomenologies of Sound*. 2nd ed. New York: State Univ. of New York Press. First edition published 1976 by Ohio Univ. Press. Page references are to the 2007 edition.

Janus, Adrienne. 2007. "In One Ear and Out the Others: Beckett. . . . Mahon. Muldoon." *Journal of Modern Literature* 30 (2): 180–96.

Jaques, Elliott. 1967. Review of *The Trickster*, by Paul Radin. *The International Journal of Psychoanalysis* 38: 429–30.

Jarniewicz, Jerzy. 2002. "Derek Mahon: History, Mute Phenomena and Beyond." In *The Poetry of Derek Mahon*, edited by Elmer Kennedy-Andrews, 83–96. Gerrards Cross, UK: Colin Smythe.

———. 2005. "Zona Media, or Paul Muldoon's 'Little Books.'" In *Paul Muldoon: Poetry, Prose, and Drama*, edited by Elmer Kennedy-Andrews, 233–47. Gerrards Cross, UK: Colin Smythe.

Jenkins, Chadwick. 2007. "Classical Radio Communities: Thoughts on Mediation." PopMatters Media. Last modified April 27. http://www.popmatters.com/pm/column/classical-radio-communities-thoughts-on-mediation/.

Johnston, Maria. 2007. "Tracing the Root of Metastasis," review of *Horse Latitudes*, by Paul Muldoon. *Contemporary Poetry Review*, July 8. http://www.cprw.com/Johnston/muldoon.htm.

Joyce, James. (1932) 2012. *Finnegans Wake*. Knoxville, TN: Wordsworth Classics.

———. (1922) 2000. *Ulysses*. Reprint, London: Penguin.

Jung, Matthias. 2001. "Ecological Criticism of Language." In *The Ecolinguistics Reader: Language, Ecology, and Environment*, edited by Alwin Fill and Peter Mühlhäusler, 270–85. London: Continuum.

Karlsson, Henrik. 2000. "The Acoustic Environment as a Public Domain." *Soundscape* 1 (2): 10–13.

Kendall, Tim. 1996. *Paul Muldoon*. Bridgend, UK: Seren Books.

Kennedy-Andrews, Elmer. 2005a. "Heaney and Muldoon: Omphalos and Diaspora." In *Paul Muldoon: Poetry, Prose, and Drama*, 101–26. Gerrards Cross, UK: Colin Smythe.

———. 2005b. "Introducing Paul Muldoon: 'Arbitrary and Contrary.'" In *Paul Muldoon: Poetry, Prose, and Drama*, 1–18. Gerrards Cross, UK: Colin Smythe.

———. 2008. *Writing Home: Poetry and Place in Northern Ireland, 1968–2008*. Suffolk, UK: Boydell & Brewer.

Kennelly, Brendan. 2000. "Irish Poetry Since Yeats." In *Irish Writing in the Twentieth Century: A Reader*, edited by David Pierce, 1098–1106. Cork, Ireland: Cork Univ. Press.

Kerrigan, John. 1998. "Earth Writing: Seamus Heaney and Ciaran Carson." *Essays in Criticism* 48 (2): 144–68.

———. 2004. "Paul Muldoon's Transits: Muddling through after *Madoc*." In *Paul Muldoon: Critical Essays*, edited by Tim Kendall and Peter McDonald, 125–49. Liverpool: Liverpool Univ. Press.

Kiely, Benedict. 1979. *Proxopera*. Dublin: Quartet/Poolbeg.

Kingsley, Charles. [1855] 1899. *Westward Ho!* Reprint, London: Frederick Warne & Co.

Kinsella, Thomas. 1970. "The Irish Writer." In *Davis, Mangan, Ferguson? Tradition and the Irish Writer*, edited by Roger McHugh, 57–70. Dublin: Dolmen.

———. 1972. *A Selected Life*. Dublin: Peppercanister.

Krause, Bernard. 1987. "Bioacoustics, Habitat Ambience in Ecological Balance." *Whole Earth Review* 57: 14–18.

———. 2012. *The Great Animal Orchestra: Finding the Origins of Music in the World's Wild Places*. Boston: Back Bay Books.

Lefebvre, Henri. (1992) 2004. *Rhythmanalysis: Space, Time and Everyday Life*. Reprint, London: Continuum.

Longley, Edna. 1995. "Derek Mahon: Extreme Religion of Art." In *Poetry in Contemporary Irish Literature*, edited by Michael Kenneally, 280–303. Gerrards Cross, UK: Colin Smythe.

———. 1994. *The Living Stream: Literature and Revisionism in Ireland*. Newcastle upon Tyne, UK: Bloodaxe.

———. 2002. “Looking Back from *The Yellow Book*.” In *The Poetry of Derek Mahon*, edited by Elmer Kennedy-Andrews, 29–48. Gerrards Cross, UK: Colin Smythe.

———. 1985. “Poetry and Politics in Northern Ireland.” *The Crane Bag* 9 (1): 26–40.

Mac Lochlainn, Gearóid. 1997. *Babylon Gaeilgeoir*. Leifear, Ireland: An Clochán.

———. 1999. *Na Scéalaithe*. Baile Átha Cliath, Ireland: Coiscéim.

———. 2003. “Speaking in Tongues: An Interview with Belfast Poet Gearóid Mac Lochlainn.” By Thomas Rain Crowe. *Asheville Poetry Review* 10 (1). http://www.ashevillepoetryreview.com/2003/issue-13/interview-with-gearoid-mac-lochlainn.

———. 2002. *Sruth Teangacha/Stream of Tongues*. Indreabhán, Ireland: Cló Iar-Chonnachta.

MacNeice, Louis. 1993. *Selected Plays*. London: Clarendon Press.

Mahon, Derek. 2006. *Adaptations*. Loughcrew, Ireland: Gallery Press.

———. 1970. *Beyond Howth Head*. Dublin: Dolmen.

———. 1999. *Collected Poems*. Loughcrew, Ireland: Gallery Press.

———. 2005. *Harbour Lights*. Loughcrew, Ireland: Gallery Press.

———. 1995. *The Hudson Letter*. Loughcrew, Ireland: Gallery Press.

———. 1983. *The Hunt by Night*. Winston-Salem, NC: Wake Forest Univ. Press.

———. 2002. “Interview with John Brown.” In *In the Chair: Interviews with Poets from the North of Ireland*, edited by John Brown, 109–24. Cliffs of Moher, Ireland: Salmon Poetry.

———. 1972a. “Introduction.” In *The Sphere Book of Modern Irish Poetry*, 1–20. London: Sphere.

———. 1997a. *Journalism: Selected Prose 1970–1995*. Loughcrew, Ireland: Gallery Press.

———. 1984. *A Kensington Notebook*. London: Anvil.

———. 2008. *Life on Earth*. Loughcrew, Ireland: Gallery Press.

———. 1972b. *Lives*. London: Oxford Univ. Press.

———. 2011. *New Collected Poems*. Loughcrew, Ireland: Gallery Press.

———. 1968. *Night-Crossing*. London: Oxford Univ. Press.

———. 1991. “Q. & A. with Derek Mahon.” By James J. Murphy. *Irish Literary Supplement* 10 (2): 27–28.

———. 2012. *Selected Prose*. Loughcrew, Ireland: Gallery Press.

———. 1975. *The Snow Party*. London: Oxford Univ. Press.

———. 2007. *Somewhere the Wave*. Loughcrew, Ireland: Gallery Press.

———. 1997b. *The Yellow Book*. Loughcrew, Ireland: Gallery Press.

McAteer, Michael. 2009. "The Word as Object: Commodification in the Poetry of Ciaran Carson." In *Ciaran Carson: Critical Essays*, edited by Elmer Kennedy-Andrews, 125–41. Dublin: Four Courts.

McCracken, Kathleen. 1995. "Ciaran Carson: Unravelling the Conditional, Mapping the Provisional." In *Poetry in Contemporary Irish Literature*, edited by Michael Kenneally, 356–72. Gerrards Cross, UK: Colin Smythe.

McDowell, Sara. 2008. "Selling Conflict Heritage through Tourism in Peacetime Northern Ireland: Transforming Conflict or Exacerbating Difference?" *International Journal of Heritage Studies* 14 (5): 405–21.

McLaughlin, Mary. 2002. *Singing in Irish Gaelic*. Essex, UK: Mel Bay.

McLiam Wilson, Robert. 1996. *Eureka Street: A Novel of Ireland like No Other*. New York: Arcade. Kindle edition.

McLuhan, Marshall. 1964. *Understanding Media*. Berkeley, CA: Gingko.

McLuhan, Marshall, and Edmund Carpenter. 1960. "Acoustic Space." In *Explorations in Communication: An Anthology*, 65–70. Toronto: Beacon.

Moi, Ruben. 2007. "Transtextual Conceptualizations of Northern Ireland: Paul Muldoon vs. Seamus Heaney." In *Readings of the Particular: The Postcolonial in the Postnational*, edited by Anne Holden Rønning and Lene Johannessen, 217–29. New York: Rodopi.

Moore, Ross. 2008. "We Don't Know the Half of It," review of *For All We Know*, by Ciaran Carson. *Culture Northern Ireland*, June 25. http://www.culturenorthernireland.org/features/literature/we-don't-know-half-it.

Moran, D. P. [1905] 2006. *The Philosophy of Irish Ireland*. Edited by Patrick Maume. Reprint, Dublin: Univ. College Dublin Press.

Muldoon, Paul. 1994a. *The Annals of Chile*. London: Faber & Faber.

———. 1985. "A Conversation with Paul Muldoon." By Michael Donaghy. *Chicago Review* 35 (1): 76–85.

———. 2006a. *The End of the Poem*. New York: Farrar, Straus and Giroux.

———, ed. 1986. *The Faber Book of Contemporary Irish Poetry*. London: Faber & Faber.

———. 2006b. *General Admission*. Loughcrew, Ireland: Gallery Press.

———. 1998a. "Getting Round: Notes towards an Ars Poetica." *Essays in Criticism* 48 (2): 107–28.

———. 2006c. Horse Latitudes. London: Faber & Faber.

———. 2008. Interview by Dillon Johnston. *Arch Literary Journal* 1. http://archjournal.wustl.edu/node/100 (site discontinued).

———. 1998b. Interview by Earl G. Ingersoll and Stan Sanvel Rubin. *Michigan Quarterly Review* 37 (1): 63–73.

———. 2009a. Interview by Frank McGuinness. *Irish Studies Review* 17 (1): 103–10.

———. 2004. Interview by John Tusa. *BBC Radio* 3, February 1. http://www.bbc.co.uk/programmes/pooncyhh.

———. 1987a. Interview by Kevin Barry. *Irish Literary Supplement* 6 (2): 36–37.

———. 1994b. Interview by Lynn Keller. *Contemporary Literature* 35: 1–29.

———. 2006d. Interview by Peter Koch. *Artvoice* 5 (8): 14.

———. 1990. *Madoc: A Mystery.* London: Faber & Faber.

———. 1987b. *Meeting the British.* London: Faber & Faber.

———. 1977. *Mules.* London: Faber & Faber.

———. 2001. *Poems, 1968–1998.* London: Faber & Faber.

———. 1983. *Quoof.* London: Faber & Faber.

———. 1995. *Six Honest Serving Men.* Loughcrew, Ireland: Gallery Press.

———. 2000. *To Ireland, I.* Oxford: Oxford Univ. Press.

———. 2009b. *Wayside Shrines.* Loughcrew, Ireland: Gallery Press.

———. 1980. *Why Brownlee Left.* London: Faber & Faber.

Muldoon, Paul, and Daron Hagen. 2007. *The Antient Concert.* New York: Carl Fischer.

———. 1998. *Bandanna.* New York: Carl Fischer.

———. 1995. *Shining Brow.* Boston: E. C. Schirmer.

———. 2009. *Shining Brow.* Buffalo Philharmonic Orchestra and Chorus, conducted by JoAnn Falletta, recorded in 2006. Naxos, compact disc.

———. 2002. *Vera of Las Vegas.* Univ. of Nevada Las Vegas Opera Theater Chorus and Orchestra, conducted by Donna Hagen, recorded in 1996. Composers Recordings, compact disc.

———. 2003. *Vera of Las Vegas.* New York: Carl Fischer.

Mullaney, Kathleen. 1989. "A Poetics of Silence: Derek Mahon 'At One Remove.'" *Journal of Irish Literature* 18 (3): 45–54.

Murtagh, Brendan. 2008. "New Spaces and Old in 'Post-conflict' Belfast." In *Divided Cities/Contested States*, Working Paper No. 5. Belfast: Queen's Univ. Belfast.

Nancy, Jean-Luc. 2007. *Listening.* Translated by Charlotte Mandell. New York: Fordham Univ. Press.

Neill, William J. V. 2004. *Urban Planning and Cultural Identity.* London: Routledge.

Ní Dhomhnaill, Nuala. 1988. "The English for Irish." *Irish Review* 4: 116–18.

———. 2002. "The Real McCoy." In *Sruth Teangacha/Stream of Tongues*, by Gearóid Mac Lochlainn, 11–20. Indreabhán, Ireland: Cló Iar-Chonnachta.

NISRA (Northern Ireland Statistics & Research Agency). 2012. *Census 2011: Key Statistics for Northern Ireland.* Belfast: United Kingdom Statistics Authority. http://www.nisra.gov.uk/Census/key_report_2011.pdf.

Ní Uallacháin, Pádraigín. 2003. *A Hidden Ulster: People, Songs, and Traditions of Oriel.* Dublin: Four Courts.

Obert, Julia C. 2006. "The Cultural Capital of Sound: *Québécité's* Acoustic Hybridity." *Postcolonial Text* 2 (4). http://postcolonial.org/index.php/pct/article/view/493/353.

O'Brien, Conor Cruise. 1995. *Ancestral Voices: Religion and Nationalism in Ireland.* Chicago: Univ. of Chicago Press.

O'Brien, Sean. 1998. *The Deregulated Muse: Essays on Contemporary Poetry in Britain and Ireland.* Newcastle upon Tyne, UK: Bloodaxe.

Ó Canainn, Tomás. 1979. *Traditional Music in Ireland.* London: Routledge.

O'Connor, Laura. 2011. "The Bilingual Routes of Paul Muldoon/Pól Ó Maoldúin." *Irish Studies Review* 19 (2): 135–55.

———. 2009. "Translation through the Macaronic: Gearóid Mac Lochlainn's *Sruth Teangacha/Stream of Tongues.*" *New Hibernia Review* 13 (1): 73–94.

O'Reilly, Camille. 2001. *Language, Ethnicity and the State, Volume 1: Minority Languages in the European Union.* New York: Palgrave.

Osborn, Andrew. 2000. "Skirmishes on the Border: The Evolution and Function of Paul Muldoon's Fuzzy Rhyme." *Contemporary Literature* 41 (2): 323–58.

Ó Tuama, Seán. 1995. *Repossessions: Selected Essays on the Irish Literary Heritage.* Cork, Ireland: Cork Univ. Press.

Papastergiadis, Nikos. 2000. *The Turbulence of Migration: Globalization, Deterritorialization, and Hybridity.* Cambridge: Blackwell.

Parini, Jay. 1999. *Robert Frost: A Life.* New York: Henry Holt.

Parker, Roger, ed. 2001. *The Oxford Illustrated History of Opera.* Oxford: Oxford Univ. Press.

Parker, Stewart. 2000. "Northern Star." In *Plays:* 2, 1–82. London: Methuen Drama.

Patke, Rajeev. 2008. "'Responsibility' and 'Difficulty' in the Poetry of Paul Muldoon." *Criticism* 50 (2): 279–99.

Patterson, Glenn. 2006. *Lapsed Protestant.* Dublin: New Island Books.

Paulin, Tom. 2003a. "The Despotism of the Eye." In *Soundscape: The School of Sound Lectures, 1998–2001*, edited by Larry Sider, Jerry Sider, and Diane Freeman, 35–48. London: Wallflower.

———. 1984. *Ireland and the English Crisis*. Newcastle upon Tyne, UK: Bloodaxe.

———. 2003b. "The Vernacular City." In *The Cities of Belfast*, edited by Nicholas Allen and Aaron Kelly, 233–42. Dublin: Four Courts.

Plantenga, Bart. 2001. "Yodeling to Rouse the Echoes." In *Writing Aloud: The Sonics of Language*, edited by Brandon LaBelle and Christof Migone, 72–81. Los Angeles: Errant Bodies.

Prochnik, George. 2010. *In Pursuit of Silence: Listening for Meaning in a World of Noise*. New York: Doubleday.

Rackett. 2006a. *Don't Try This at Home*. Scamafone, compact disc.

———. 2007. *Resistance*. Scamafone, compact disc.

———. 2006b. *Standing Room Only*. Scamafone, compact disc.

Radin, Paul. 1956. *The Trickster: A Study in Native American Mythology*. New York: Schocken.

Ramazani, Jahan. 2009. *A Transnational Poetics*. Chicago: Univ. of Chicago Press.

Rankin Russell, Richard. 2010. *Poetry and Peace: Michael Longley, Seamus Heaney, and Northern Ireland*. Notre Dame, IN: Univ. of Notre Dame Press.

Reik, Theodor. 1953. *The Haunting Melody: Psychoanalytic Experiences in Life and Music*. New York: Farrar, Strauss and Young.

Rodaway, Paul. 1994. *Sensuous Geographies: Body, Sense, and Place*. New York: Routledge.

Rumens, Carol. 2007. *Self into Song*. Newcastle upon Tyne, UK: Bloodaxe.

Rushdie, Salman. 1992. *Imaginary Homelands: Essays and Criticism 1981–1991*. New York: Penguin.

Sacks, Oliver. 2008. *Musicophilia: Tales of Music and the Brain*. New York: Random House.

Said, Edward. 2002. "Between Worlds." In *Reflections on Exile and Other Essays*, 554–68. Cambridge, MA: Harvard Univ. Press.

———. 1993. *Culture and Imperialism*. New York: Knopf.

Schafer, R. Murray. 1997. "On Acoustic Design" (lecture), recorded in 1973, on *The Vancouver Soundscape 1973/Soundscape Vancouver 1996*. Cambridge Street Records, compact disc.

———. 1977. *The Tuning of the World*. New York: Random House.

Shields, Kathleen. 1994. "Derek Mahon's Poetry of Belonging." *Irish University Review* 24 (1): 67–79.

Smith, Stan. 2005. *Irish Poetry and the Construction of Modern Identity.* Dublin: Irish Academic.

Smyth, Gerry. 2001. *Space and the Irish Cultural Imagination.* New York: Palgrave.

Spenser, Edmund. 1633. *A View of the Present State of Ireland.* Cork, Ireland: CELT, Univ. College. http://www.ucc.ie/celt/published/E500000-001/index.html.

Stewart, Bruce. 2000. "On the Necessity of De-Hydifying Irish Cultural Criticism." *New Hibernia Review* 4 (1): 23–44.

Stewart, Garrett. 1990. *Reading Voices: Literature and the Phonotext.* Berkeley, CA: Univ. of California Press.

Stewart, Susan. 2002. *Poetry and the Fate of the Senses.* Chicago: Univ. of Chicago Press.

Stokes, Martin. 1994. *Ethnicity, Identity and Music: The Musical Construction of Place.* Providence, RI: Berg.

Stoler, Ann Laura. 2002. *Carnal Knowledge and Imperial Power: Race and the Intimate in Colonial Rule.* Berkeley, CA: Univ. of California Press.

Tell, Carol. 2004. *Part-Time Exiles: Contemporary Irish Poets and Their Migrations.* Bethesda, MD: Academica.

Terada, Rei. 2001. *Feeling in Theory: Emotion after the 'Death of the Subject.'* Cambridge, MA: Harvard Univ. Press.

Tillinghast, Richard. 2008. "Derek Mahon: Exile and Stranger." In *Finding Ireland: A Poet's Explorations of Irish Literature and Culture,* 179–92. Notre Dame, IN: Univ. of Notre Dame Press.

Truax, Barry. 2001. *Acoustic Communication.* 2nd ed. Westport, CT: Ablex.

Tyler, Meg. 2013. *A Singing Contest: Conventions of Sound in the Poetry of Seamus Heaney.* 2nd ed. London: Routledge.

Tymoczko, Maria, and Colin Ireland. 2003. "Language and Identity in Twentieth-Century Ireland." *Éire-Ireland* (1–2): 4–22.

Vallely, Fintan. 1999. *Companion to Irish Traditional Music.* New York: New York Univ. Press.

———. 2008. *Tuned Out: Traditional Music and Identity in Northern Ireland.* Cork, Ireland: Cork Univ. Press.

Wagner, Richard. (1893) 1995. *Richard Wagner's Prose Works.* Vol. 2, *Opera and Drama.* Translated by William Ashton Ellis. Reprint, Lincoln, NE: Univ. of Nebraska Press. http://users.belgacom.net/wagnerlibrary/prose/wlpro063.htm.

Wallis, Geoff, and Sue Wilson. 2005. *The Rough Guide to Irish Music*. London: Rough Guides.

Ward, Paul. 2004. *Britishness Since 1870*. London: Routledge.

Westerkamp, Hildegard. 2000. "Editorial." *Soundscape* 1 (1): 3–4.

Wheatley, David. 2004. "All Art Is a Collaboration: Paul Muldoon as Librettist." In *Paul Muldoon: Critical Essays*, edited by Tim Kendall and Peter McDonald, 150–69. Liverpool: Liverpool Univ. Press.

———. 1999. "An Irish Poet in America." *Raritan* 18 (4): 145–57.

———. 2009. "'Pushed Next to Nothing': Ciaran Carson's *Breaking News*." In *Ciaran Carson: Critical Essays*, edited by Elmer Kennedy-Andrews, 45–65. Dublin: Four Courts.

Whitman, Walt. [1855] 2001. *Song of Myself*. Reprint, New York: Dover.

Wills, Clair. 1998. *Reading Paul Muldoon*. Newcastle upon Tyne, UK: Bloodaxe.

Wrightson, Kendall. 2000. "An Introduction to Acoustic Ecology." *Soundscape* 1 (1): 10–13.

Yeats, W. B. (1937) 1991. "Cathleen Ní Houlihan." In *Modern Irish Drama*, edited by John P. Harrington, 3–11. London: W. W. Norton.

Zamorano Llena, Carmen. 2007. "'It's Time for Some New Coinage': Derek Mahon's Redefinition of Identity and the Memory of Place in a Postnationalist Context." In *Recovering Memory: Irish Representations of Past and Present*, edited by Hedda Friberg, Irene Gilsenan Nordin, and Lene Yding Pedersen, 98–114. Newcastle upon Tyne, UK: Cambridge Scholars.

INDEX

JULIA C. OBERT is assistant professor and assistant chair in the Department of English at the University of Wyoming. She researches and teaches in the areas of Irish studies, post-colonial literature and theory, poetry and poetics, twentieth-century British literature, and contemporary critical theory (in particular, sound theory and acoustic ecology, affect theory, and theories of spatiality).